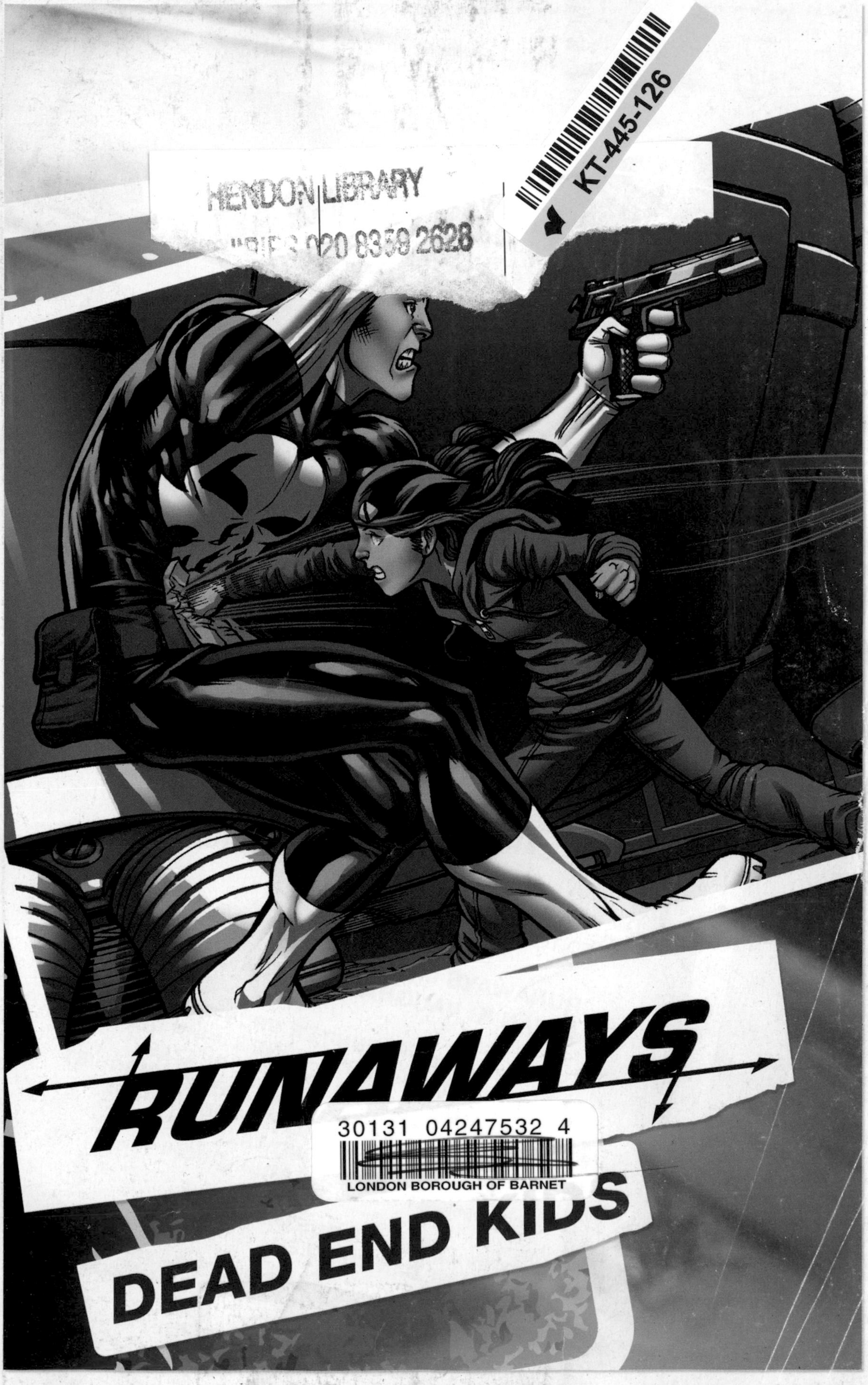
RUNAWAYS
DEAD END KIDS

RUNAWAYS

DEAD END KIDS

WRITER: **JOSS WHEDON**

PENCILER: **MICHAEL RYAN**

INKER: **RICK KETCHAM** WITH **JAY LEISTEN, ANDREW HENNESSY, VICTOR OLAZABA & ROLAND PARIS**

COLORIST: **CHRISTINA STRAIN**

LETTERER: **VC'S RANDY GENTILE, JOE CARAMAGNA & CORY PETIT**

COVER ARTIST: **JO CHEN**

ASSISTANT EDITOR: **DANIEL KETCHUM**

EDITOR: **NICK LOWE**

RUNAWAYS CREATED BY **BRIAN K. VAUGHAN & ADRIAN ALPHONA**

COLLECTION EDITOR: **JENNIFER GRÜNWALD**

ASSISTANT EDITORS: **CORY LEVINE & JOHN DENNING**

EDITOR, SPECIAL PROJECTS: **MARK D. BEAZLEY**

SENIOR EDITOR, SPECIAL PROJECTS: **JEFF YOUNGQUIST**

SENIOR VICE PRESIDENT OF SALES: **DAVID GABRIEL**

PRODUCTION: **JERRY KALINOWSKI**

BOOK DESIGNER: **RODOLFO MURAGUCHI**

EDITOR IN CHIEF: **JOE QUESADA**

PUBLISHER: **DAN BUCKLEY**

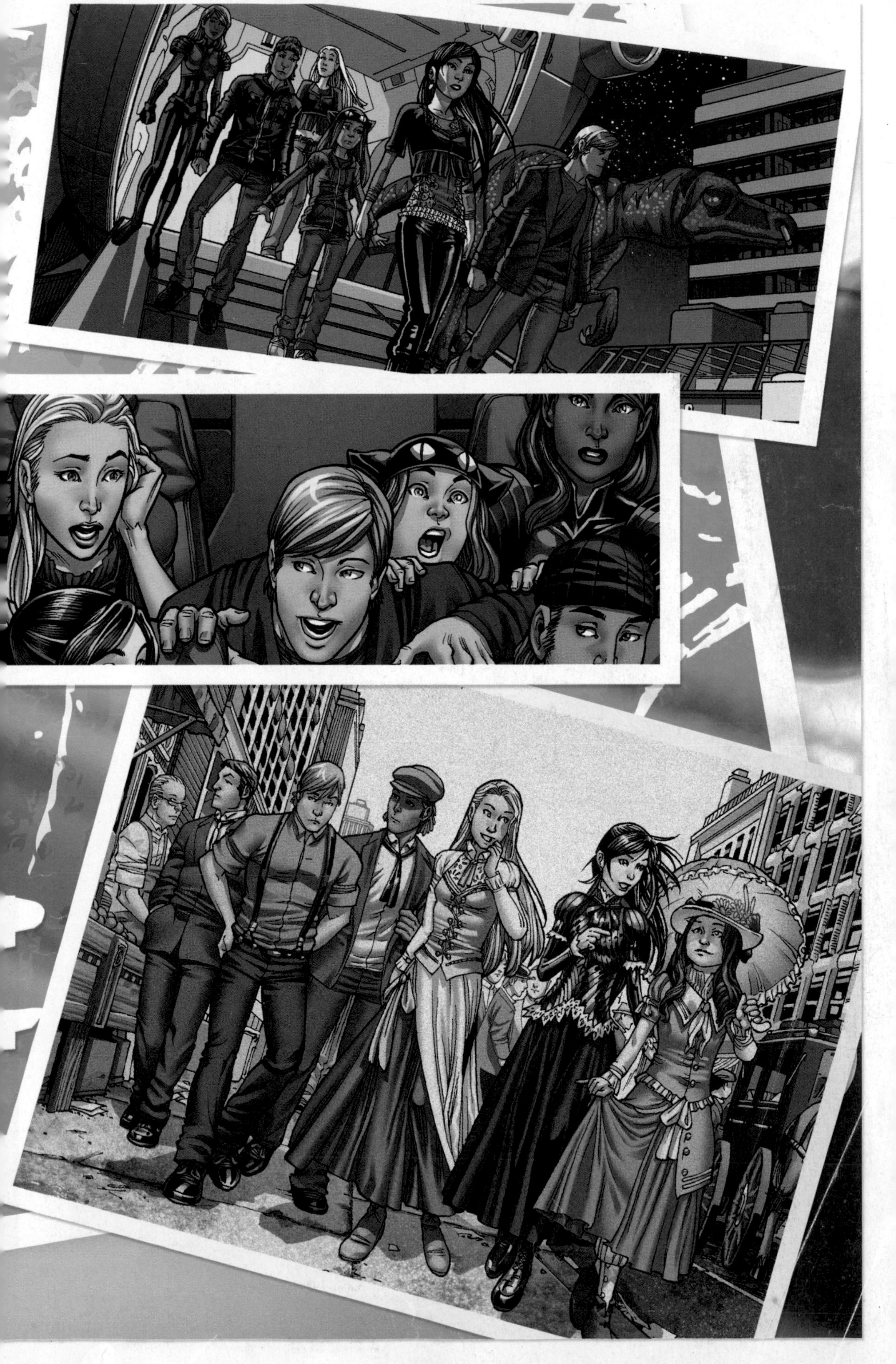

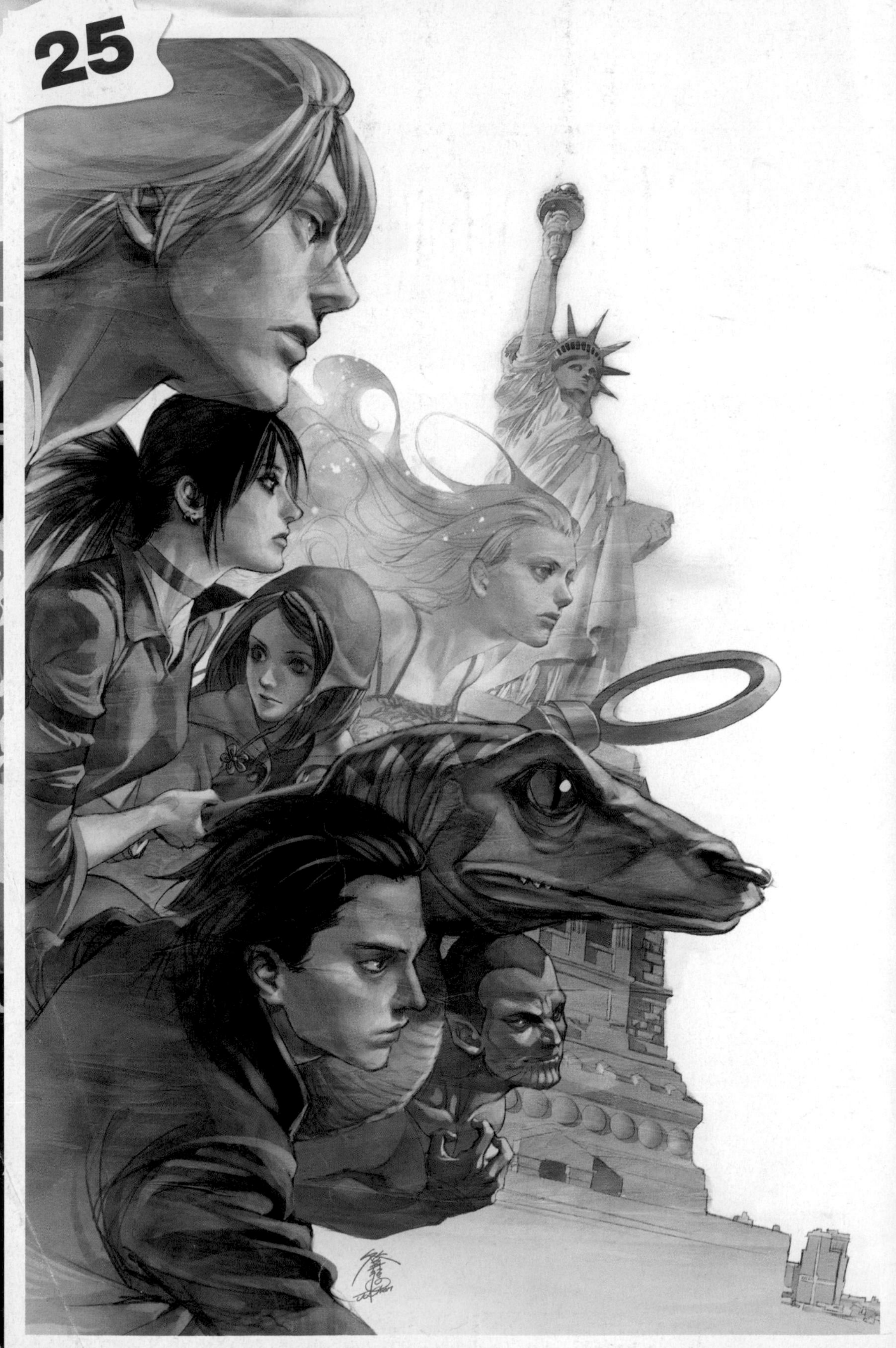
25

DEAD-END KIDS

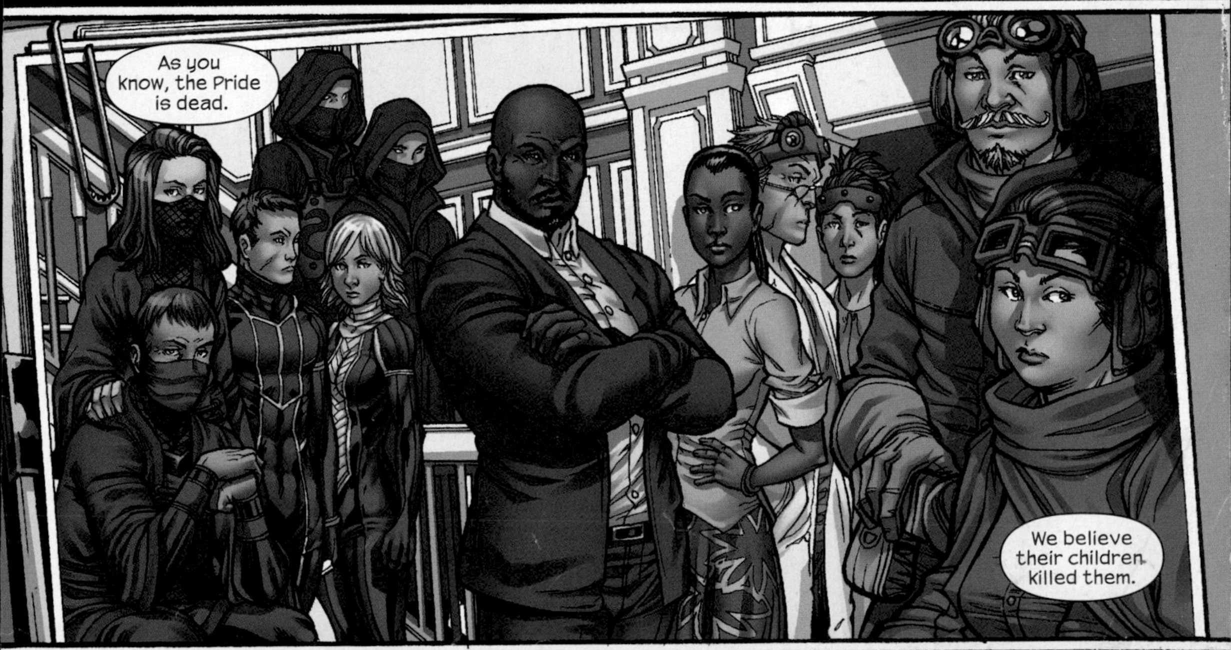
As you know, the Pride is dead.
We believe their children killed them.

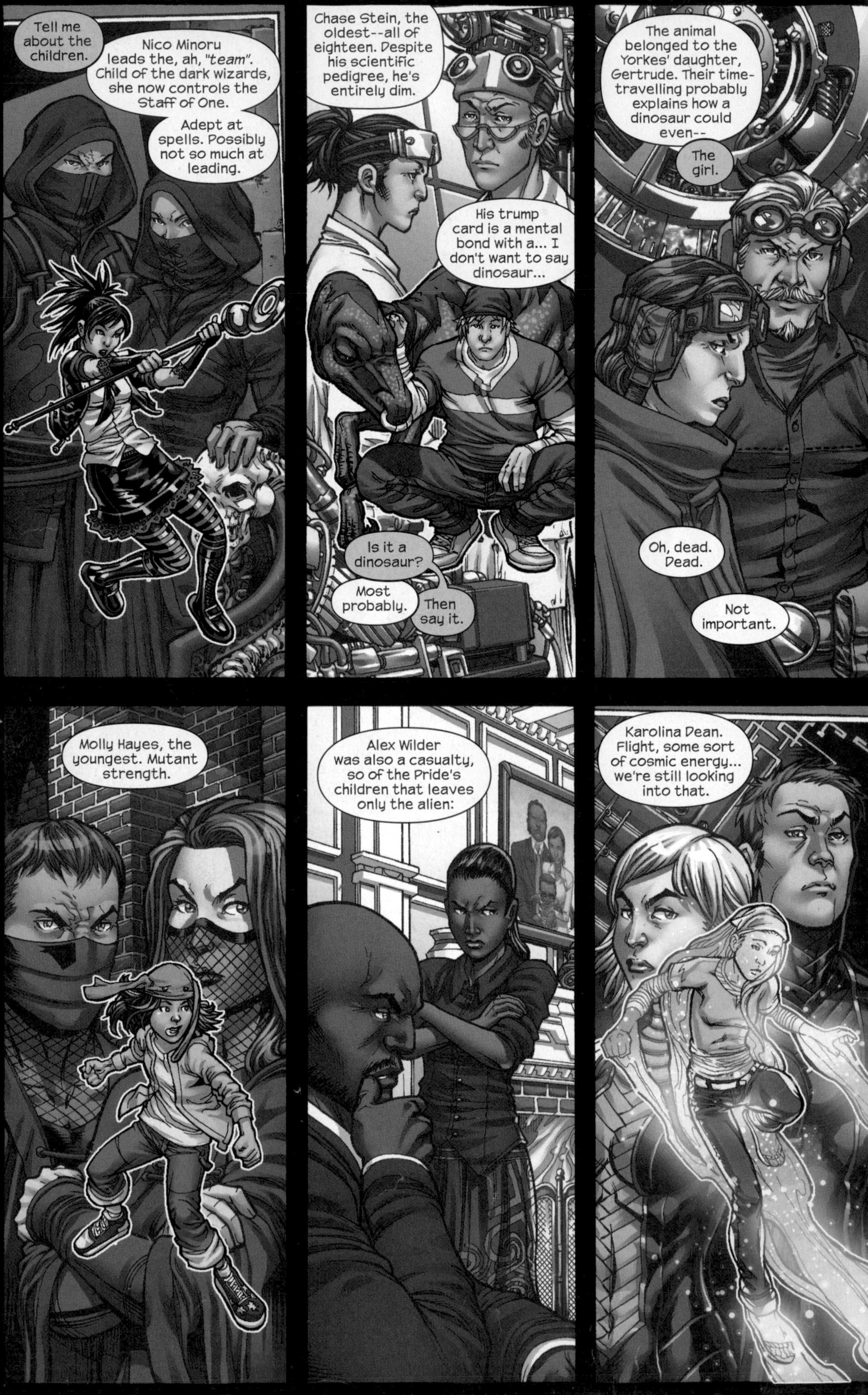
Tell me about the children.
Nico Minoru leads the, ah, "team". Child of the dark wizards, she now controls the Staff of One.
Adept at spells. Possibly not so much at leading.
Chase Stein, the oldest--all of eighteen. Despite his scientific pedigree, he's entirely dim.
His trump card is a mental bond with a... I don't want to say dinosaur...
Is it a dinosaur?
Most probably.
Then say it.
The animal belonged to the Yorkes' daughter, Gertrude. Their time-travelling probably explains how a dinosaur could even--
The girl.
Oh, dead. Dead.
Not important.
Molly Hayes, the youngest. Mutant strength.
Alex Wilder was also a casualty, so of the Pride's children that leaves only the alien:
Karolina Dean. Flight, some sort of cosmic energy... we're still looking into that.

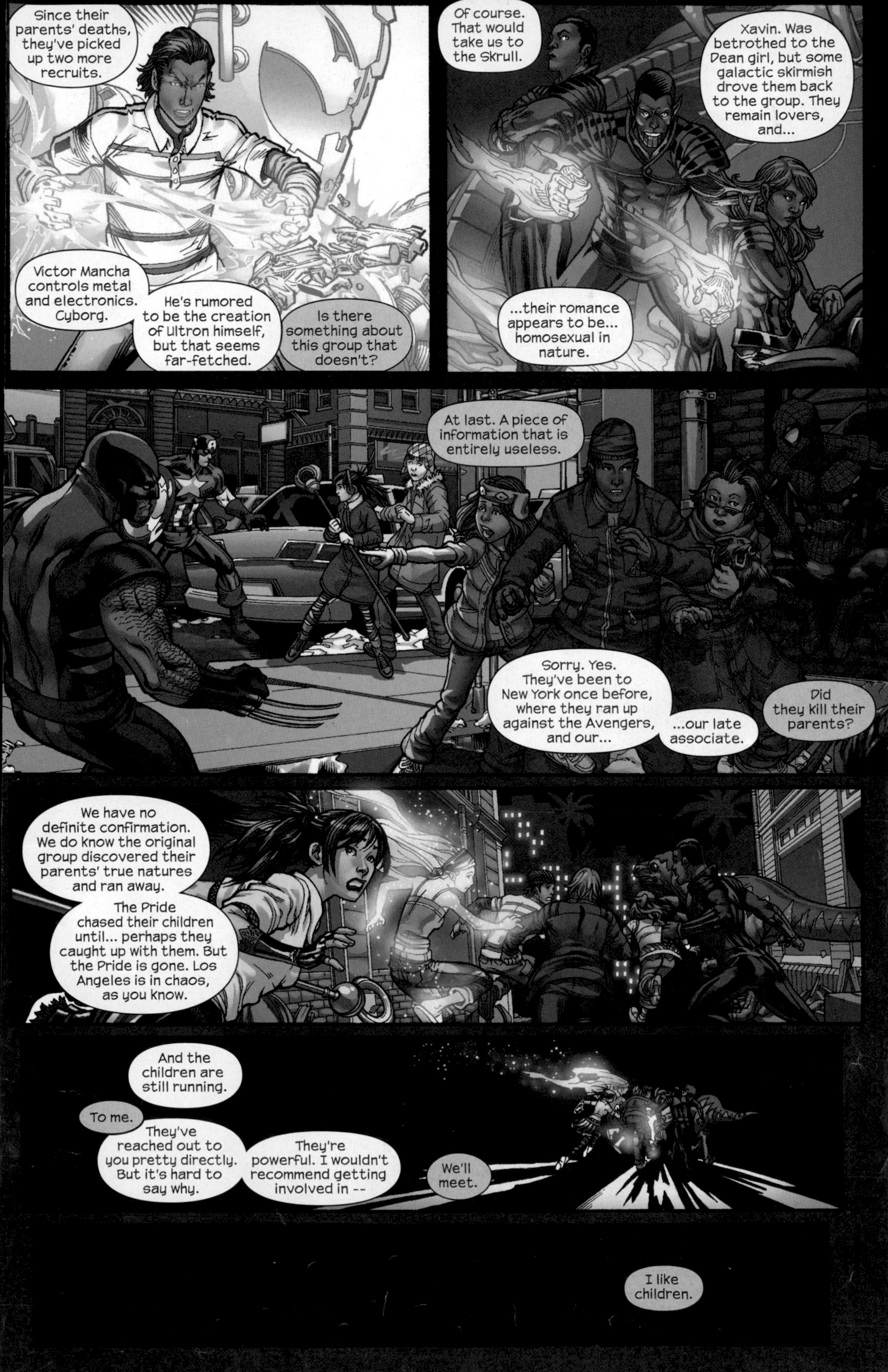
Since their parents' deaths, they've picked up two more recruits.
Victor Mancha controls metal and electronics. Cyborg.
He's rumored to be the creation of Ultron himself, but that seems far-fetched.
Is there something about this group that doesn't?
Of course. That would take us to the Skrull.
Xavin. Was betrothed to the Dean girl, but some galactic skirmish drove them back to the group. They remain lovers, and...
...their romance appears to be... homosexual in nature.
At last. A piece of information that is entirely useless.
Sorry. Yes. They've been to New York once before, where they ran up against the Avengers, and our...
...our late associate.
Did they kill their parents?
We have no definite confirmation. We do know the original group discovered their parents' true natures and ran away.
The Pride chased their children until... perhaps they caught up with them. But the Pride is gone. Los Angeles is in chaos, as you know.
And the children are still running.
To me.
They've reached out to you pretty directly. But it's hard to say why.
They're powerful. I wouldn't recommend getting involved in --
We'll meet.
I like children.

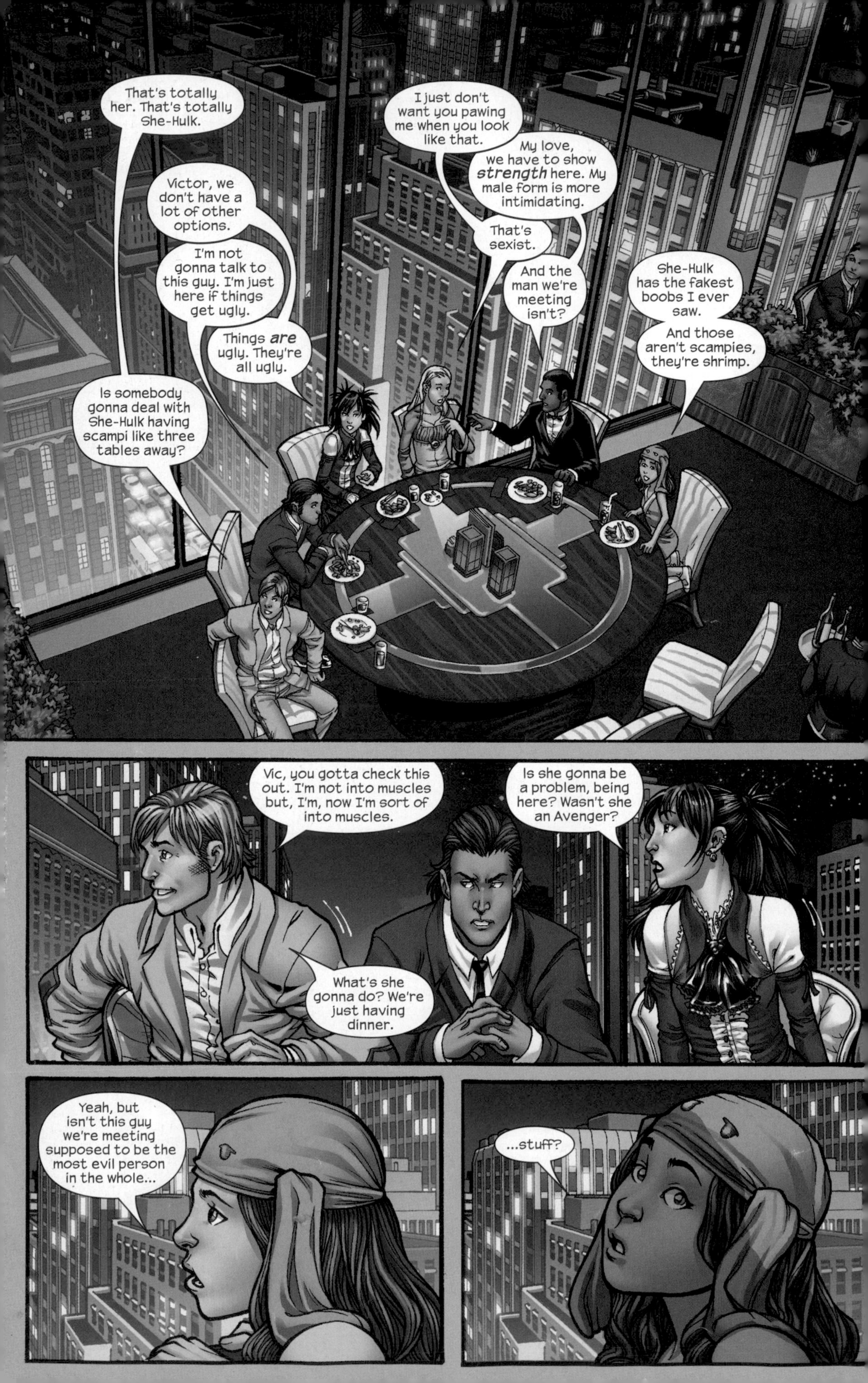

That's totally her. That's totally She-Hulk.
Victor, we don't have a lot of other options.
I'm not gonna talk to this guy. I'm just here if things get ugly.
Things *are* ugly. They're all ugly.
Is somebody gonna deal with She-Hulk having scampi like three tables away?
I just don't want you pawing me when you look like that.
My love, we have to show *strength* here. My male form is more intimidating.
That's sexist.
And the man we're meeting isn't?
She-Hulk has the fakest boobs I ever saw.
And those aren't scampies, they're shrimp.
Vic, you gotta check this out. I'm not into muscles but, I'm, now I'm sort of into muscles.
What's she gonna do? We're just having dinner.
Is she gonna be a problem, being here? Wasn't she an Avenger?
Yeah, but isn't this guy we're meeting supposed to be the most evil person in the whole...
...stuff?

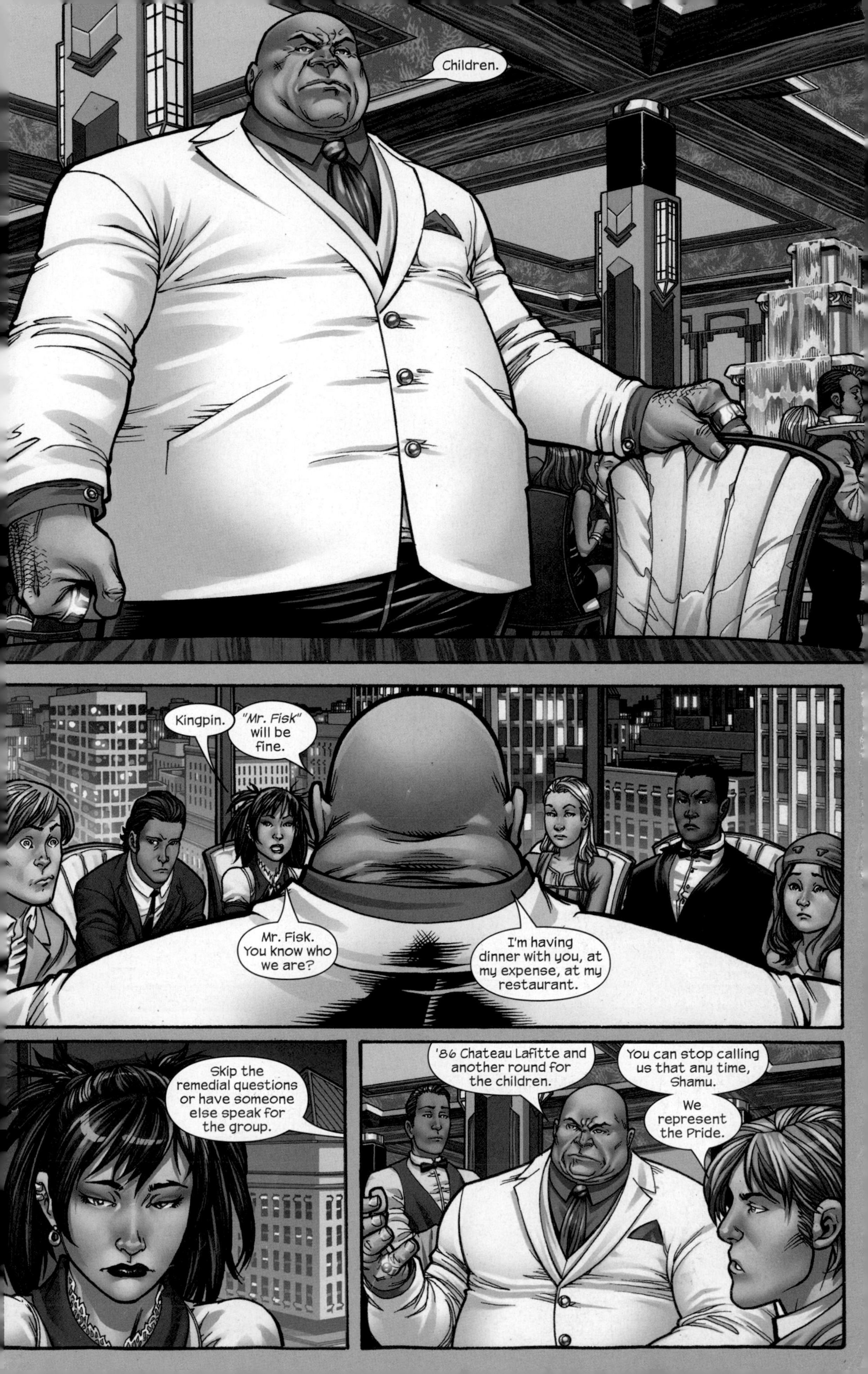
Children.
Kingpin.
"Mr. Fisk" will be fine.
Mr. Fisk. You know who we are?
I'm having dinner with you, at my expense, at my restaurant.
Skip the remedial questions or have someone else speak for the group.
'86 Chateau Lafitte and another round for the children.
You can stop calling us that any time, Shamu.
We represent the Pride.

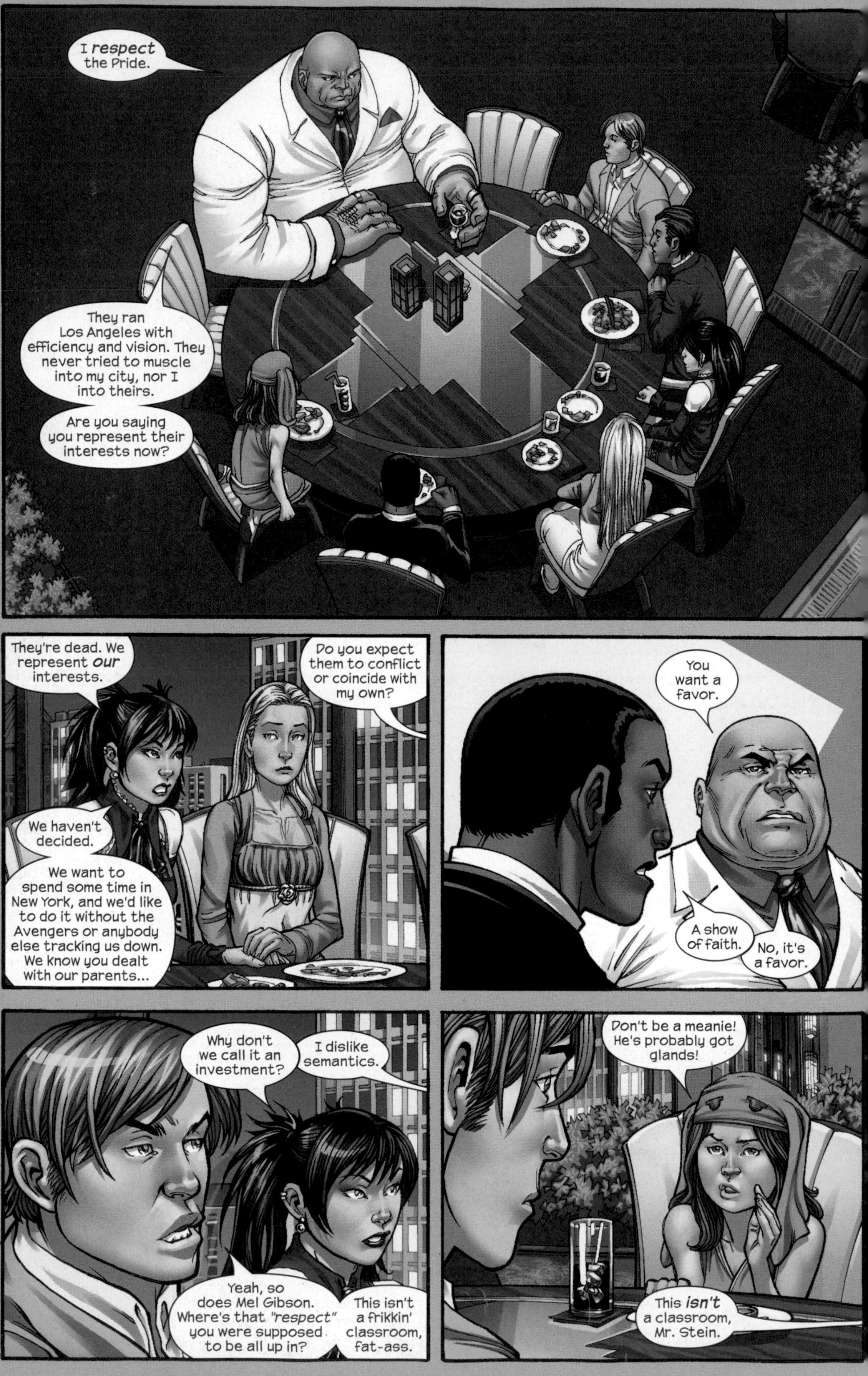
I respect the Pride.
They ran Los Angeles with efficiency and vision. They never tried to muscle into my city, nor I into theirs.
Are you saying you represent their interests now?
They're dead. We represent our interests.
Do you expect them to conflict or coincide with my own?
We haven't decided.
We want to spend some time in New York, and we'd like to do it without the Avengers or anybody else tracking us down. We know you dealt with our parents...
You want a favor.
A show of faith.
No, it's a favor.
Why don't we call it an investment?
I dislike semantics.
Yeah, so does Mel Gibson. Where's that "respect" you were supposed to be all up in?
This isn't a frikkin' classroom, fat-ass.
Don't be a meanie! He's probably got glands!
This isn't a classroom, Mr. Stein.

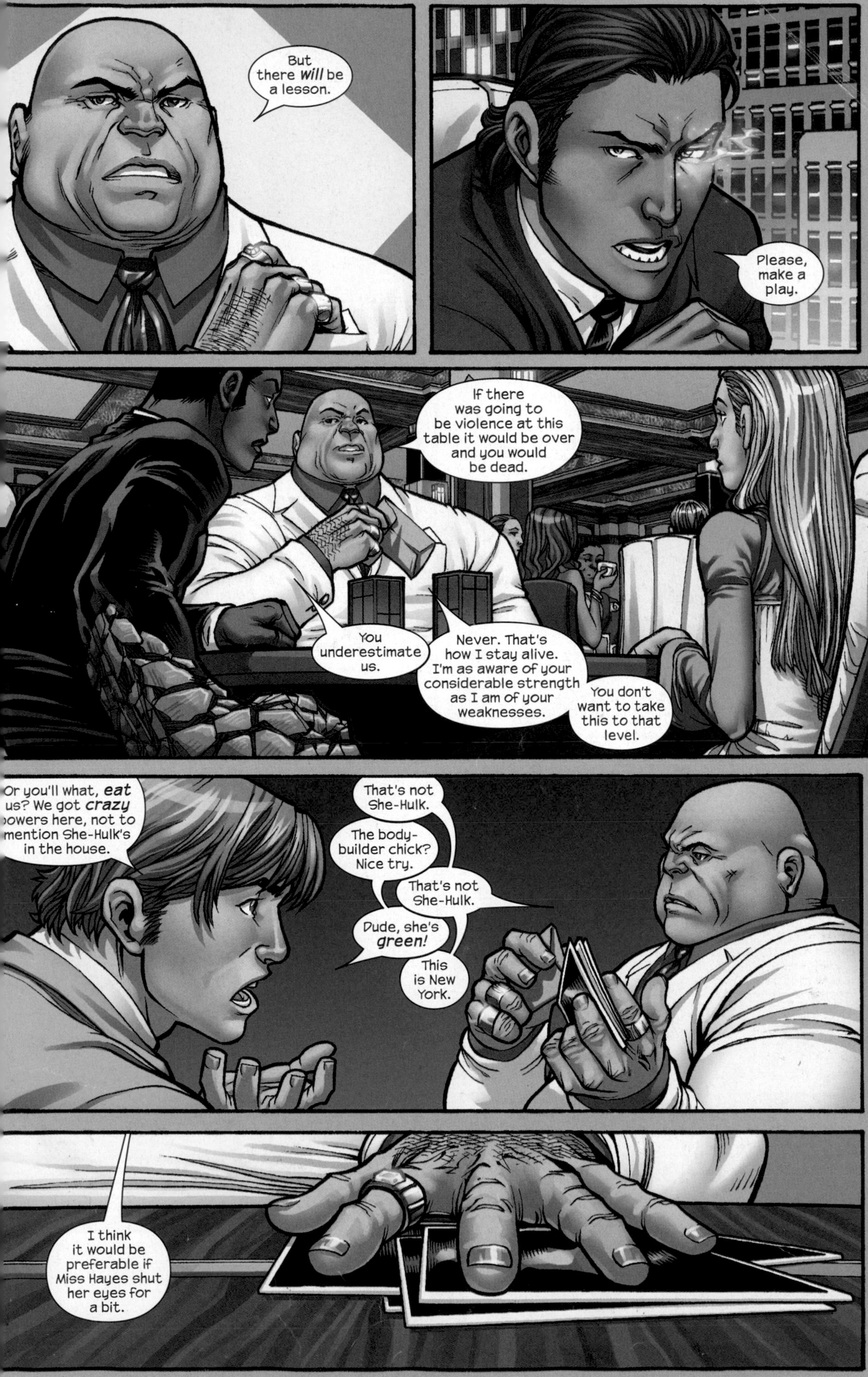
But there *will* be a lesson.
Please, make a play.
If there was going to be violence at this table it would be over and you would be dead.
You underestimate us.
Never. That's how I stay alive. I'm as aware of your considerable strength as I am of your weaknesses.
You don't want to take this to that level.
Or you'll what, *eat* us? We got *crazy* powers here, not to mention She-Hulk's in the house.
That's not She-Hulk.
The body-builder chick? Nice try.
That's not She-Hulk.
Dude, she's *green!*
This is New York.
I think it would be preferable if Miss Hayes shut her eyes for a bit.

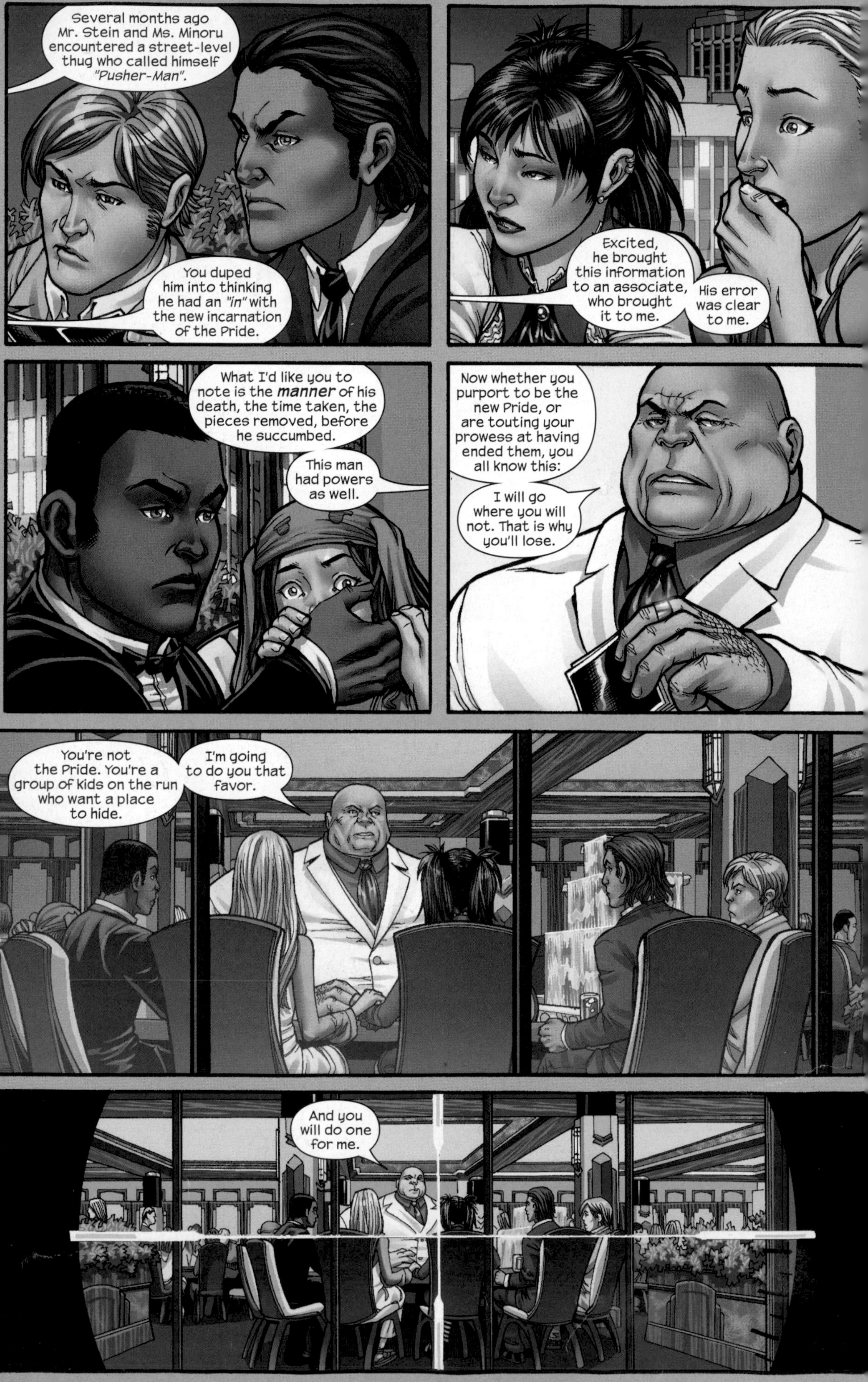
Several months ago Mr. Stein and Ms. Minoru encountered a street-level thug who called himself "Pusher-Man".
You duped him into thinking he had an "in" with the new incarnation of the Pride.
Excited, he brought this information to an associate, who brought it to me.
His error was clear to me.
What I'd like you to note is the manner of his death, the time taken, the pieces removed, before he succumbed.
This man had powers as well.
Now whether you purport to be the new Pride, or are touting your prowess at having ended them, you all know this:
I will go where you will not. That is why you'll lose.
You're not the Pride. You're a group of kids on the run who want a place to hide.
I'm going to do you that favor.
And you will do one for me.

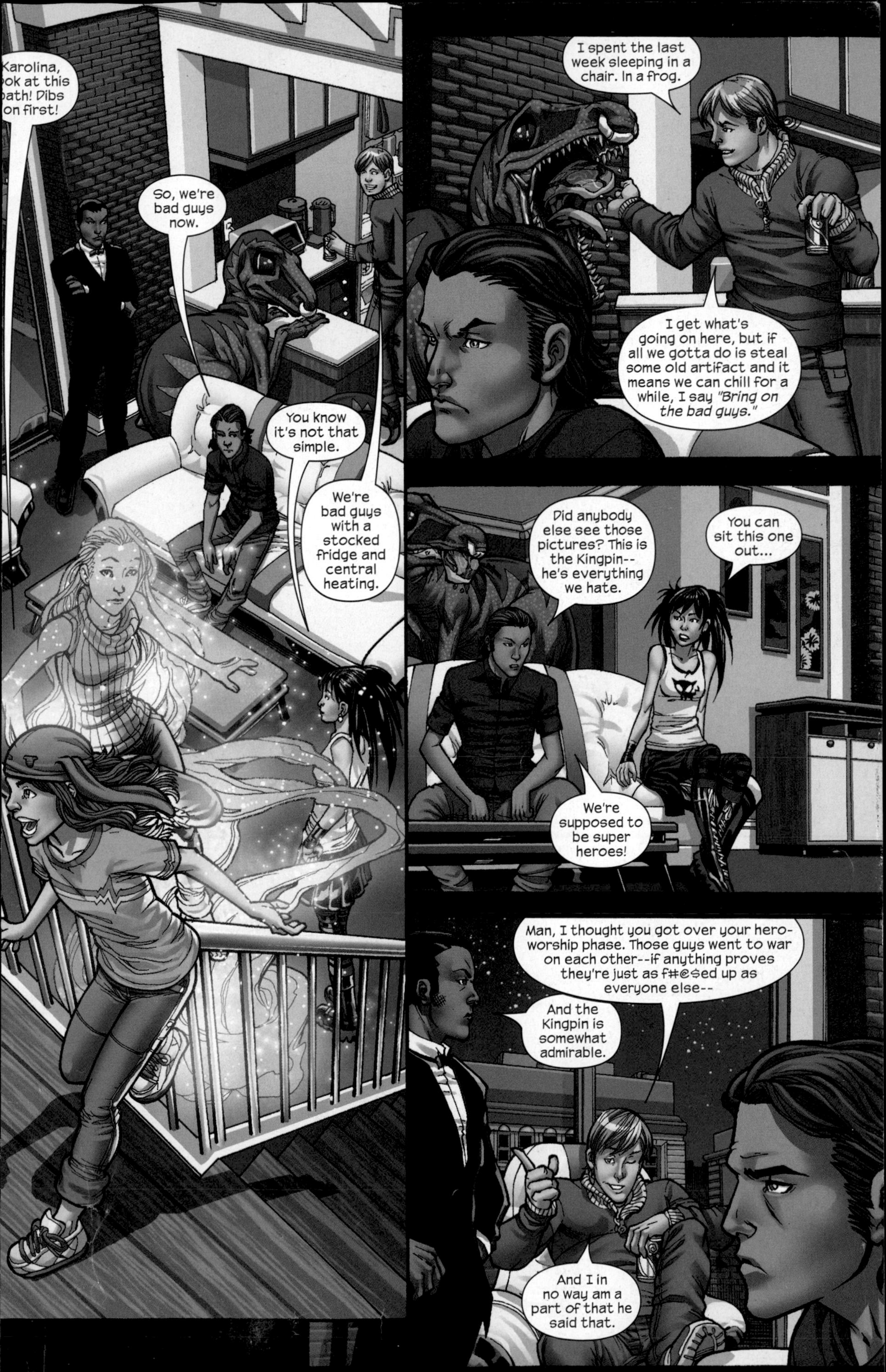
Karolina, ook at this bath! Dibs on first!
So, we're bad guys now.
You know it's not that simple.
We're bad guys with a stocked fridge and central heating.
I spent the last week sleeping in a chair. In a frog.
I get what's going on here, but if all we gotta do is steal some old artifact and it means we can chill for a while, I say "Bring on the bad guys."
Did anybody else see those pictures? This is the Kingpin--he's everything we hate.
You can sit this one out...
We're supposed to be super heroes!
Man, I thought you got over your hero-worship phase. Those guys went to war on each other--if anything proves they're just as f#@$ed up as everyone else--
And the Kingpin is somewhat admirable.
And I in no way am a part of that he said that.

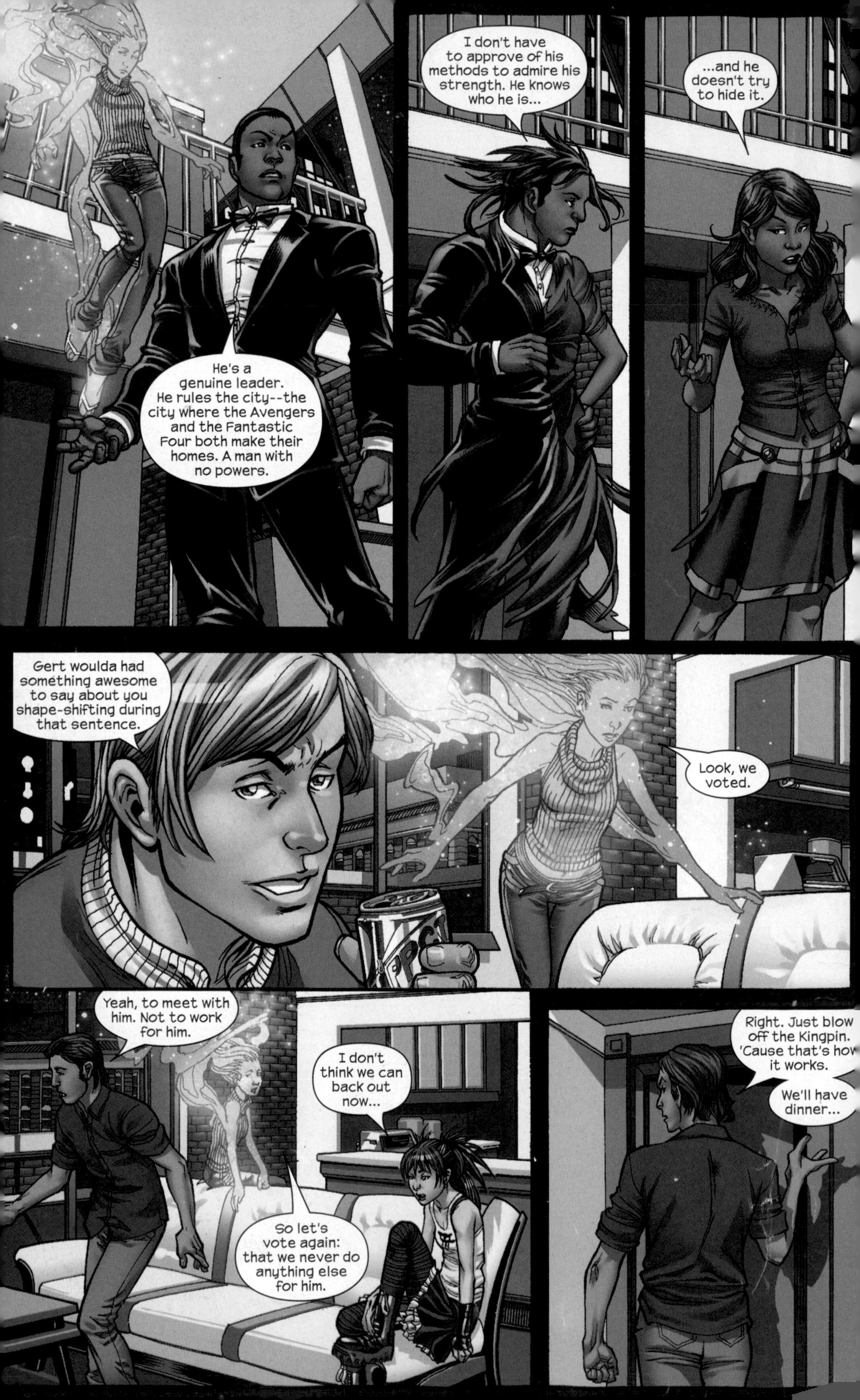
He's a genuine leader. He rules the city--the city where the Avengers and the Fantastic Four both make their homes. A man with no powers.
I don't have to approve of his methods to admire his strength. He knows who he is...
...and he doesn't try to hide it.
Gert woulda had something awesome to say about you shape-shifting during that sentence.
Look, we voted.
Yeah, to meet with him. Not to work for him.
I don't think we can back out now...
So let's vote again: that we never do anything else for him.
Right. Just blow off the Kingpin. 'Cause that's how it works.
We'll have dinner...

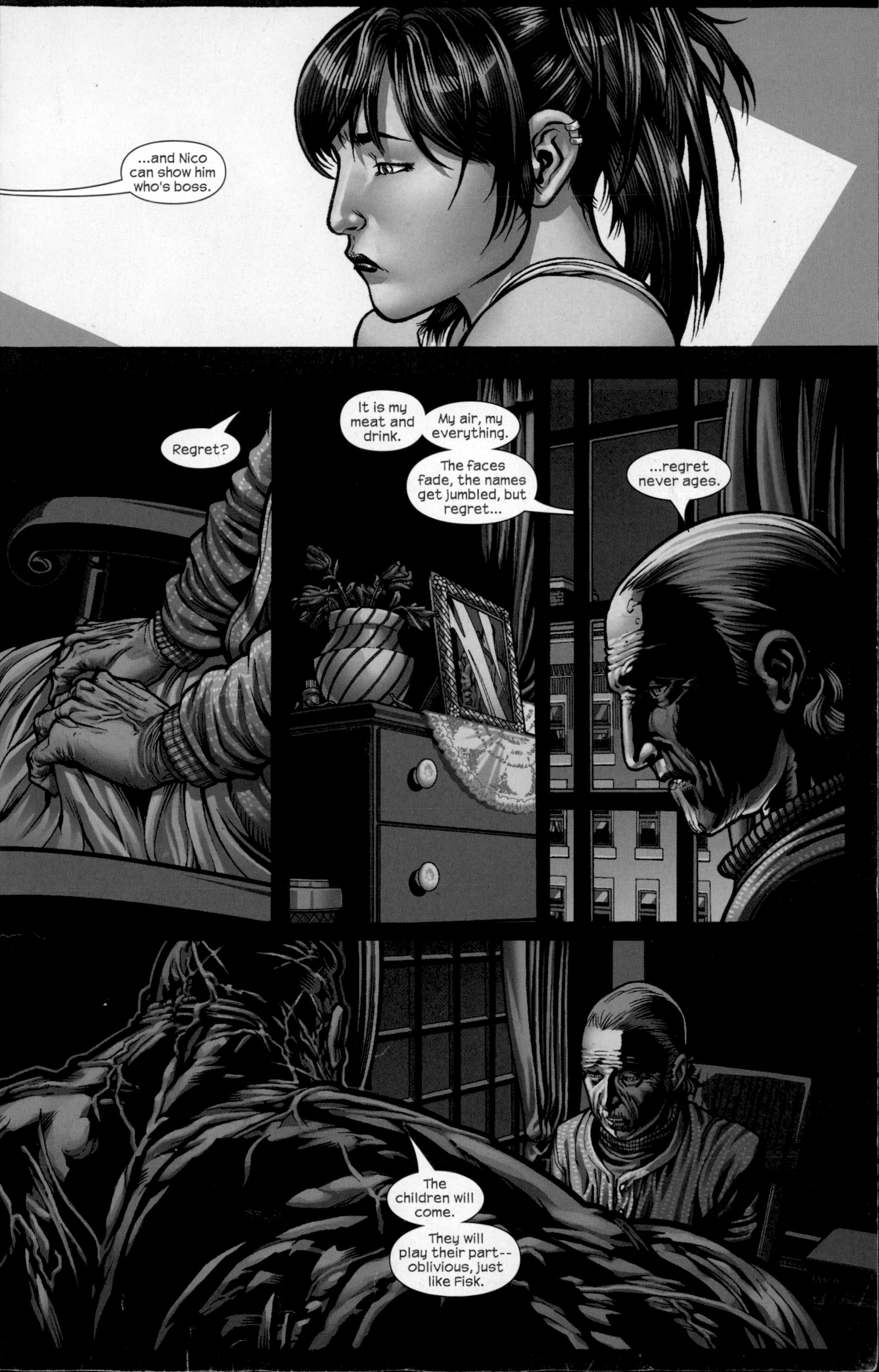
...and Nico can show him who's boss.
Regret?
It is my meat and drink.
My air, my everything.
The faces fade, the names get jumbled, but regret...
...regret never ages.
The children will come.
They will play their part-- oblivious, just like Fisk.

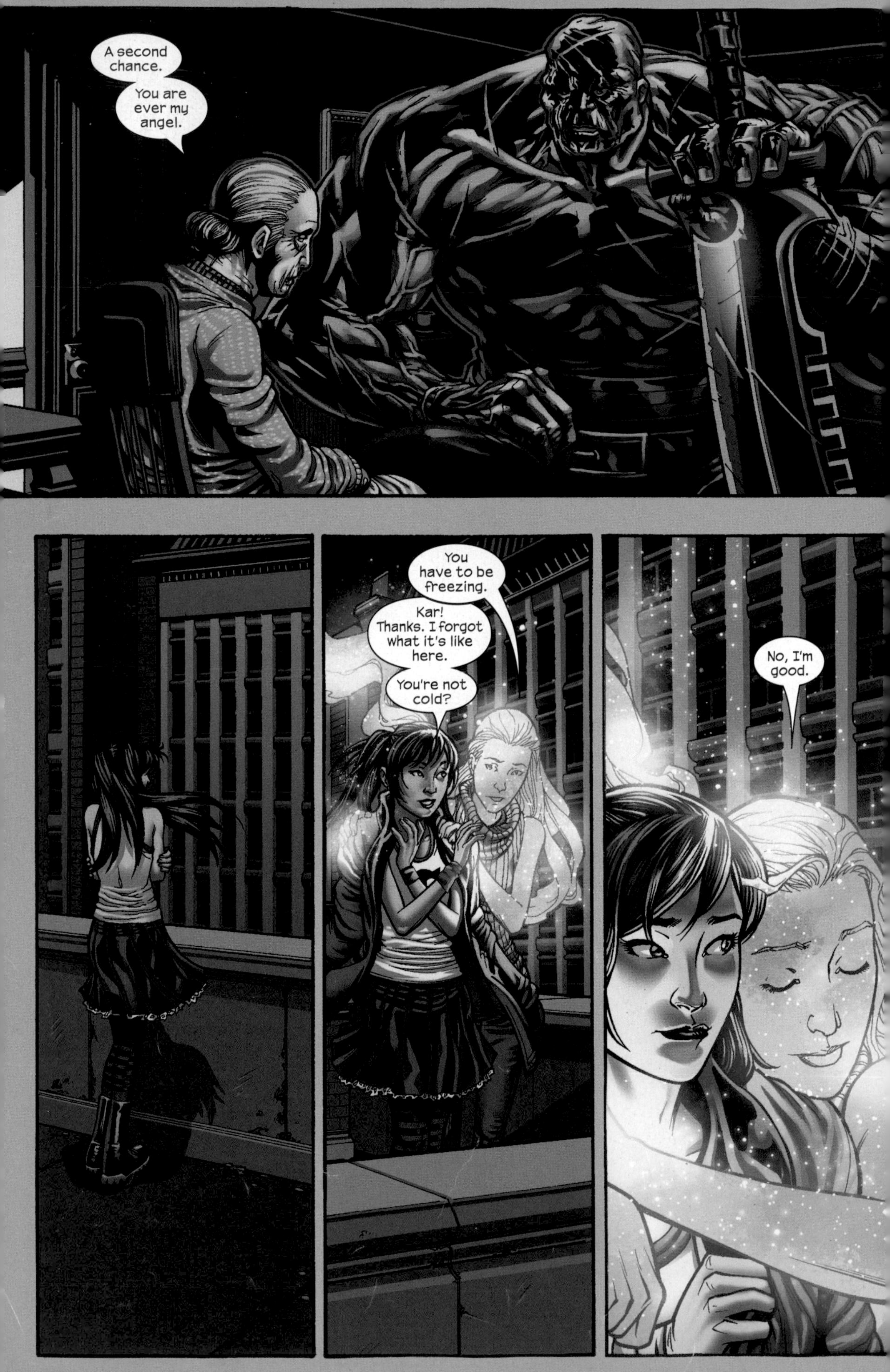
A second chance.
You are ever my angel.
You have to be freezing.
Kar! Thanks. I forgot what it's like here.
You're not cold?
No, I'm good.

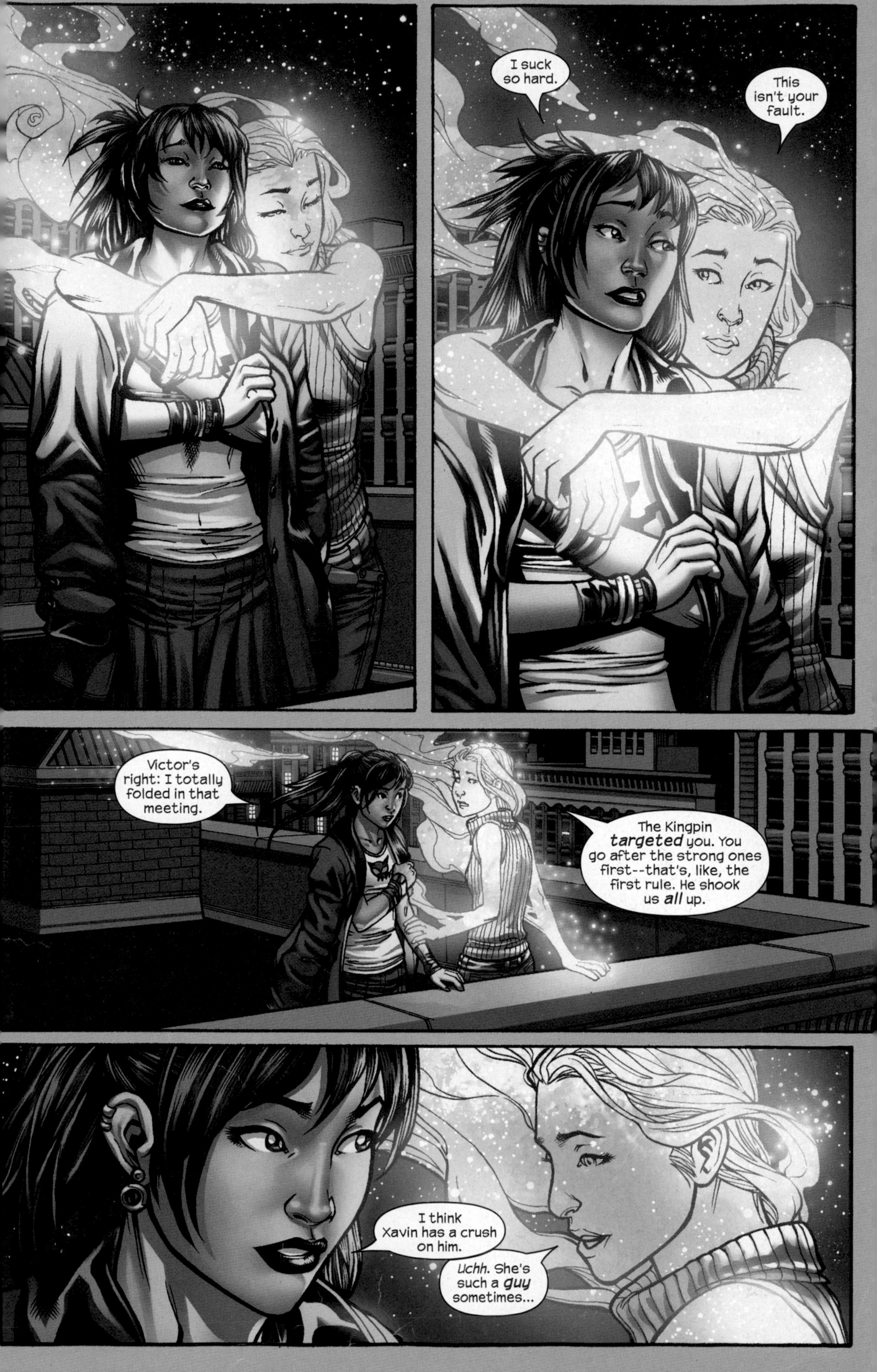
I suck so hard.
This isn't your fault.
Victor's right: I totally folded in that meeting.
The Kingpin *targeted* you. You go after the strong ones first--that's, like, the first rule. He shook us *all* up.
I think Xavin has a crush on him.
Uchh. She's such a *guy* sometimes...

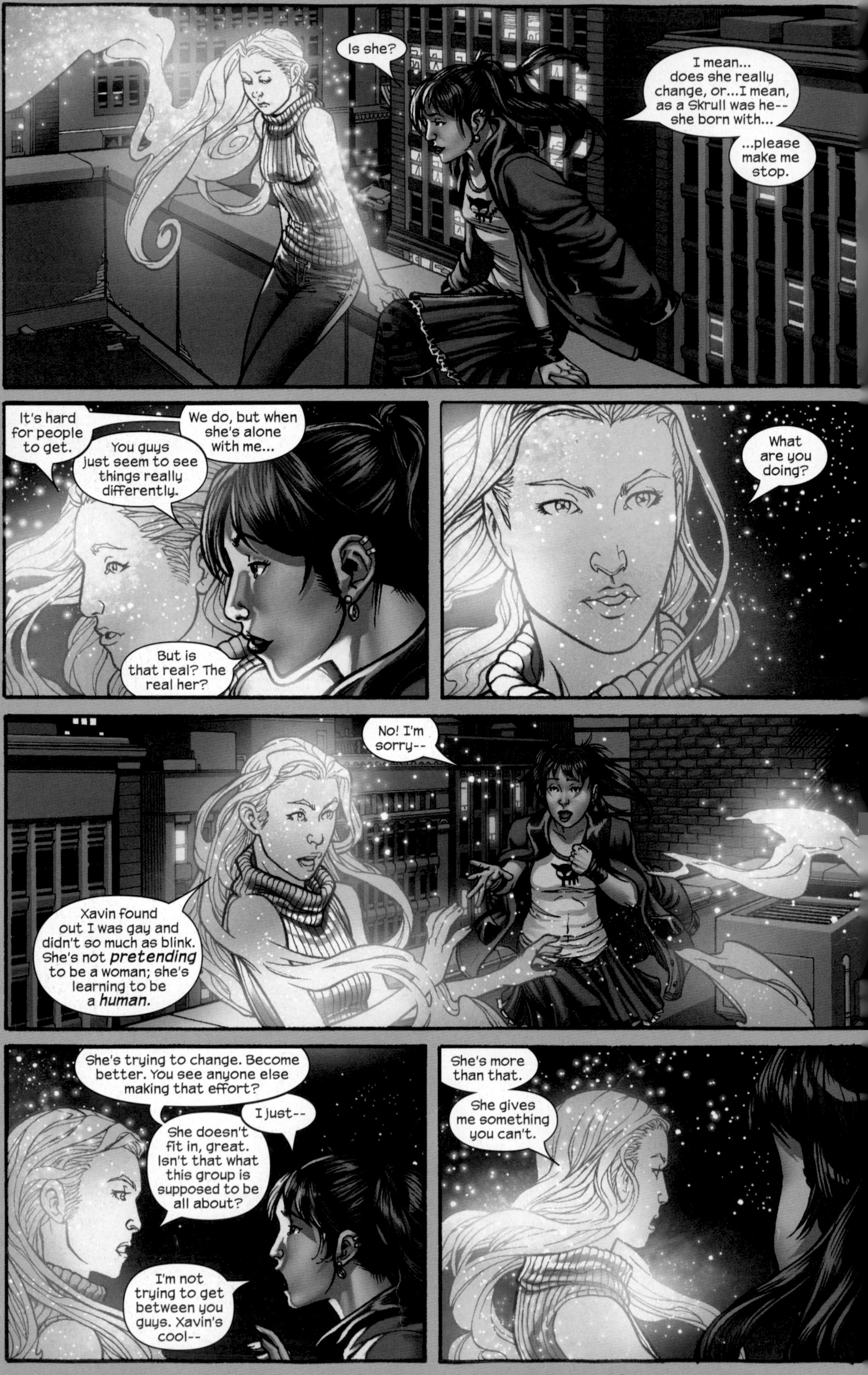
Is she?
I mean... does she really change, or...I mean, as a Skrull was he--she born with...
...please make me stop.
It's hard for people to get.
We do, but when she's alone with me...
You guys just seem to see things really differently.
But is that real? The real her?
What are you doing?
No! I'm sorry--
Xavin found out I was gay and didn't so much as blink. She's not *pretending* to be a woman; she's learning to be a ***human.***
She's trying to change. Become better. You see anyone else making that effort?
I just--
She doesn't fit in, great. Isn't that what this group is supposed to be all about?
I'm not trying to get between you guys. Xavin's cool--
She's more than that.
She gives me something you can't.

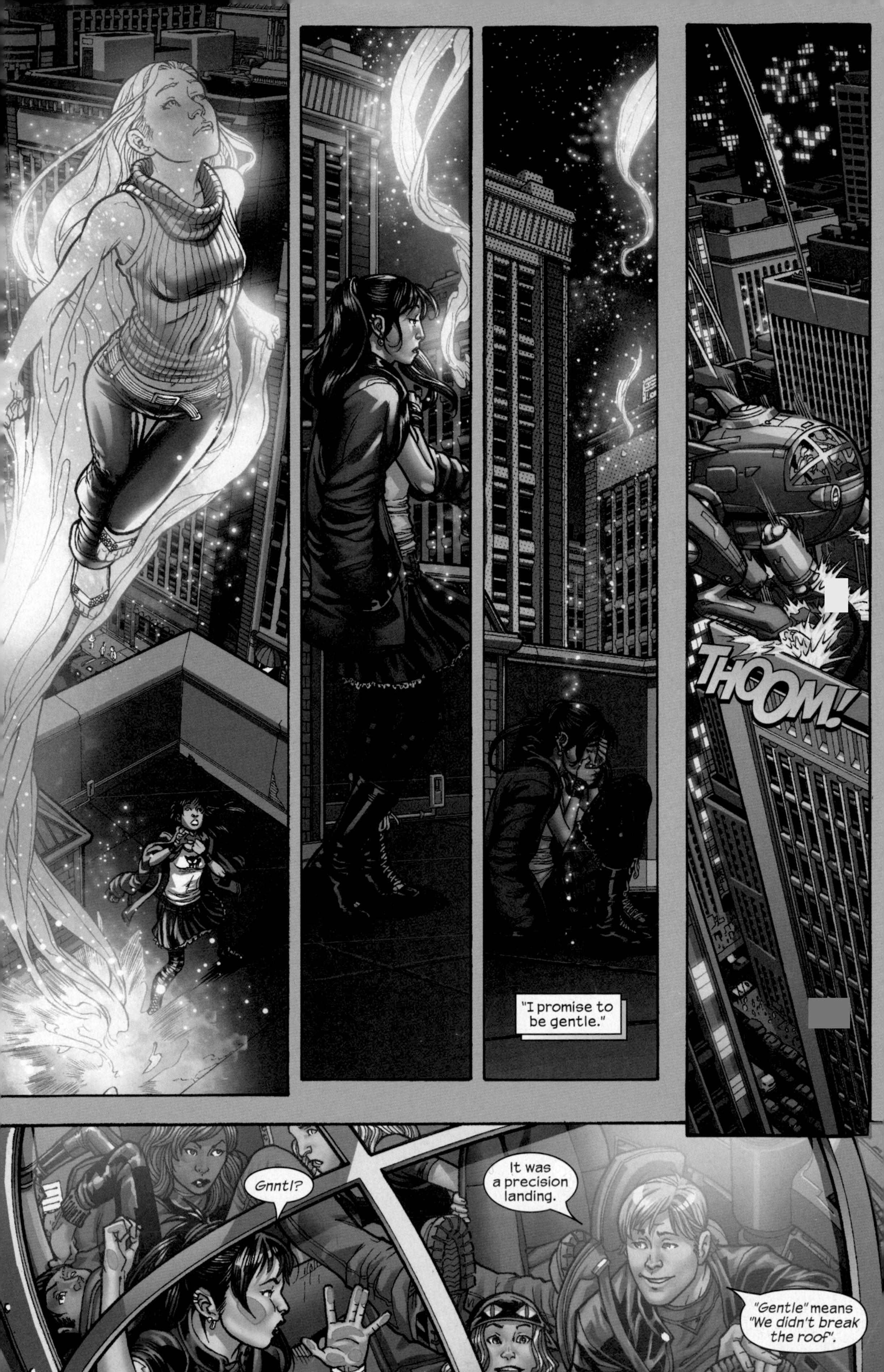
"I promise to be gentle."
THOOM!
Gnntl!?
It was a precision landing.
"Gentle" means "We didn't break the roof".

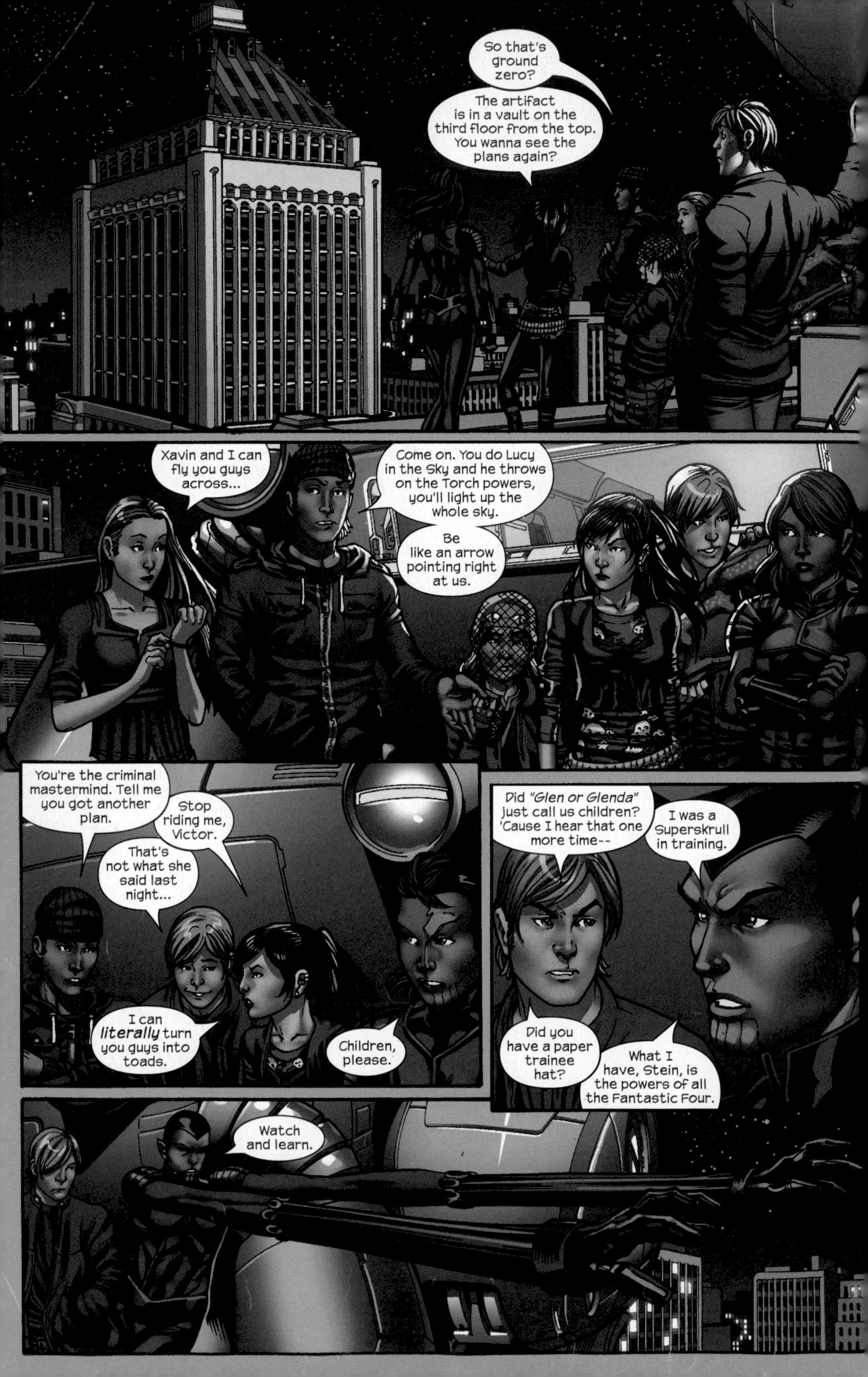

So that's ground zero?
The artifact is in a vault on the third floor from the top. You wanna see the plans again?
Xavin and I can fly you guys across...
Come on. You do Lucy in the Sky and he throws on the Torch powers, you'll light up the whole sky.
Be like an arrow pointing right at us.
You're the criminal mastermind. Tell me you got another plan.
Stop riding me, Victor.
That's not what she said last night...
I can *literally* turn you guys into toads.
Children, please.
Did *"Glen or Glenda"* just call us children? 'Cause I hear that one more time--
I was a Superskrull in training.
Did you have a paper trainee hat?
What I have, Stein, is the powers of all the Fantastic Four.
Watch and learn.

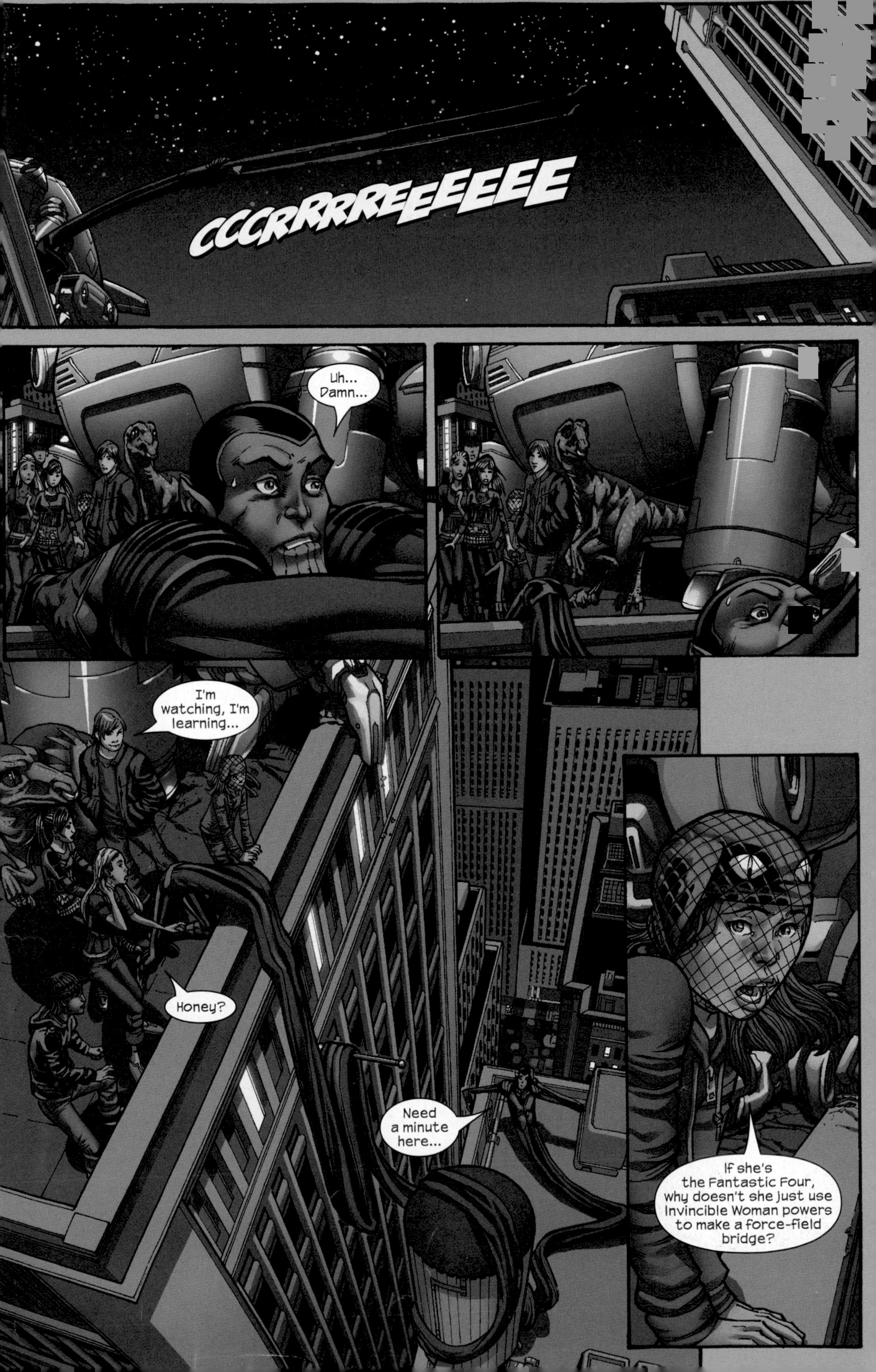
CCCRRRREEEEEE
Uh... Damn...
I'm watching, I'm learning...
Honey?
Need a minute here...
If she's the Fantastic Four, why doesn't she just use Invincible Woman powers to make a force-field bridge?

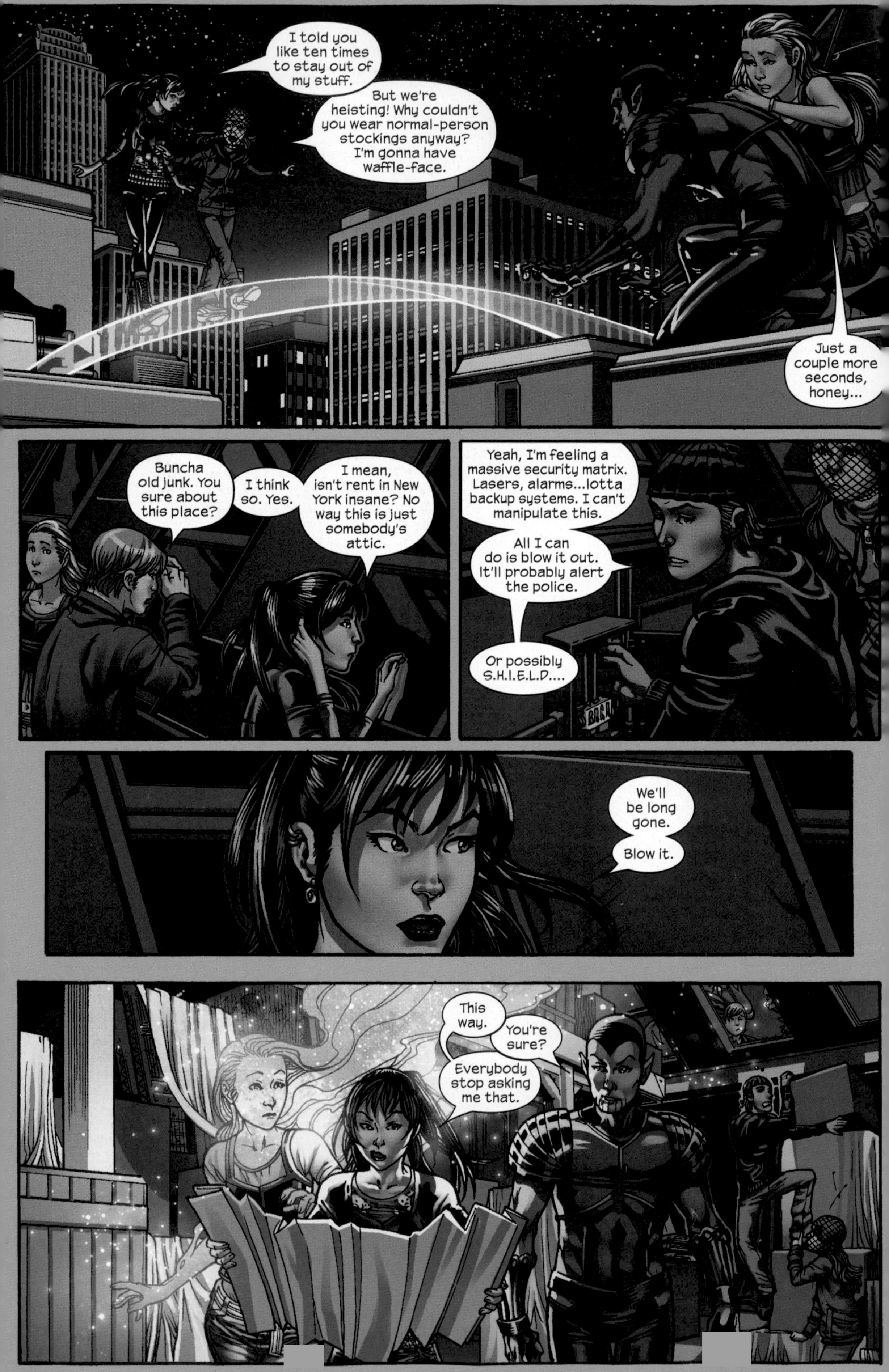
I told you like ten times to stay out of my stuff.
But we're heisting! Why couldn't you wear normal-person stockings anyway? I'm gonna have waffle-face.
Just a couple more seconds, honey...
Buncha old junk. You sure about this place?
I think so. Yes.
I mean, isn't rent in New York insane? No way this is just somebody's attic.
Yeah, I'm feeling a massive security matrix. Lasers, alarms...lotta backup systems. I can't manipulate this.
All I can do is blow it out. It'll probably alert the police.
Or possibly S.H.I.E.L.D....
We'll be long gone.
Blow it.
This way.
You're sure?
Everybody stop asking me that.

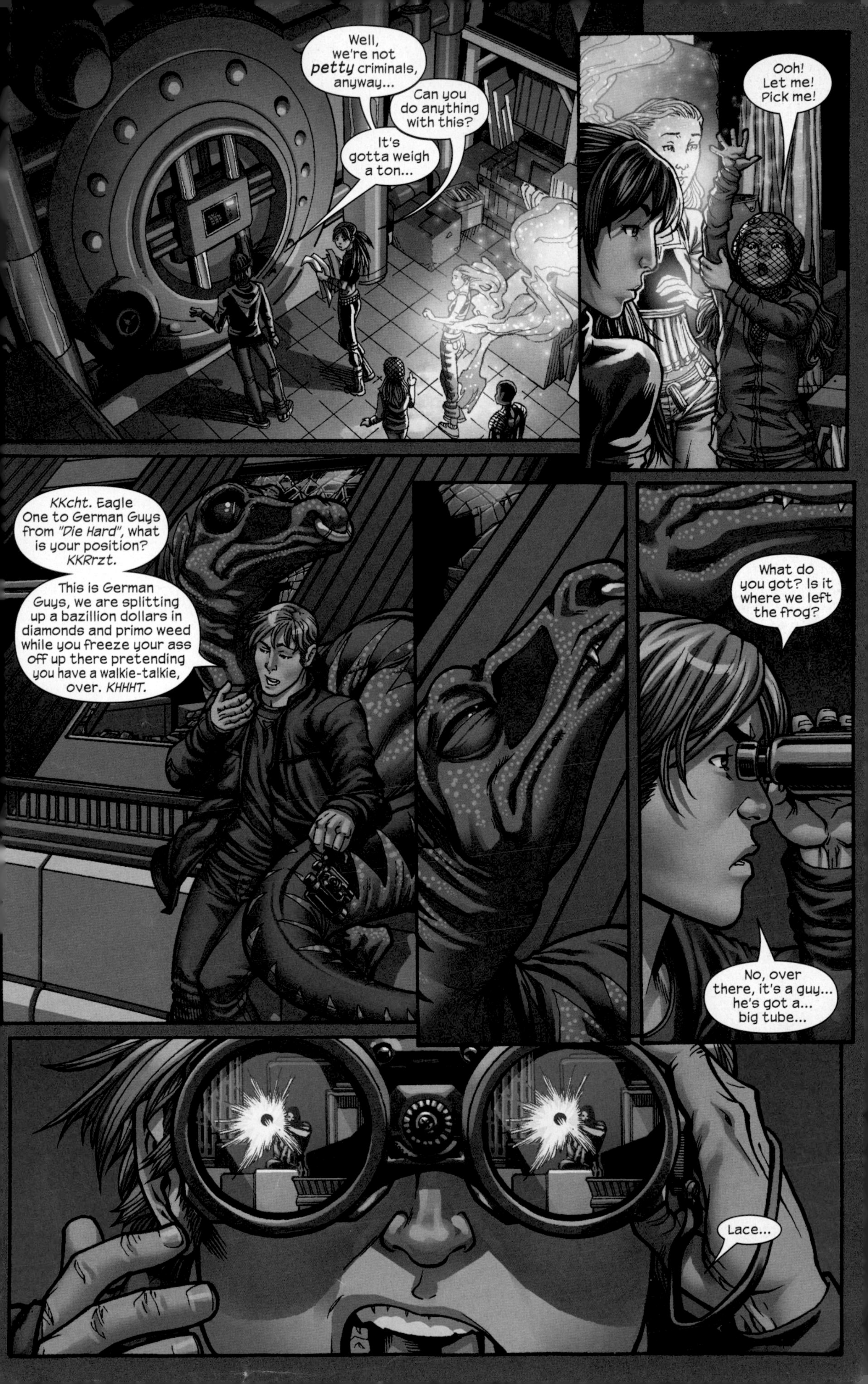
Well, we're not *petty* criminals, anyway...
Can you do anything with this?
It's gotta weigh a ton...
Ooh! Let me! Pick me!
KKcht. Eagle One to German Guys from *"Die Hard"*, what is your position? *KKRrzt.*
This is German Guys, we are splitting up a bazillion dollars in diamonds and primo weed while you freeze your ass off up there pretending you have a walkie-talkie, over. *KHHHT.*
What do you got? Is it where we left the frog?
No, over there, it's a guy... he's got a... big tube...
Lace...

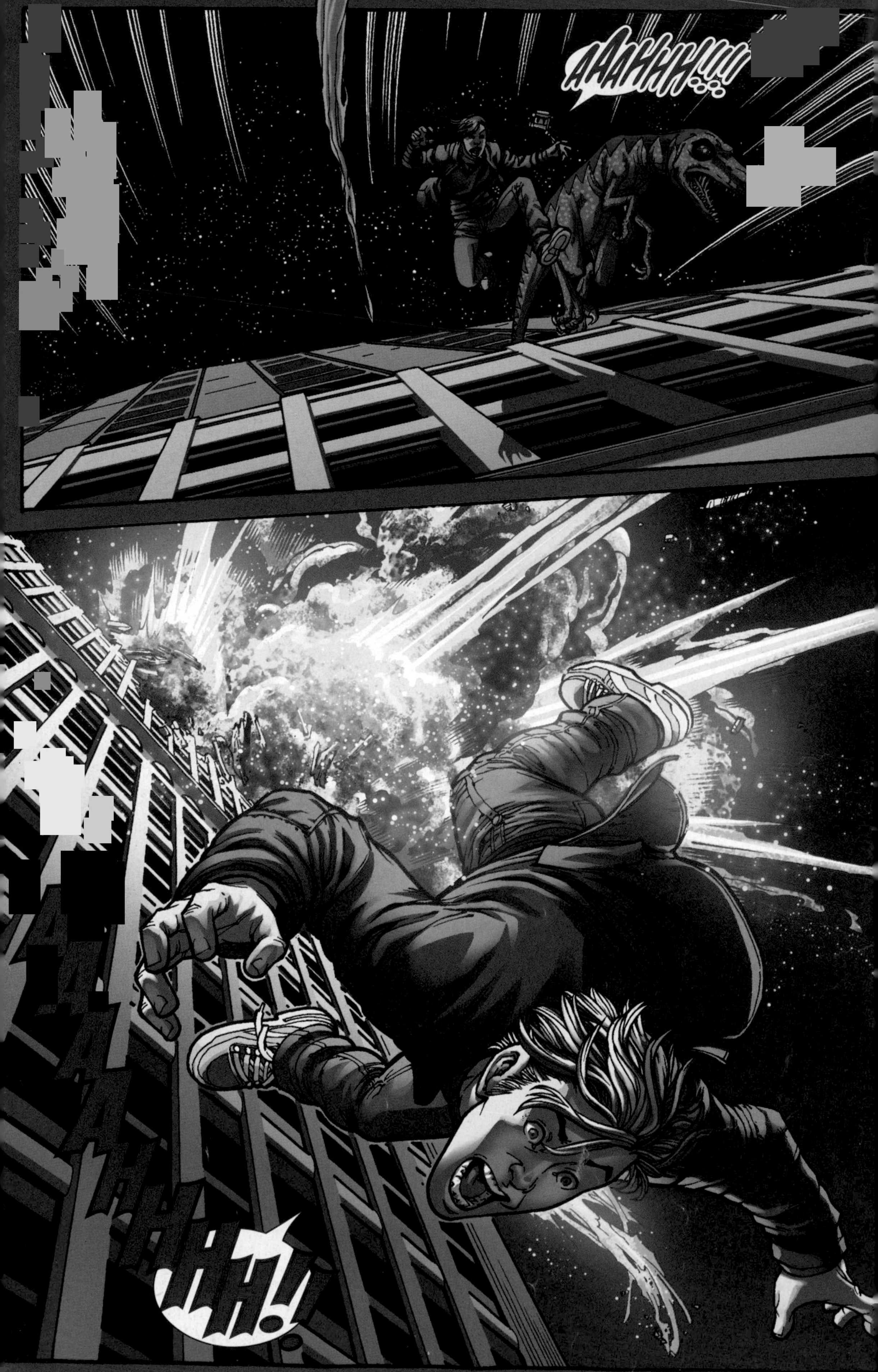
AAAHHH!!!
[redacted]AAAAHHHH!

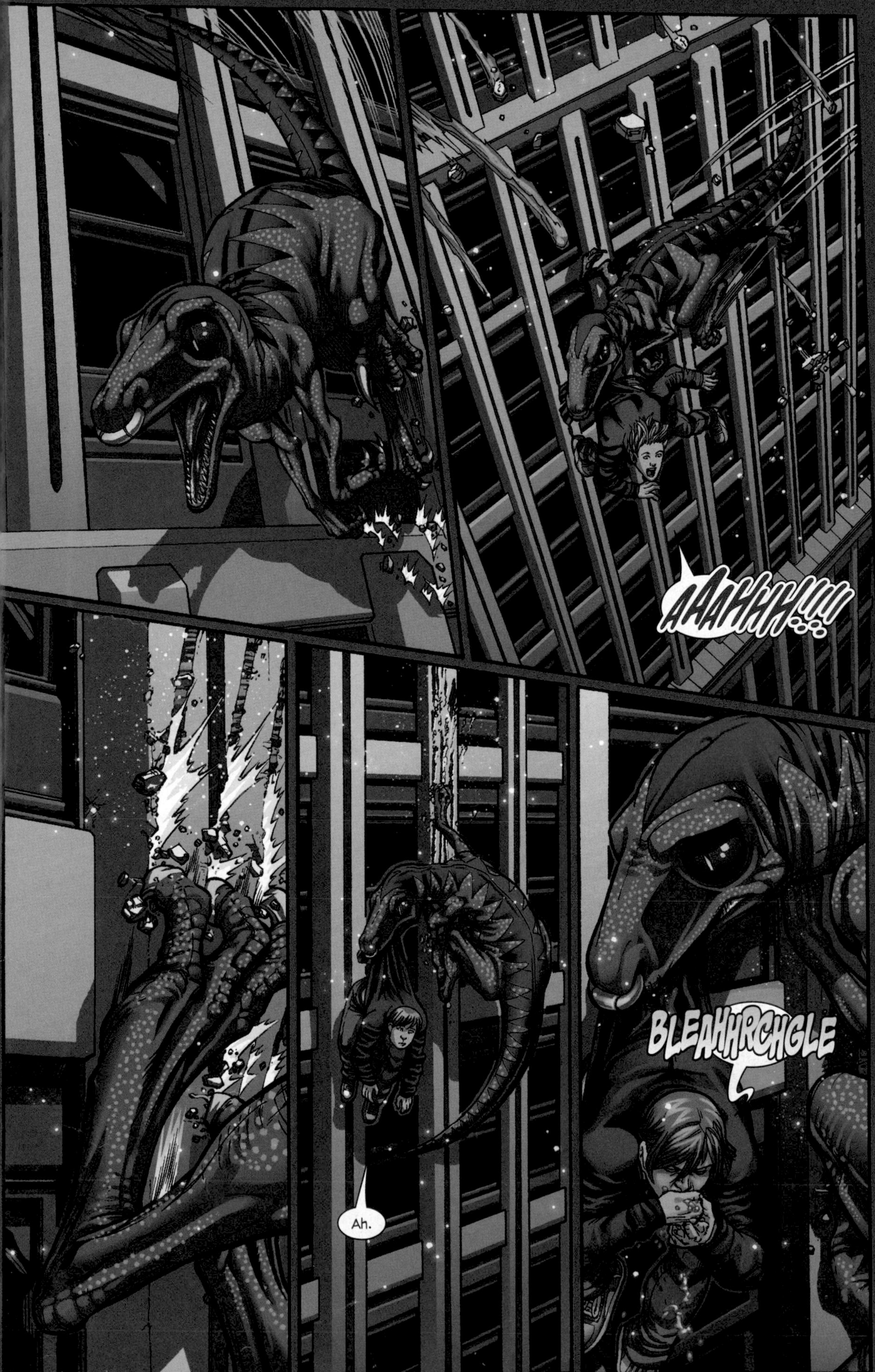
AAAHHH!!!!
Ah.
BLEAHHRCHGLE

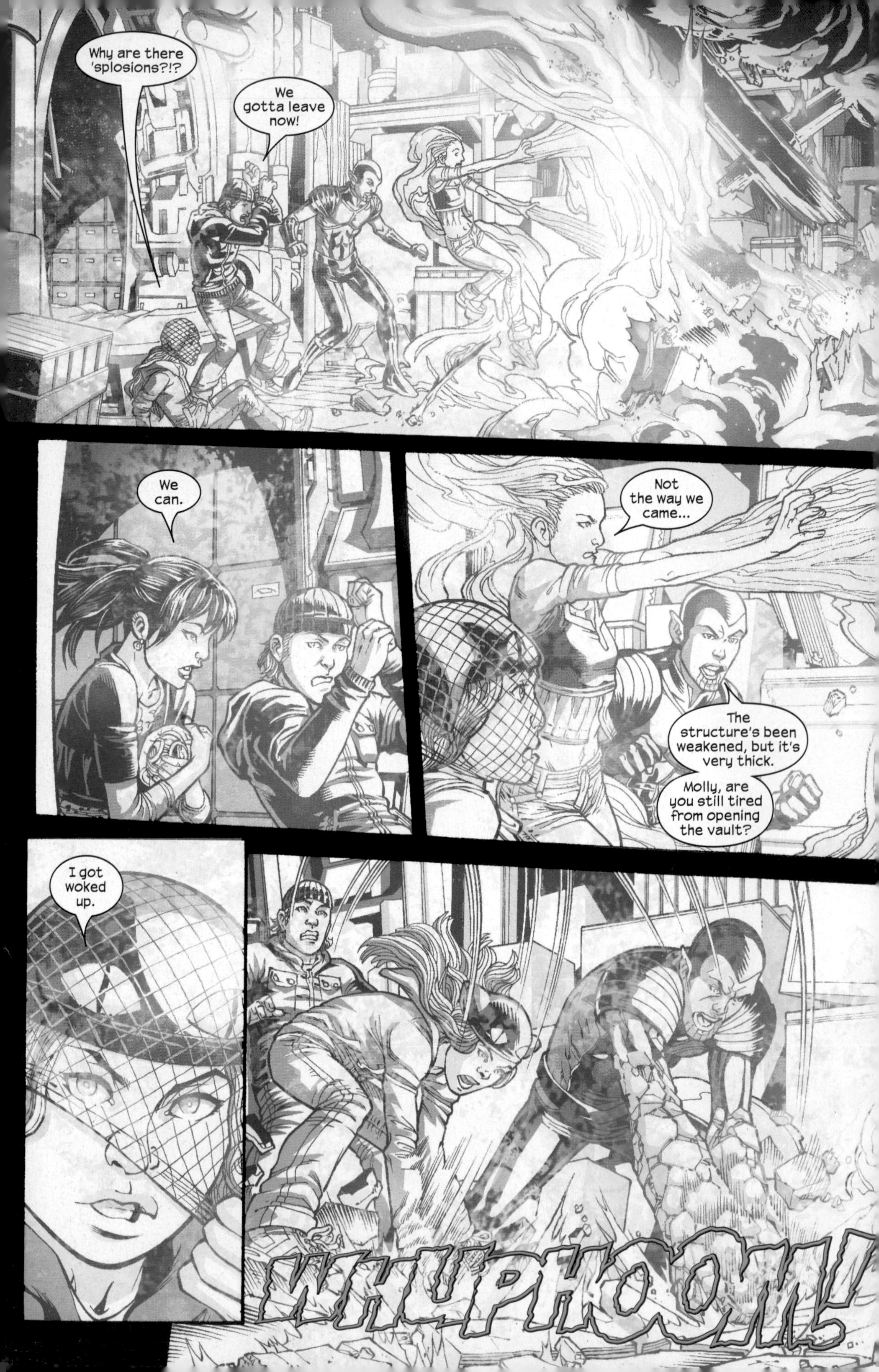
Why are there 'splosions?!?
We gotta leave now!
We can.
Not the way we came...
The structure's been weakened, but it's very thick.
Molly, are you still tired from opening the vault?
I got woked up.
WHUPHOOM!

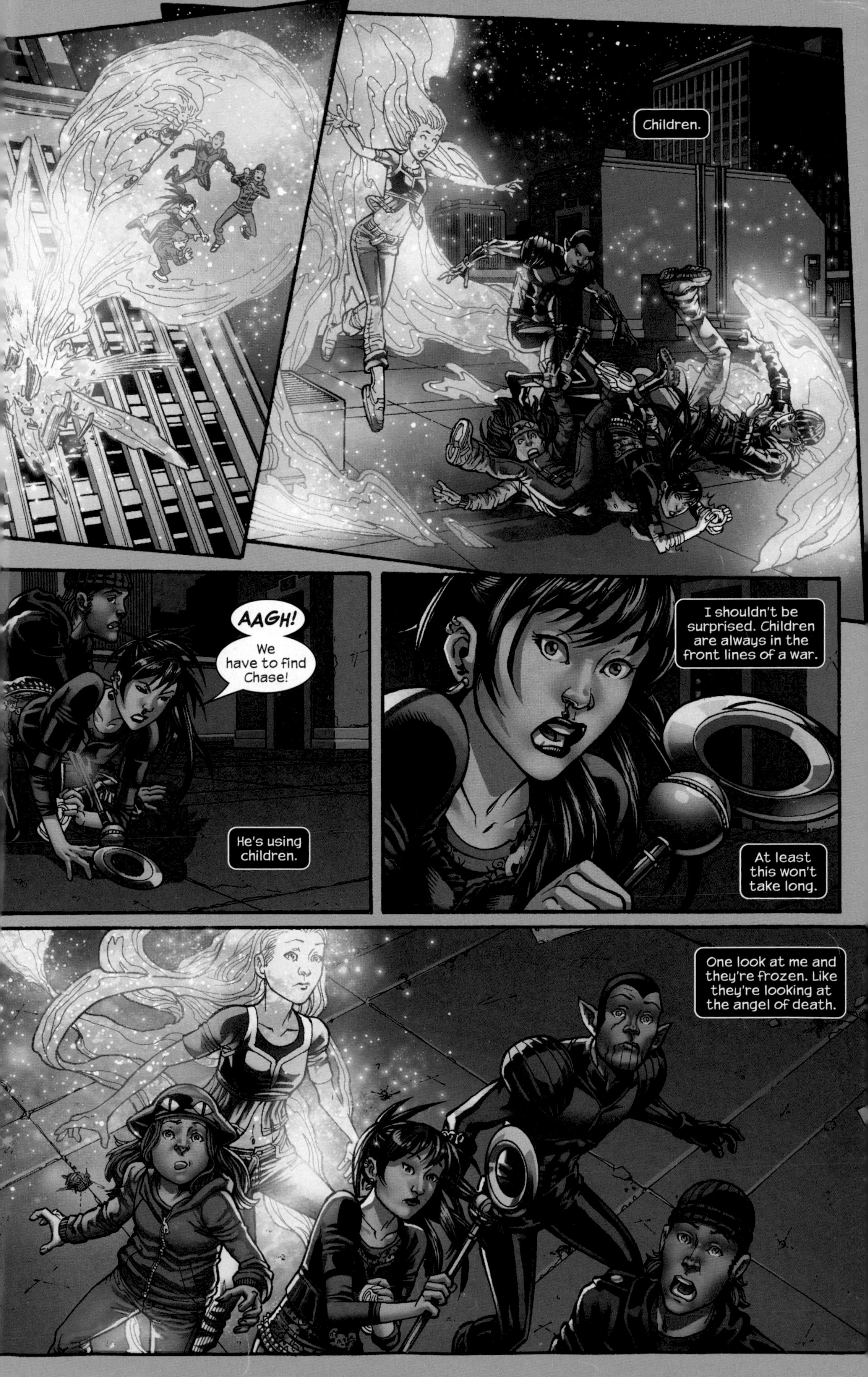
Children.
AAGH!
We have to find Chase!
He's using children.
I shouldn't be surprised. Children are always in the front lines of a war.
At least this won't take long.
One look at me and they're frozen. Like they're looking at the angel of death.

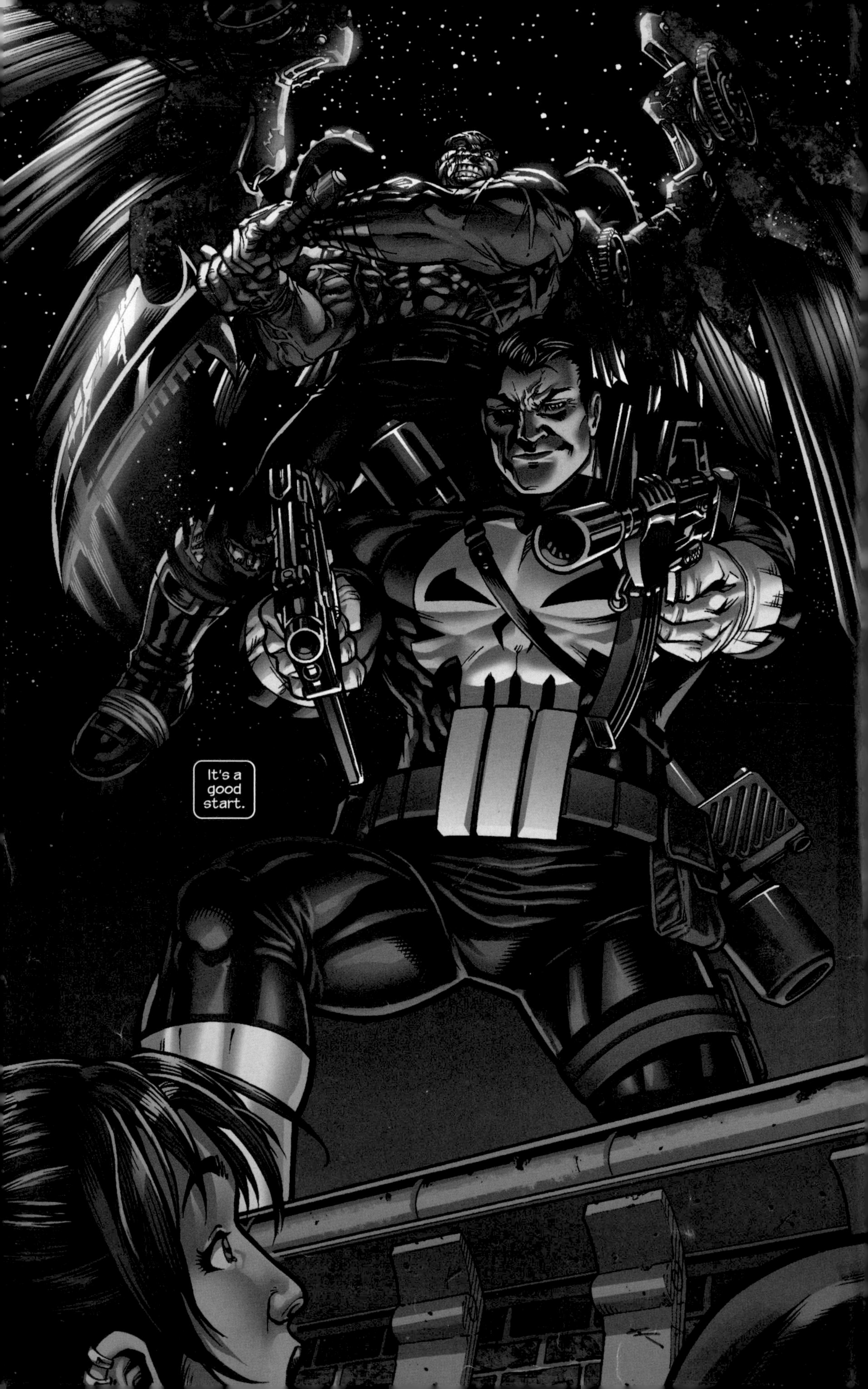
It's a good start.

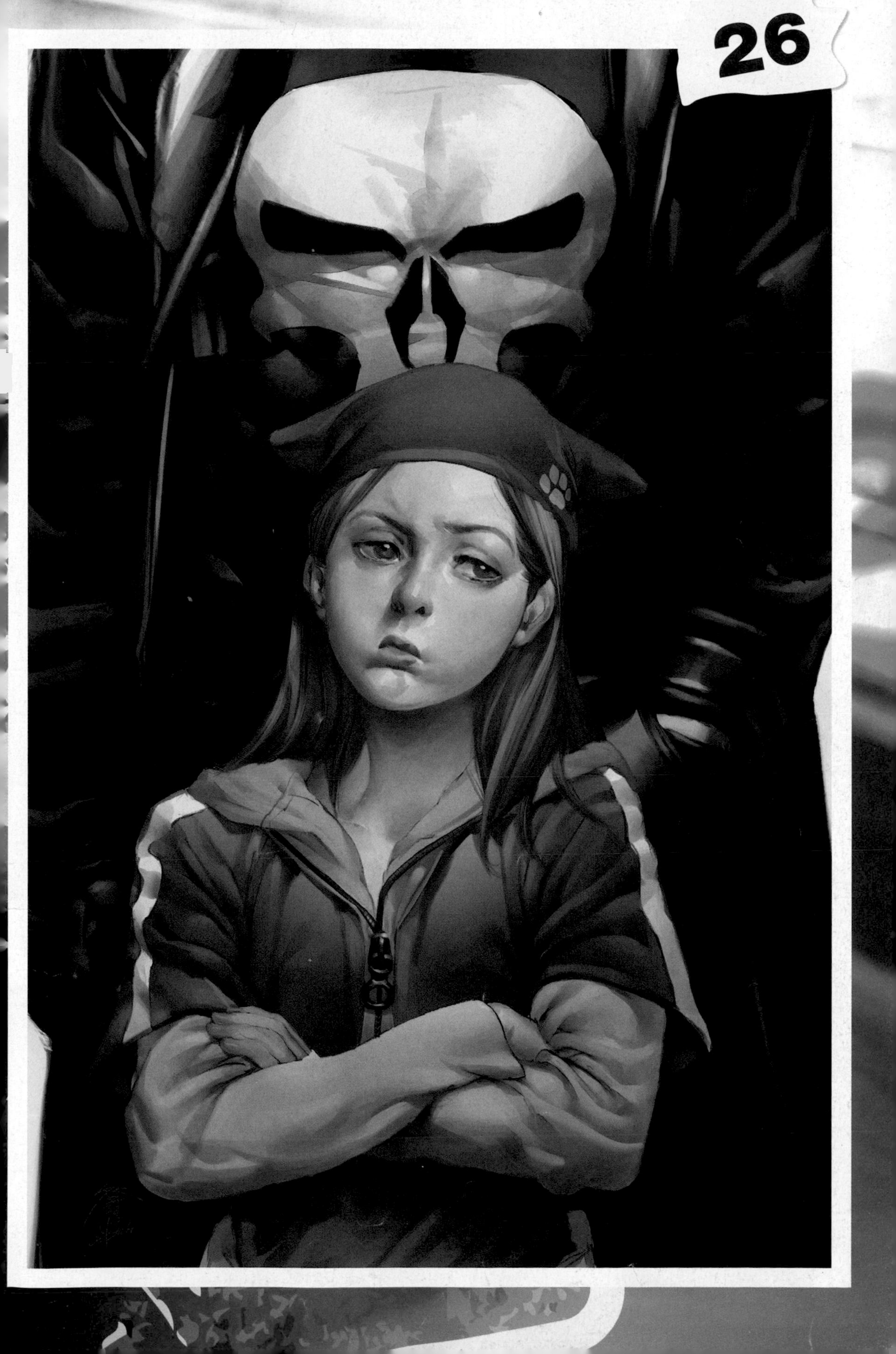
26

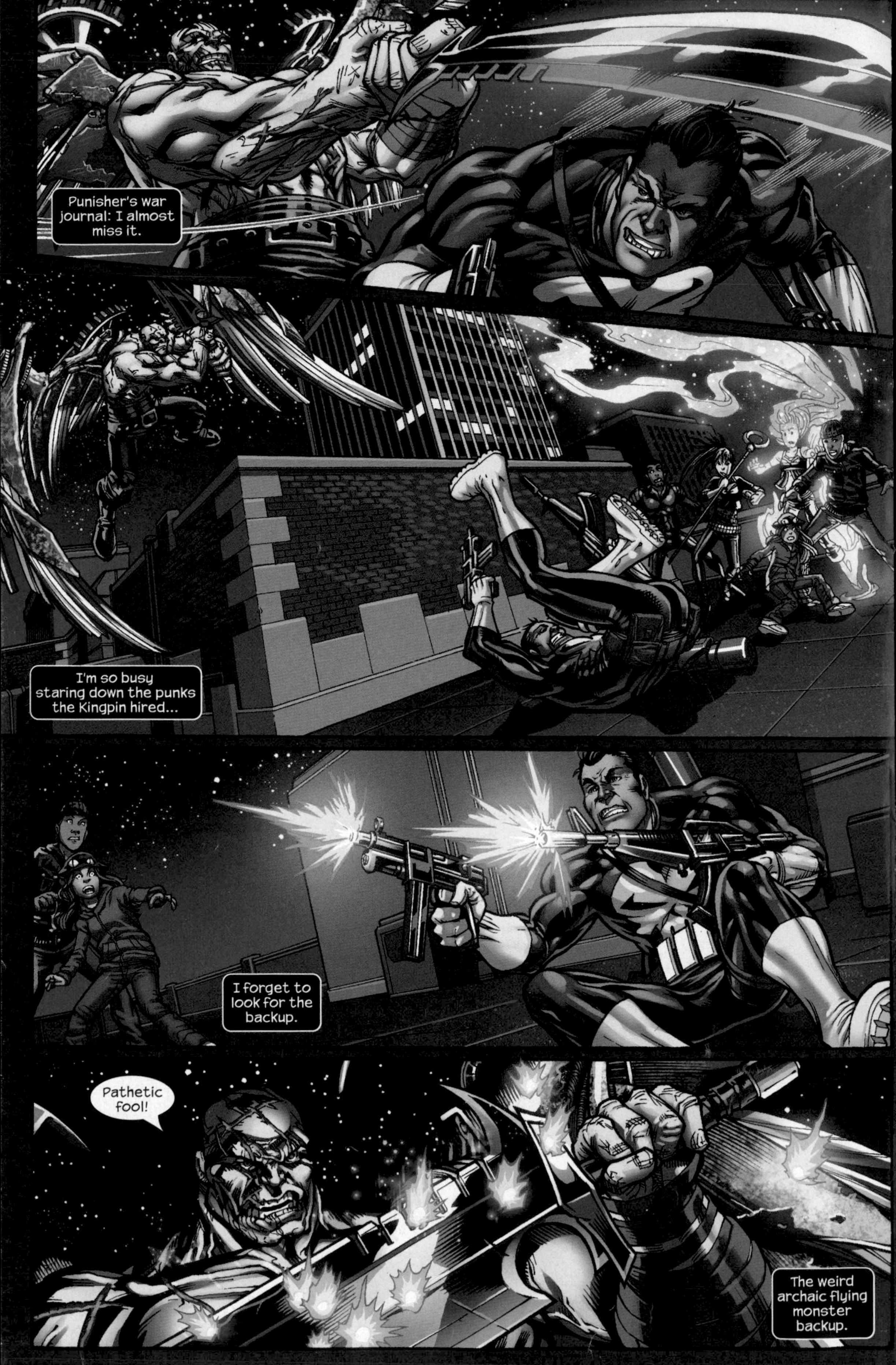
Punisher's war journal: I almost miss it.
I'm so busy staring down the punks the Kingpin hired...
I forget to look for the backup.
Pathetic fool!
The weird archaic flying monster backup.

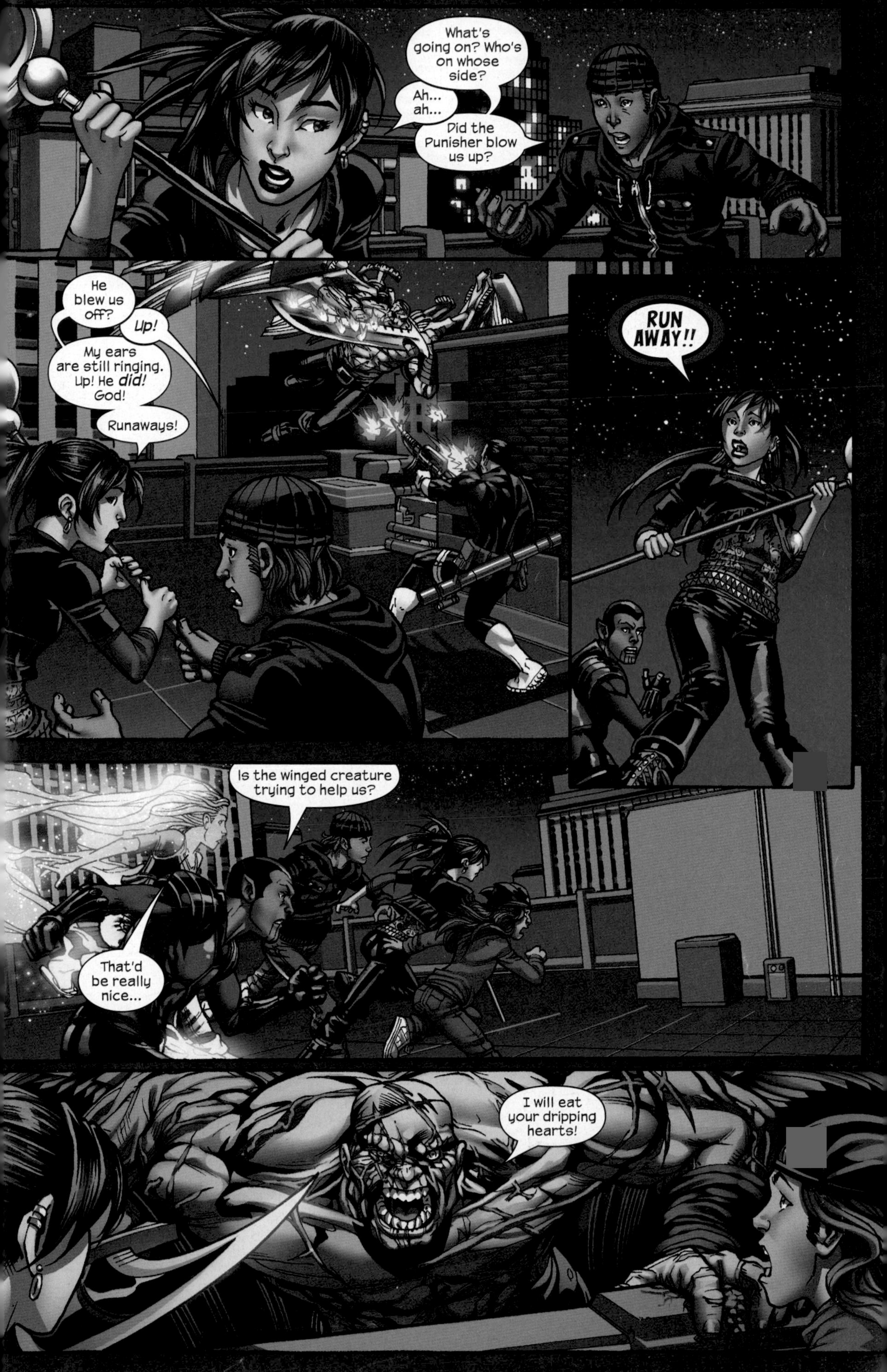
What's going on? Who's on whose side?
Ah... ah...
Did the Punisher blow us up?
He blew us off?
Up!
My ears are still ringing. Up! He *did!* God!
Runaways!
RUN AWAY!!
Is the winged creature trying to help us?
That'd be really nice...
I will eat your dripping hearts!

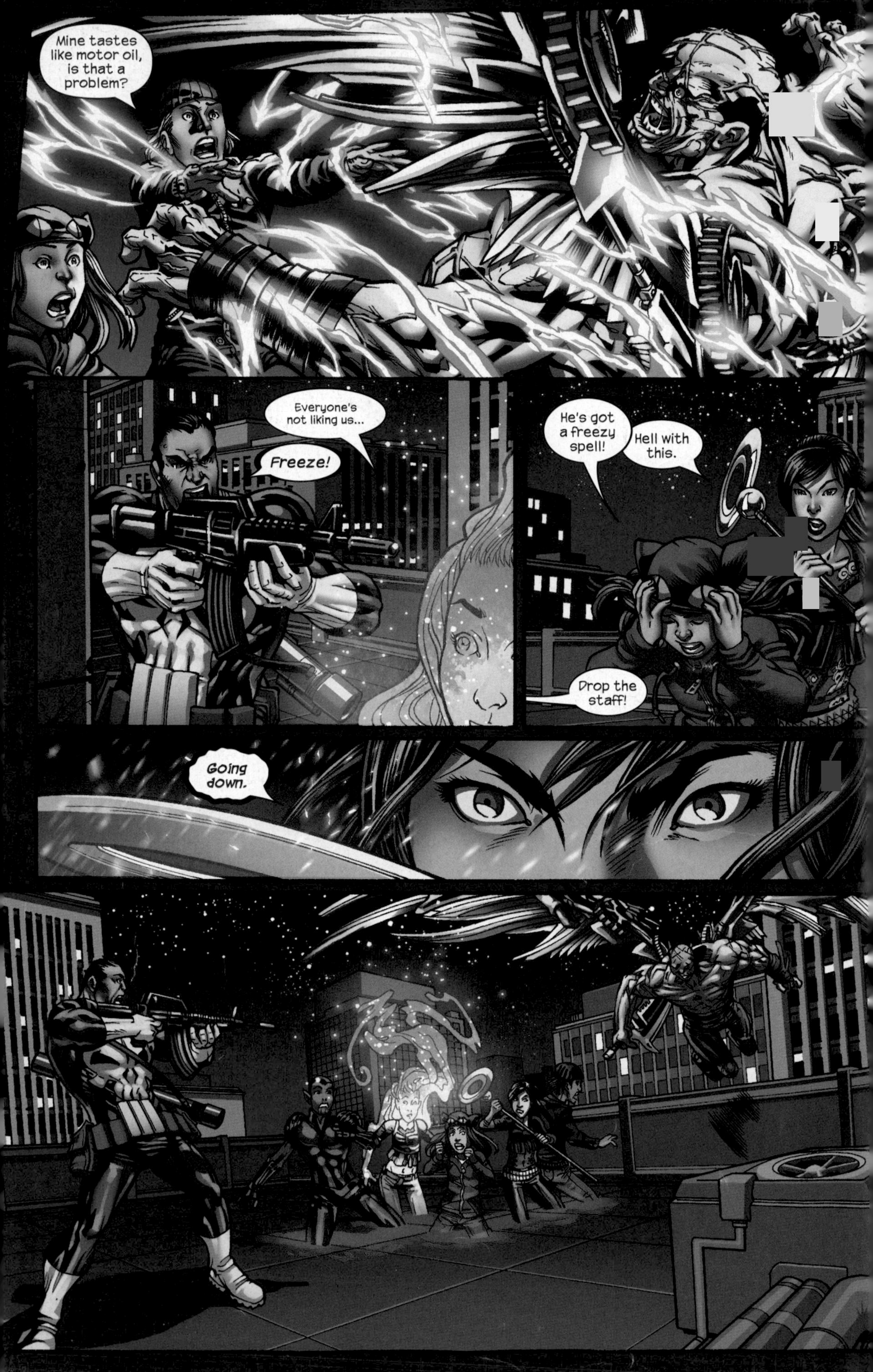
Mine tastes like motor oil, is that a problem?
Everyone's not liking us...
Freeze!
He's got a freezy spell!
Hell with this.
Drop the staff!
Going down.

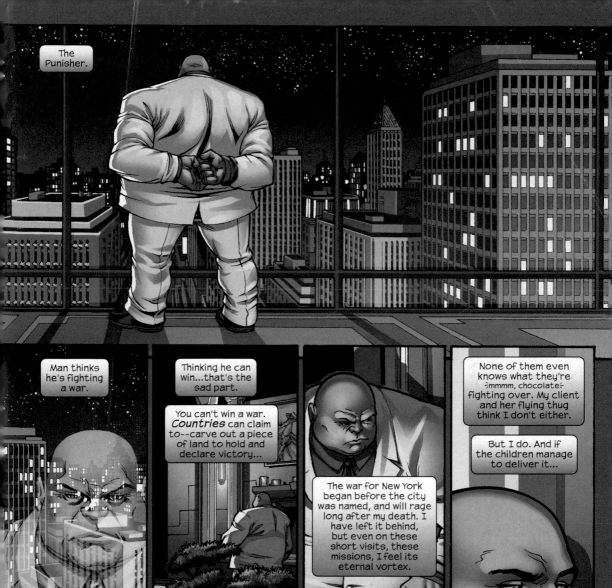

The Punisher.

Man thinks he's fighting a war.

Which is the only thing about him I admire.

Thinking he can win...that's the sad part.

You can't win a war. *Countries* can claim to--carve out a piece of land to hold and declare victory...

But no *man* wins.

The best he can do is thrive.

The war for New York began before the city was named, and will rage long after my death. I have left it behind, but even on these short visits, these missions, I feel its eternal vortex.

Castle lacks that perspective. He's as myopic and impulsive as...as those children.

None of them even knows what they're ⌇mmmm, chocolate⌇ fighting over. My client and her flying thug think I don't either.

But I do. And if the children manage to deliver it...

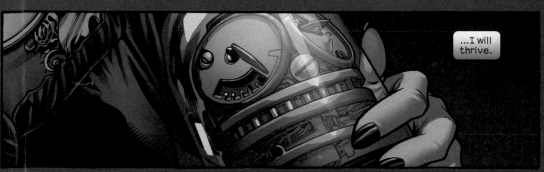

...I will thrive.

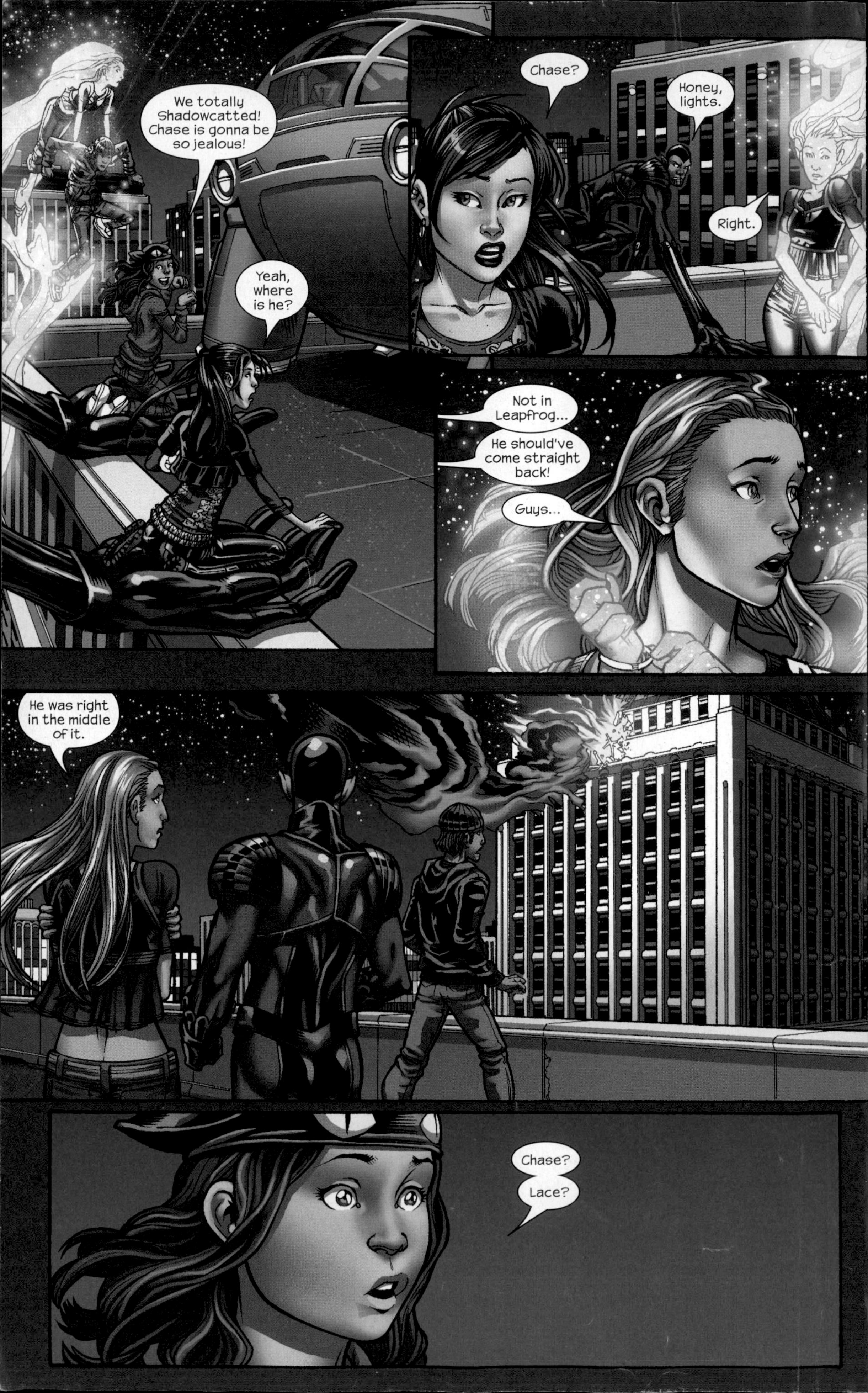
We totally Shadowcatted! Chase is gonna be so jealous!
Yeah, where is he?
Chase?
Honey, lights.
Right.
Not in Leapfrog...
He should've come straight back!
Guys...
He was right in the middle of it.
Chase?
Lace?

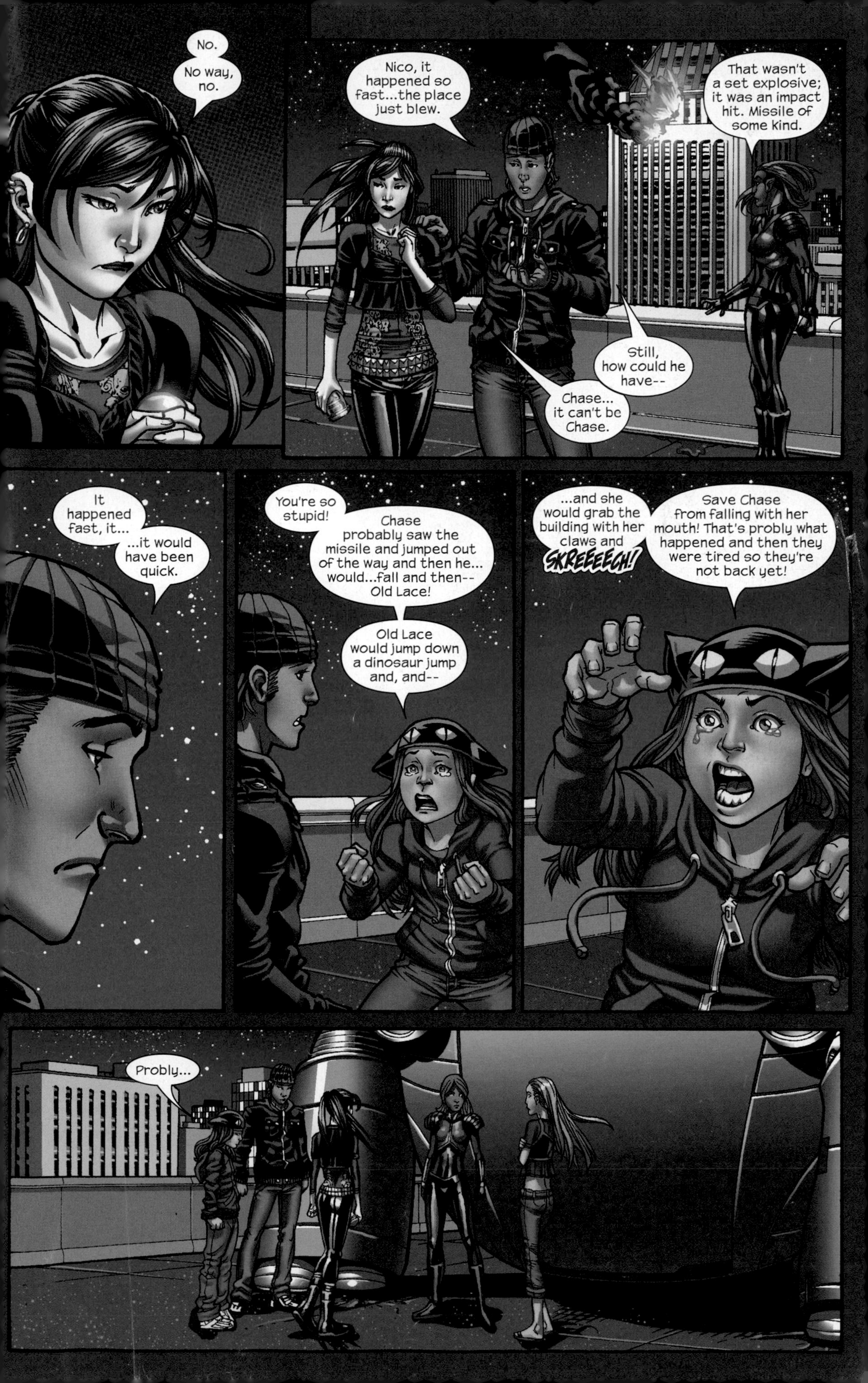
No.
No way, no.
Nico, it happened so fast...the place just blew.
That wasn't a set explosive; it was an impact hit. Missile of some kind.
Still, how could he have--
Chase... it can't be Chase.
It happened fast, it...
...it would have been quick.
You're so stupid!
Chase probably saw the missile and jumped out of the way and then he... would...fall and then-- Old Lace!
Old Lace would jump down a dinosaur jump and, and--
...and she would grab the building with her claws and SKREEEECH!
Save Chase from falling with her mouth! That's probly what happened and then they were tired so they're not back yet!
Probly...

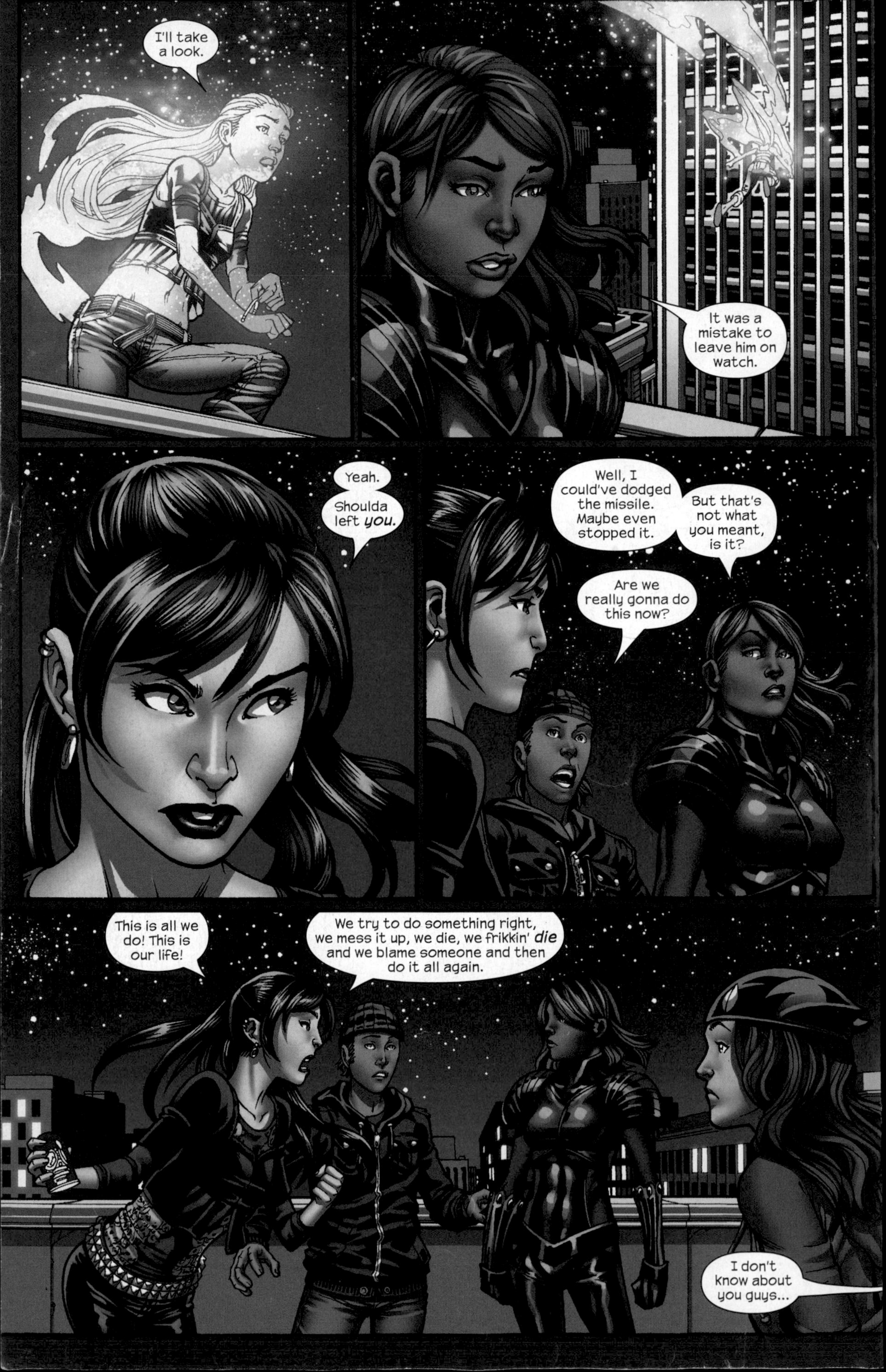
I'll take a look.
It was a mistake to leave him on watch.
Yeah. Shoulda left *you.*
Well, I could've dodged the missile. Maybe even stopped it.
But that's not what you meant, is it?
Are we really gonna do this now?
This is all we do! This is our life!
We try to do something right, we mess it up, we die, we frikkin' *die* and we blame someone and then do it all again.
I don't know about you guys...

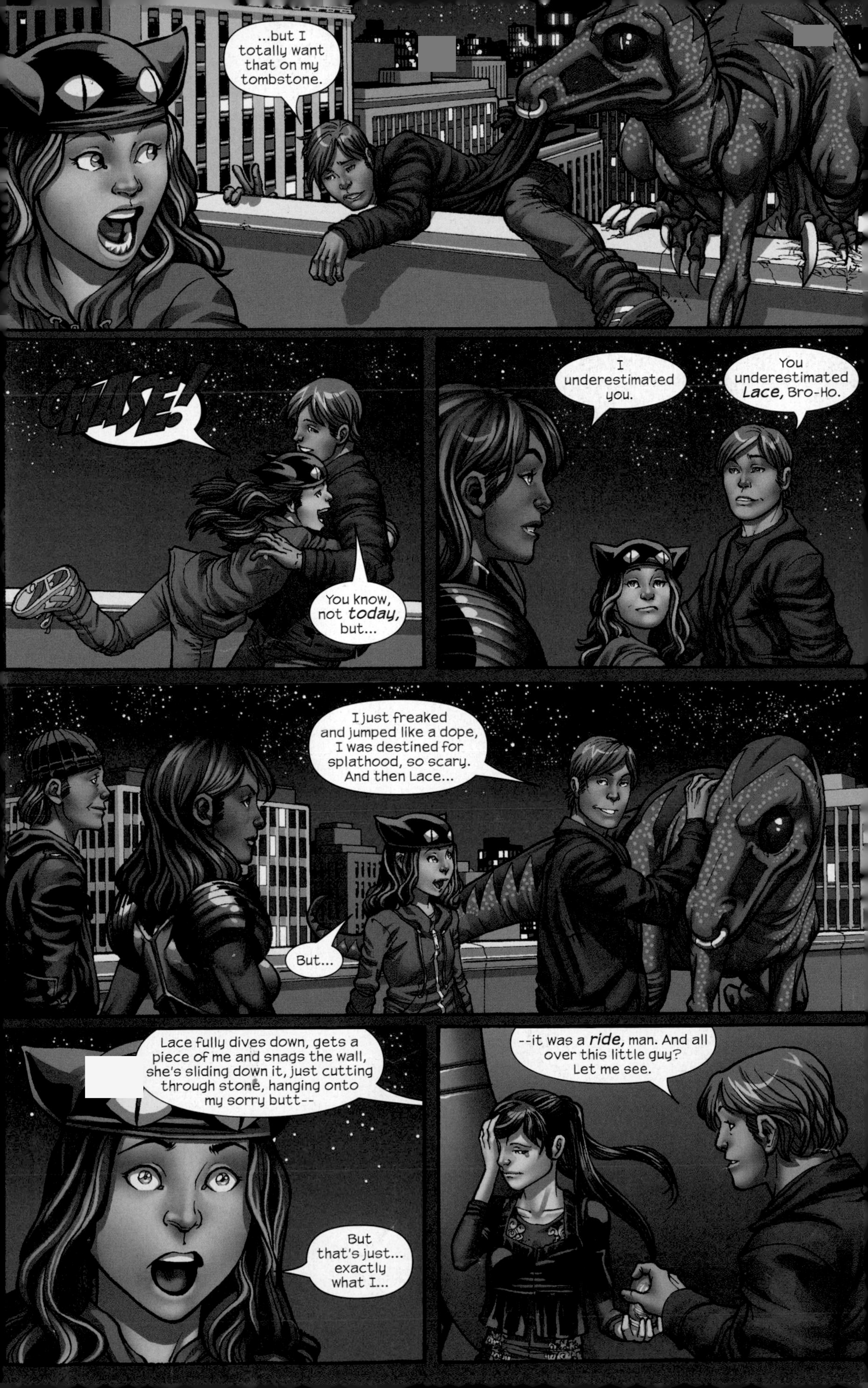
...but I totally want that on my tombstone.
CHASE!
You know, not *today,* but...
I underestimated you.
You underestimated *Lace,* Bro-Ho.
I just freaked and jumped like a dope, I was destined for splathood, so scary. And then Lace...
But...
Lace fully dives down, gets a piece of me and snags the wall, she's sliding down it, just cutting through stone, hanging onto my sorry butt--
But that's just... exactly what I...
--it was a *ride,* man. And all over this little guy? Let me see.

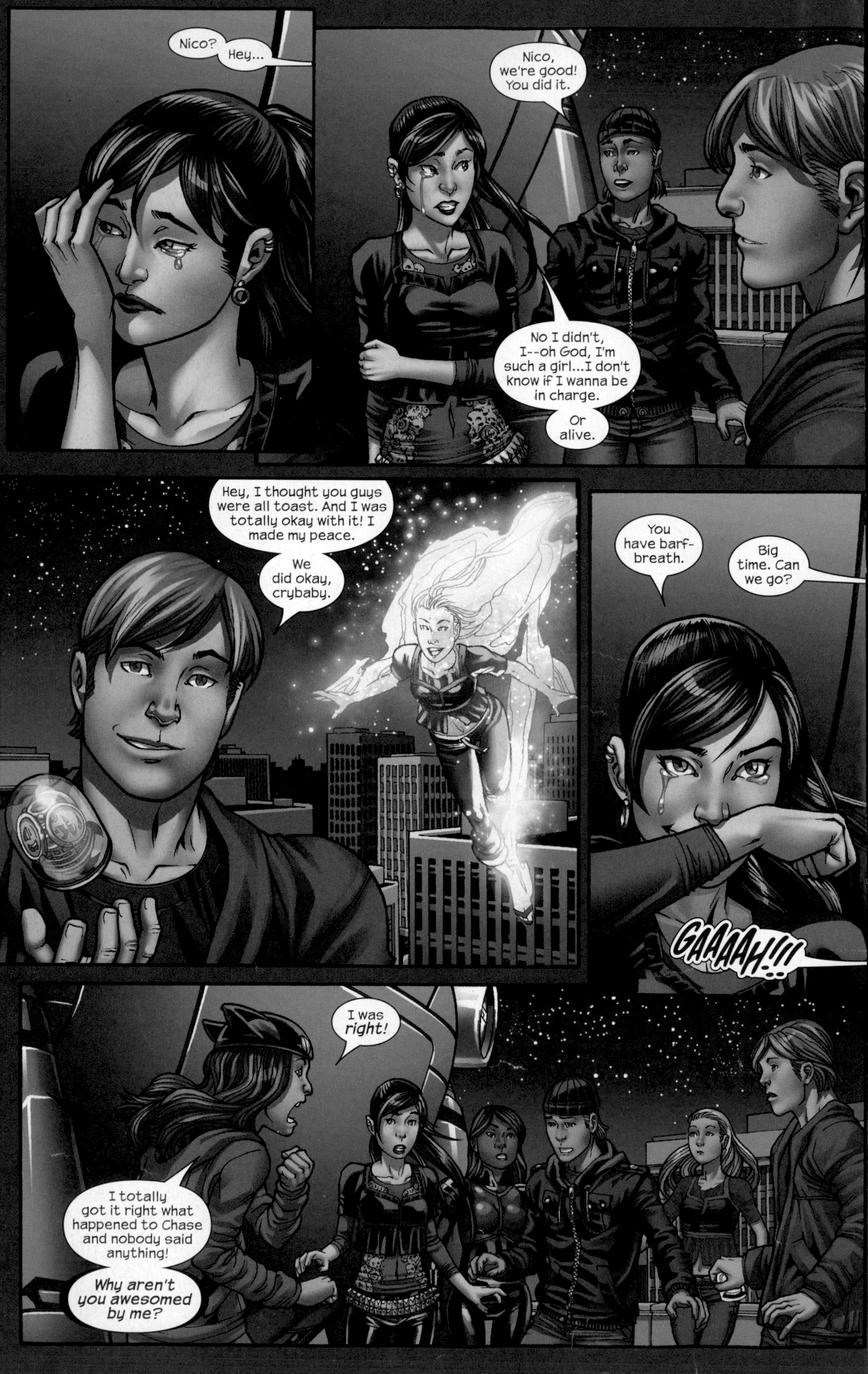
Nico?
Hey...
Nico, we're good! You did it.
No I didn't, I--oh God, I'm such a girl...I don't know if I wanna be in charge.
Or alive.
Hey, I thought you guys were all toast. And I was totally okay with it! I made my peace.
We did okay, crybaby.
You have barf-breath.
Big time. Can we go?
GAAAAH!!!
I was *right!*
I totally got it right what happened to Chase and nobody said anything!
Why aren't you awesomed by me?

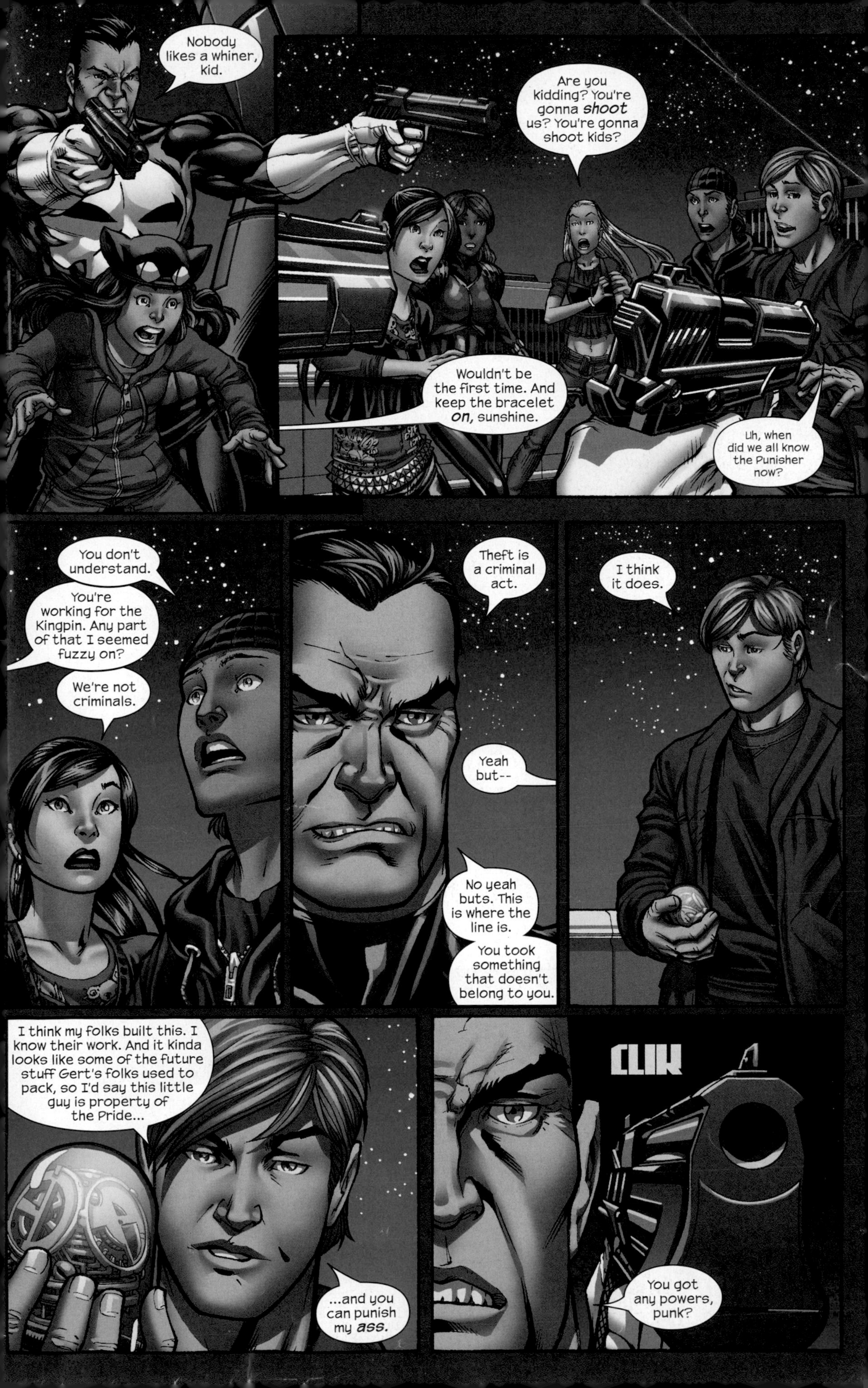
Nobody likes a whiner, kid.
Are you kidding? You're gonna shoot us? You're gonna shoot kids?
Wouldn't be the first time. And keep the bracelet on, sunshine.
Uh, when did we all know the Punisher now?
You don't understand.
You're working for the Kingpin. Any part of that I seemed fuzzy on?
We're not criminals.
Theft is a criminal act.
Yeah but--
No yeah buts. This is where the line is.
You took something that doesn't belong to you.
I think it does.
I think my folks built this. I know their work. And it kinda looks like some of the future stuff Gert's folks used to pack, so I'd say this little guy is property of the Pride...
...and you can punish my ass.
CLIK
You got any powers, punk?

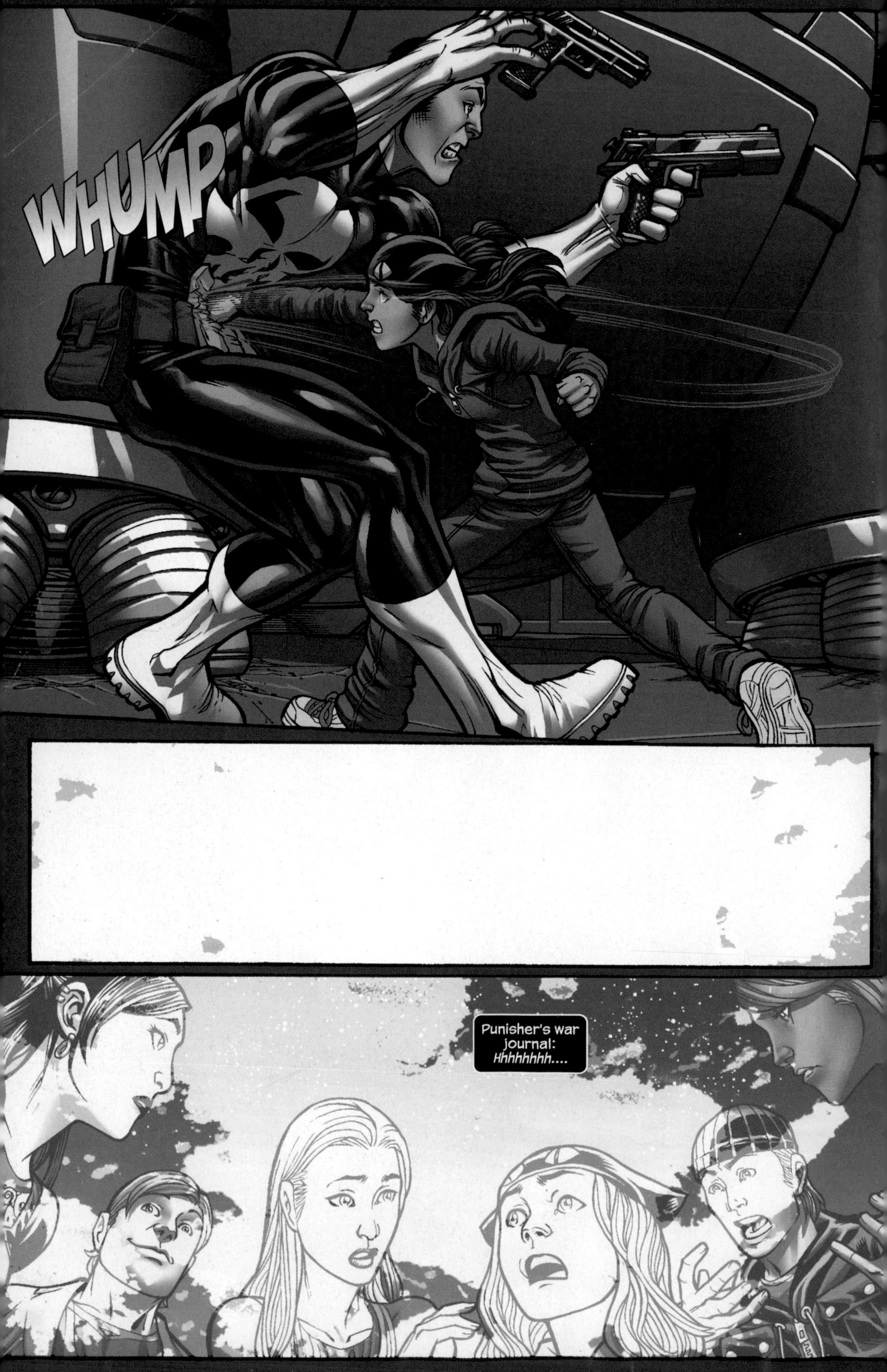
WHUMP
Punisher's war journal: *Hhhhhhhh....*

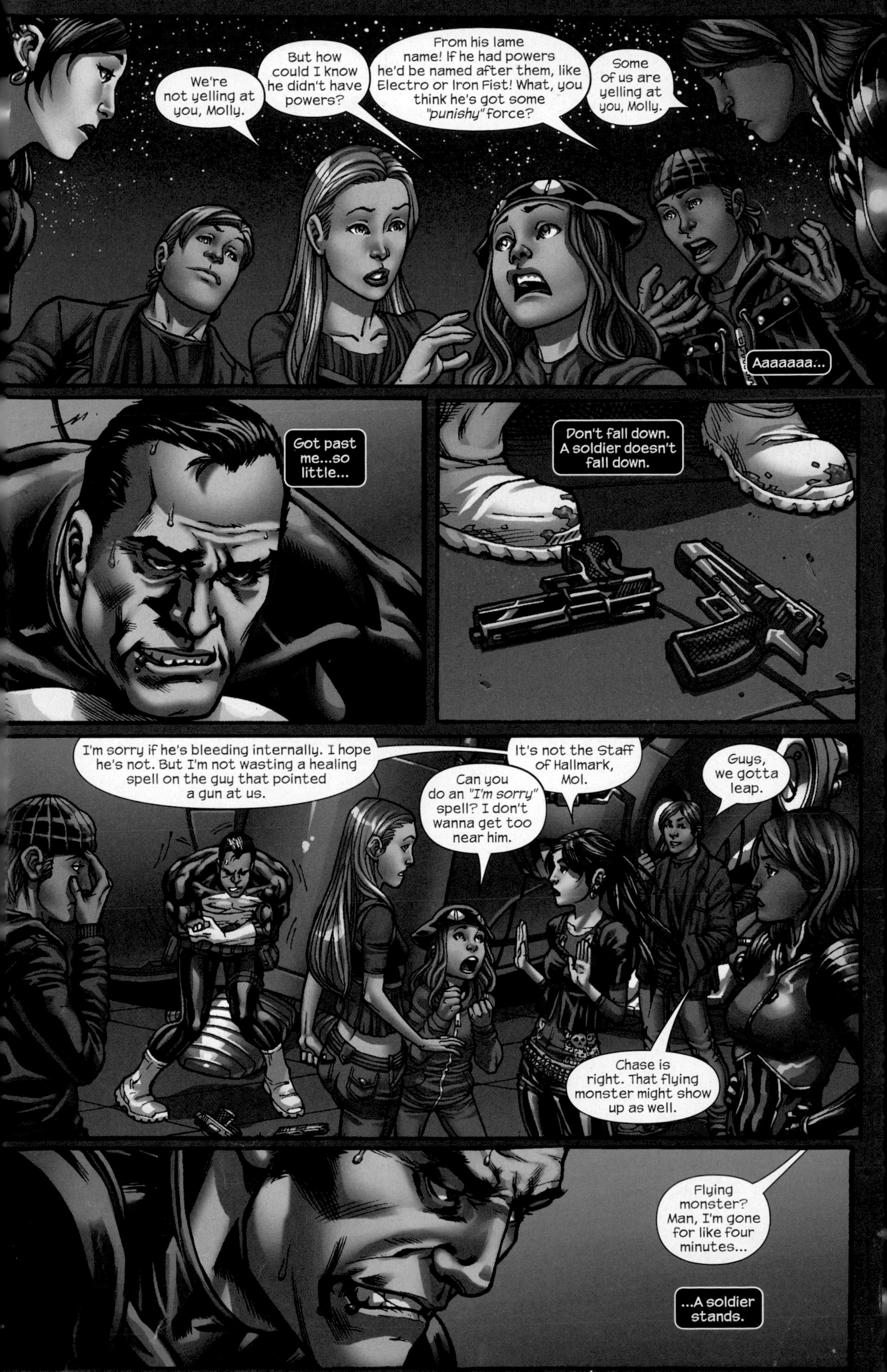
We're not yelling at you, Molly.
But how could I know he didn't have powers?
From his lame name! If he had powers he'd be named after them, like Electro or Iron Fist! What, you think he's got some "punishy" force?
Some of us are yelling at you, Molly.
Aaaaaaa...
Got past me...so little...
Don't fall down. A soldier doesn't fall down.
I'm sorry if he's bleeding internally. I hope he's not. But I'm not wasting a healing spell on the guy that pointed a gun at us.
It's not the Staff of Hallmark, Mol.
Can you do an "I'm sorry" spell? I don't wanna get too near him.
Guys, we gotta leap.
Chase is right. That flying monster might show up as well.
Flying monster? Man, I'm gone for like four minutes...
...A soldier stands.

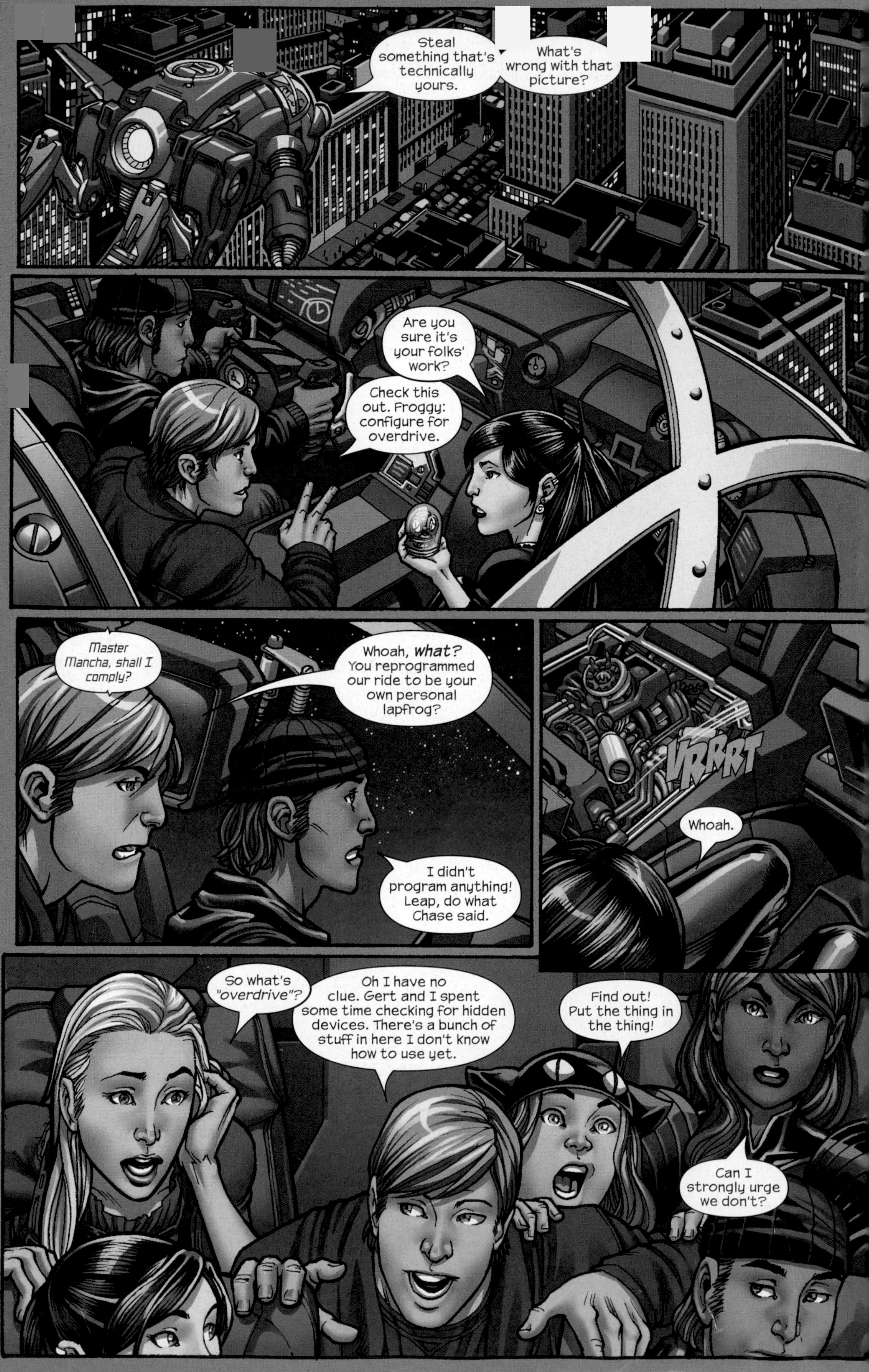
Steal something that's technically yours.
What's wrong with that picture?
Are you sure it's your folks' work?
Check this out. Froggy: configure for overdrive.
Master Mancha, shall I comply?
Whoah, *what?* You reprogrammed our ride to be your own personal lapfrog?
I didn't program anything! Leap, do what Chase said.
VRRRT
Whoah.
So what's *"overdrive"*?
Oh I have no clue. Gert and I spent some time checking for hidden devices. There's a bunch of stuff in here I don't know how to use yet.
Find out! Put the thing in the thing!
Can I strongly urge we don't?

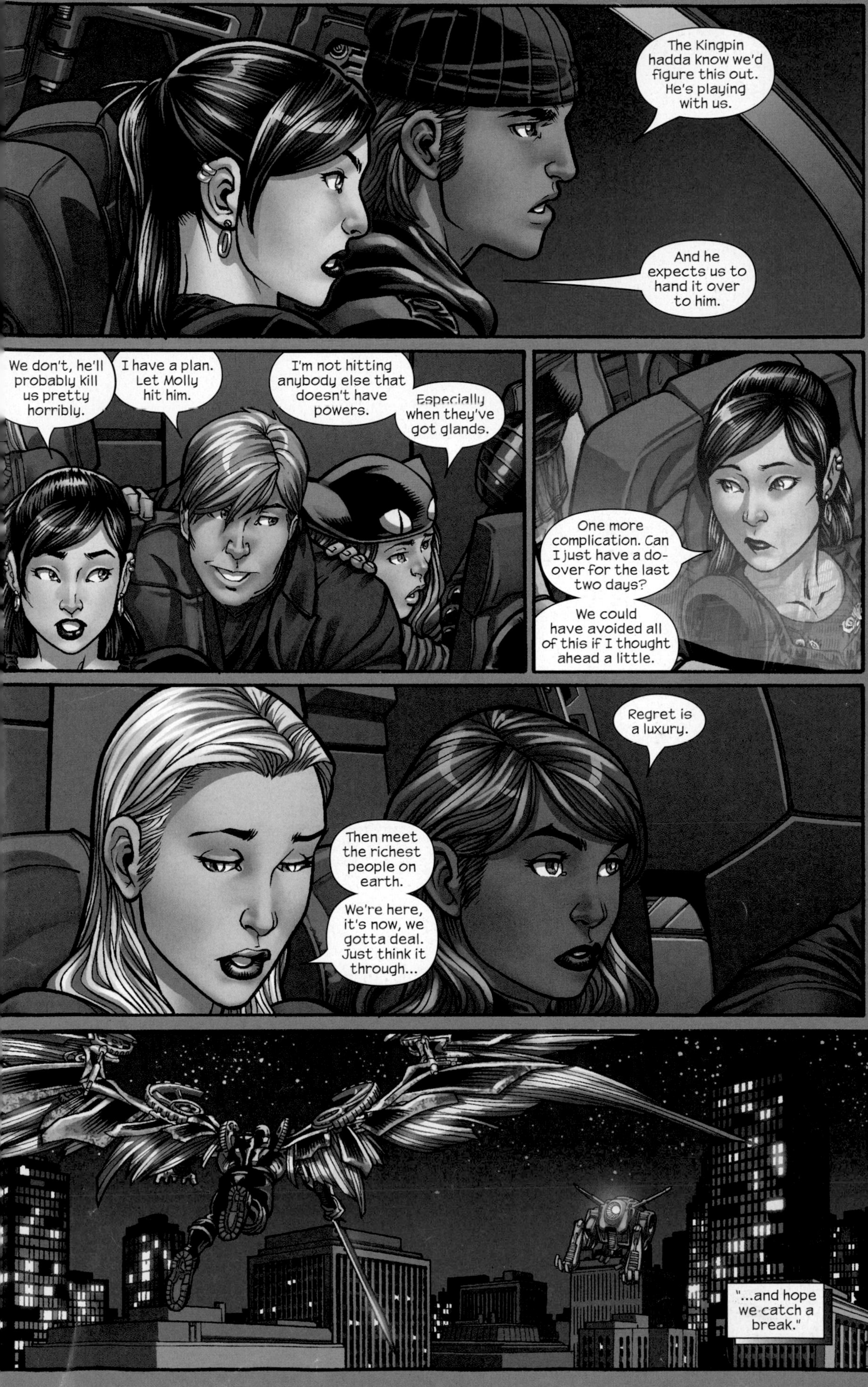
The Kingpin hadda know we'd figure this out. He's playing with us.
And he expects us to hand it over to him.
We don't, he'll probably kill us pretty horribly.
I have a plan. Let Molly hit him.
I'm not hitting anybody else that doesn't have powers.
Especially when they've got glands.
One more complication. Can I just have a do-over for the last two days?
We could have avoided all of this if I thought ahead a little.
Regret is a luxury.
Then meet the richest people on earth.
We're here, it's now, we gotta deal. Just think it through...
"...and hope we catch a break."

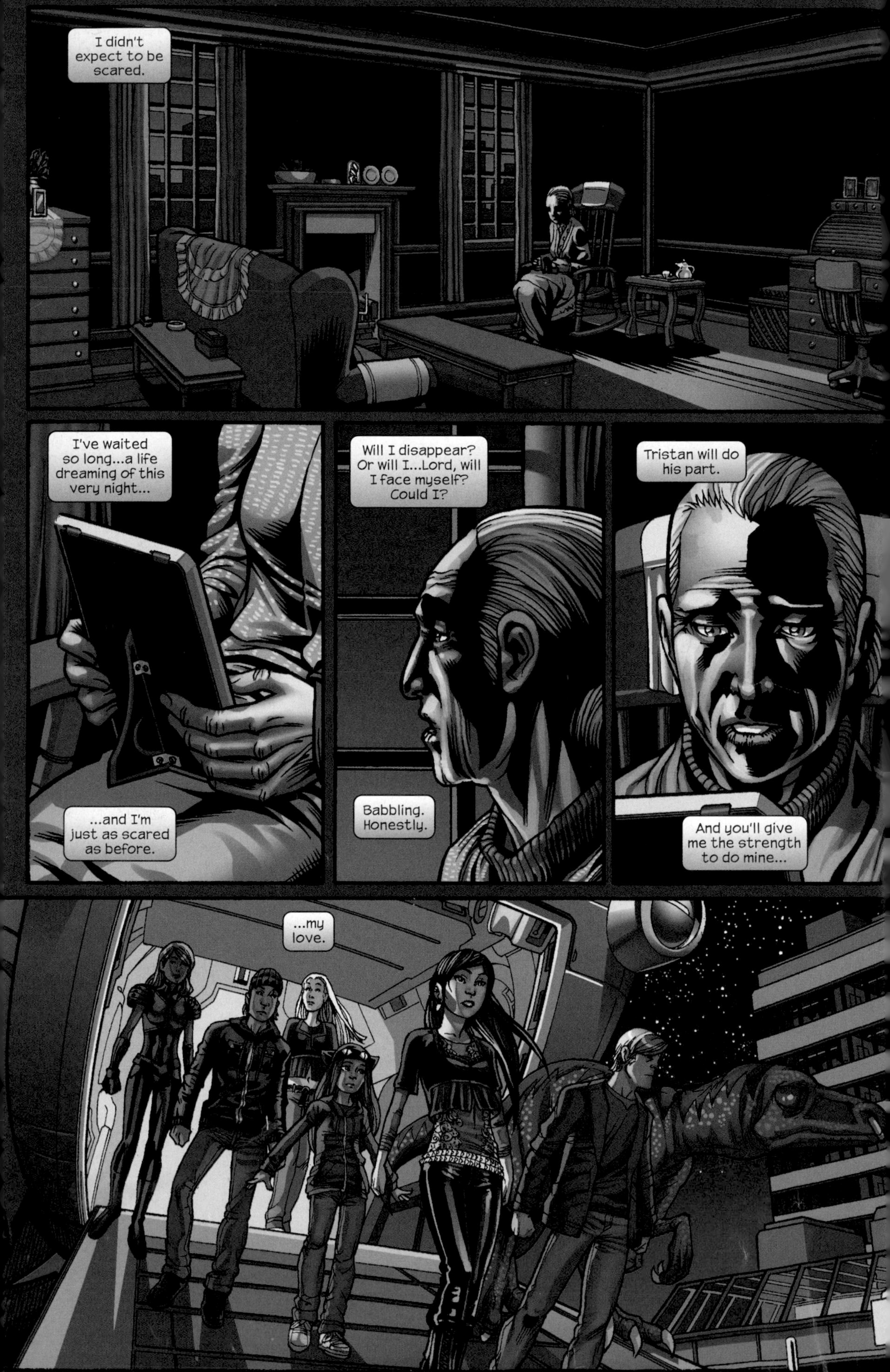
I didn't expect to be scared.
I've waited so long...a life dreaming of this very night...
...and I'm just as scared as before.
Will I disappear? Or will I...Lord, will I face myself? Could I?
Babbling. Honestly.
Tristan will do his part.
And you'll give me the strength to do mine...
...my love.

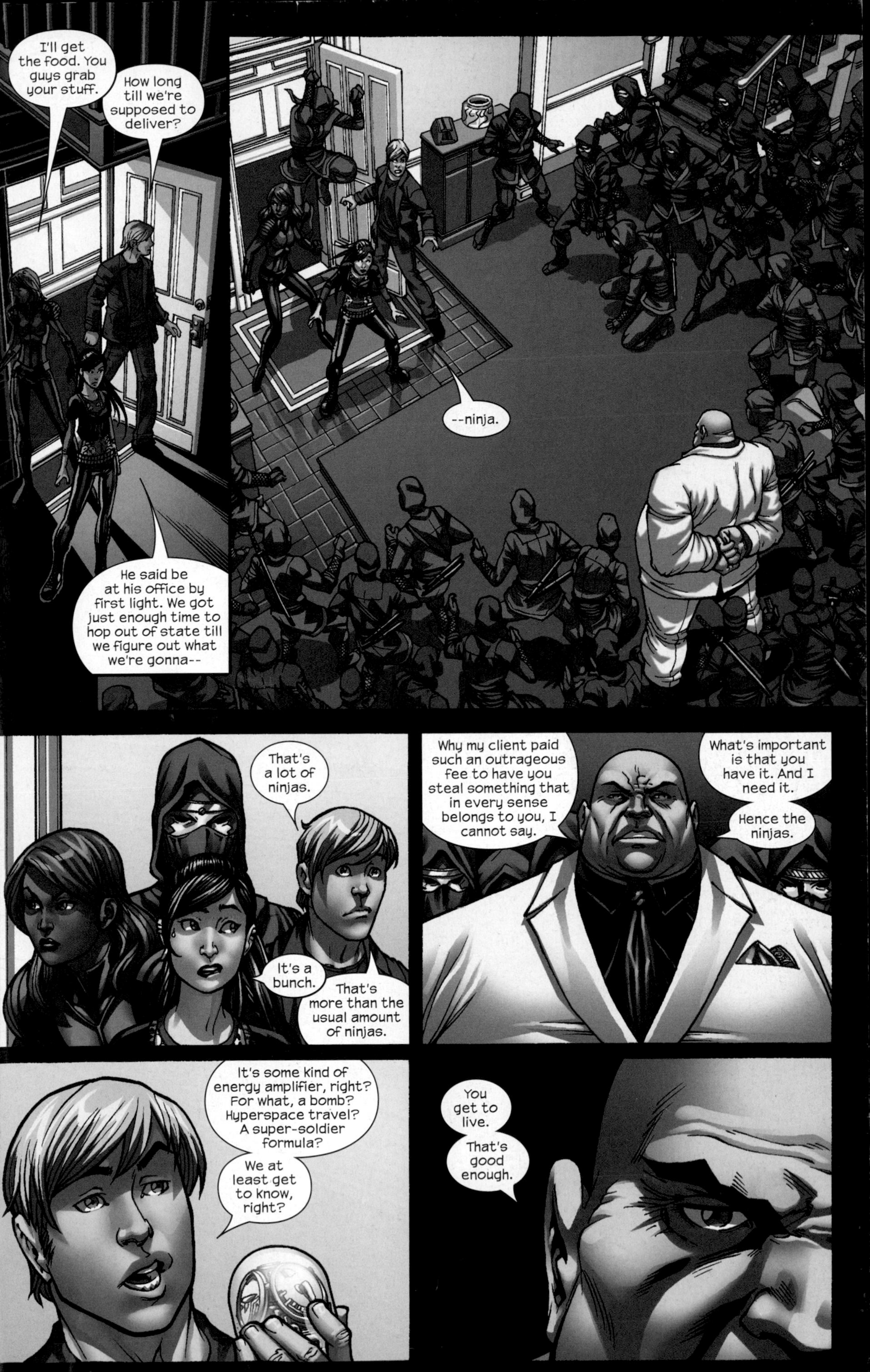
I'll get the food. You guys grab your stuff.
How long till we're supposed to deliver?
He said be at his office by first light. We got just enough time to hop out of state till we figure out what we're gonna--
--ninja.
That's a lot of ninjas.
It's a bunch.
That's more than the usual amount of ninjas.
Why my client paid such an outrageous fee to have you steal something that in every sense belongs to you, I cannot say.
What's important is that you have it. And I need it.
Hence the ninjas.
It's some kind of energy amplifier, right? For what, a bomb? Hyperspace travel? A super-soldier formula?
We at least get to know, right?
You get to live.
That's good enough.

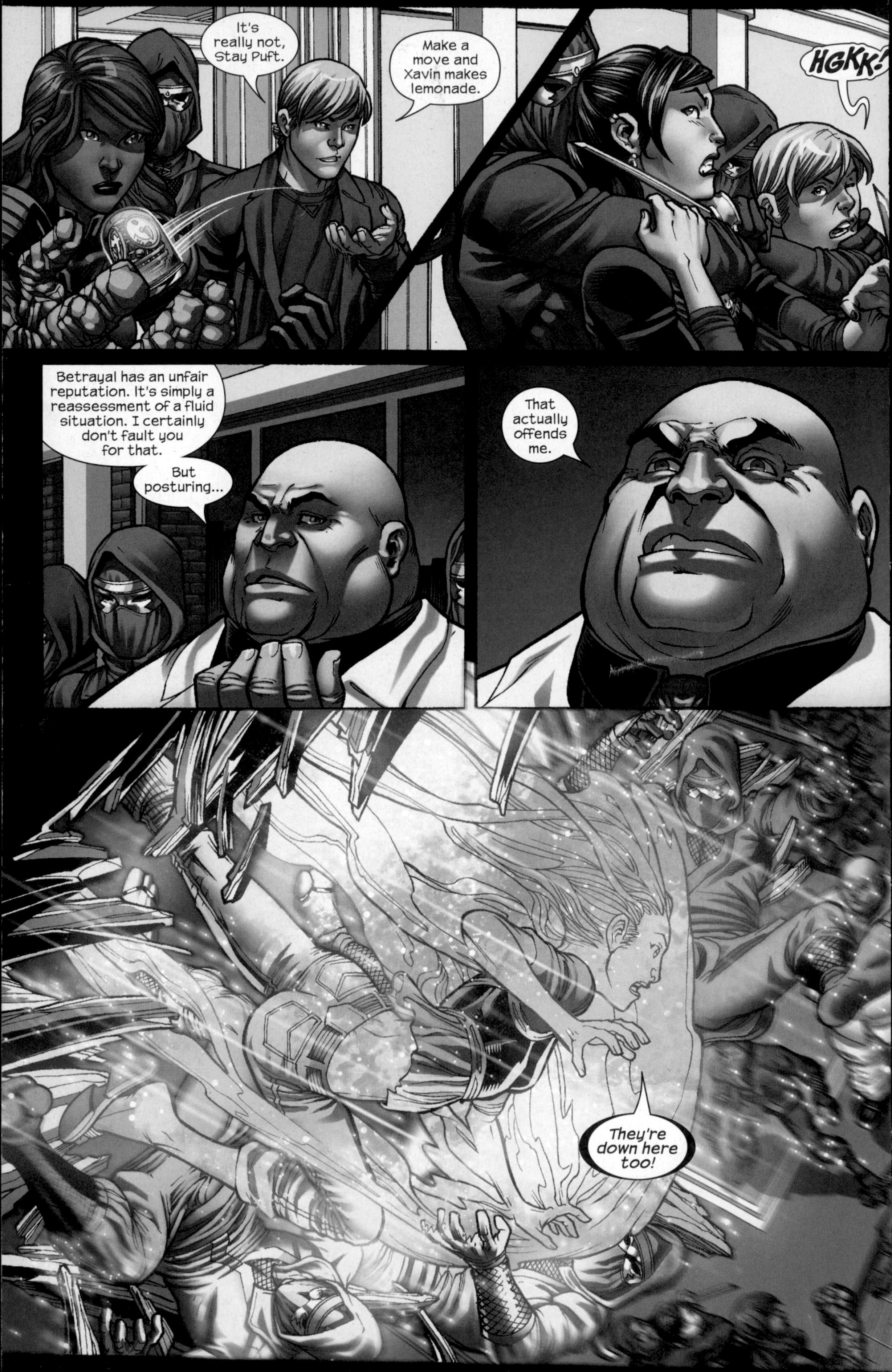
It's really not, Stay Puft.
Make a move and Xavin makes lemonade.
HGKK!
Betrayal has an unfair reputation. It's simply a reassessment of a fluid situation. I certainly don't fault you for that.
But posturing...
That actually offends me.
They're down here too!

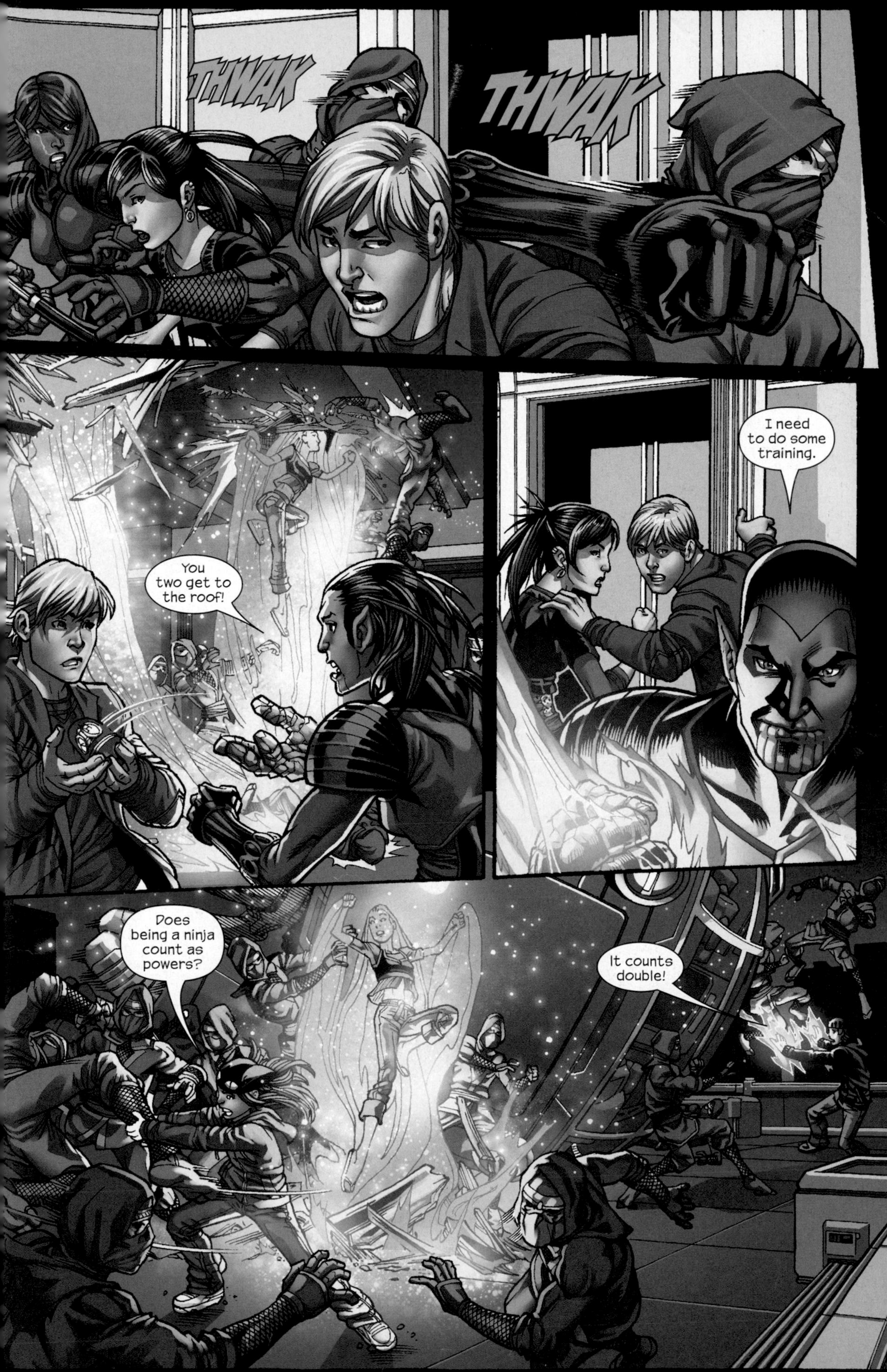
THWAK
THWAK
You two get to the roof!
I need to do some training.
Does being a ninja count as powers?
It counts double!

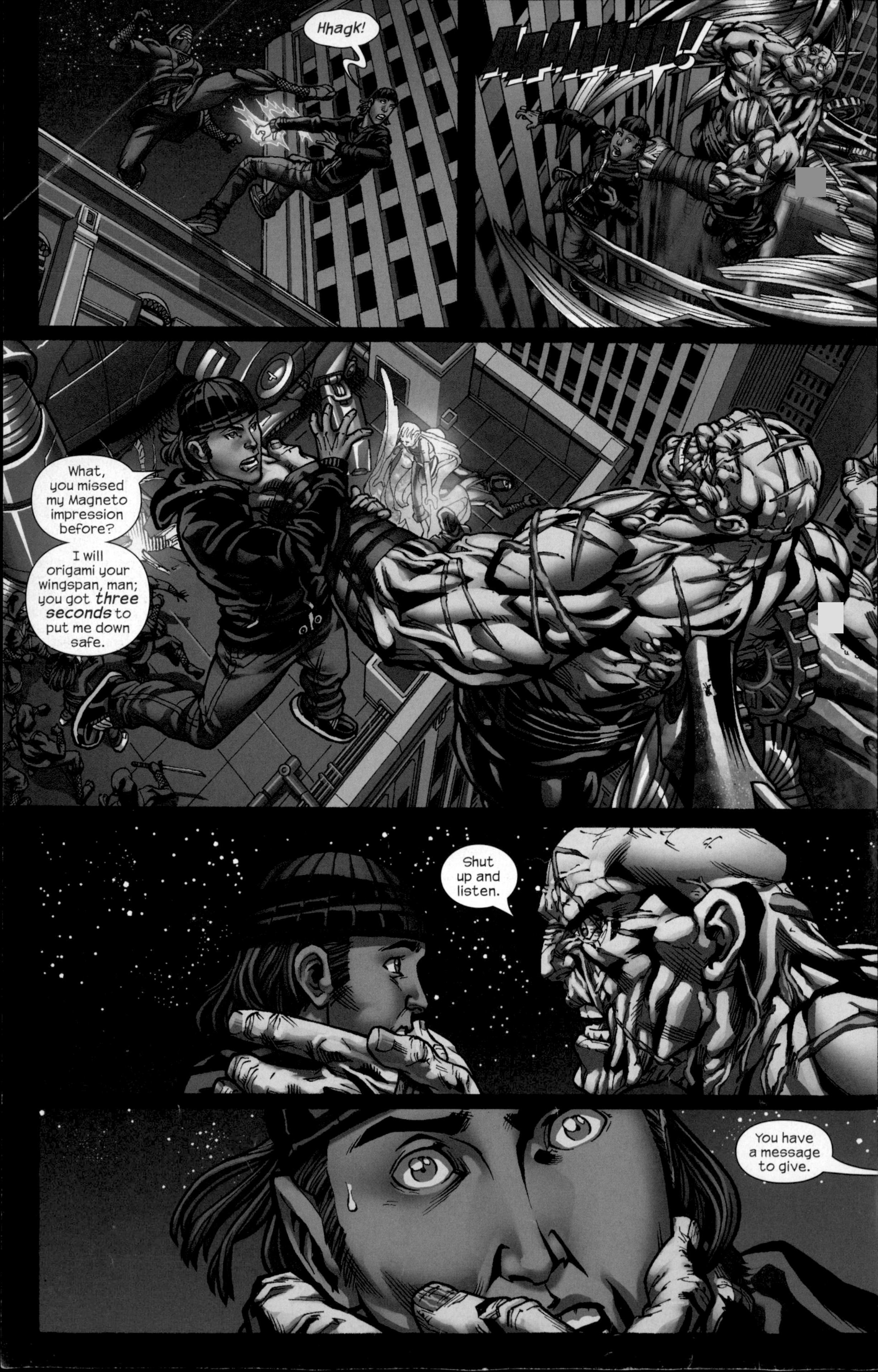
Hhagk!
What, you missed my Magneto impression before?
I will origami your wingspan, man; you got *three seconds* to put me down safe.
Shut up and listen.
You have a message to give.

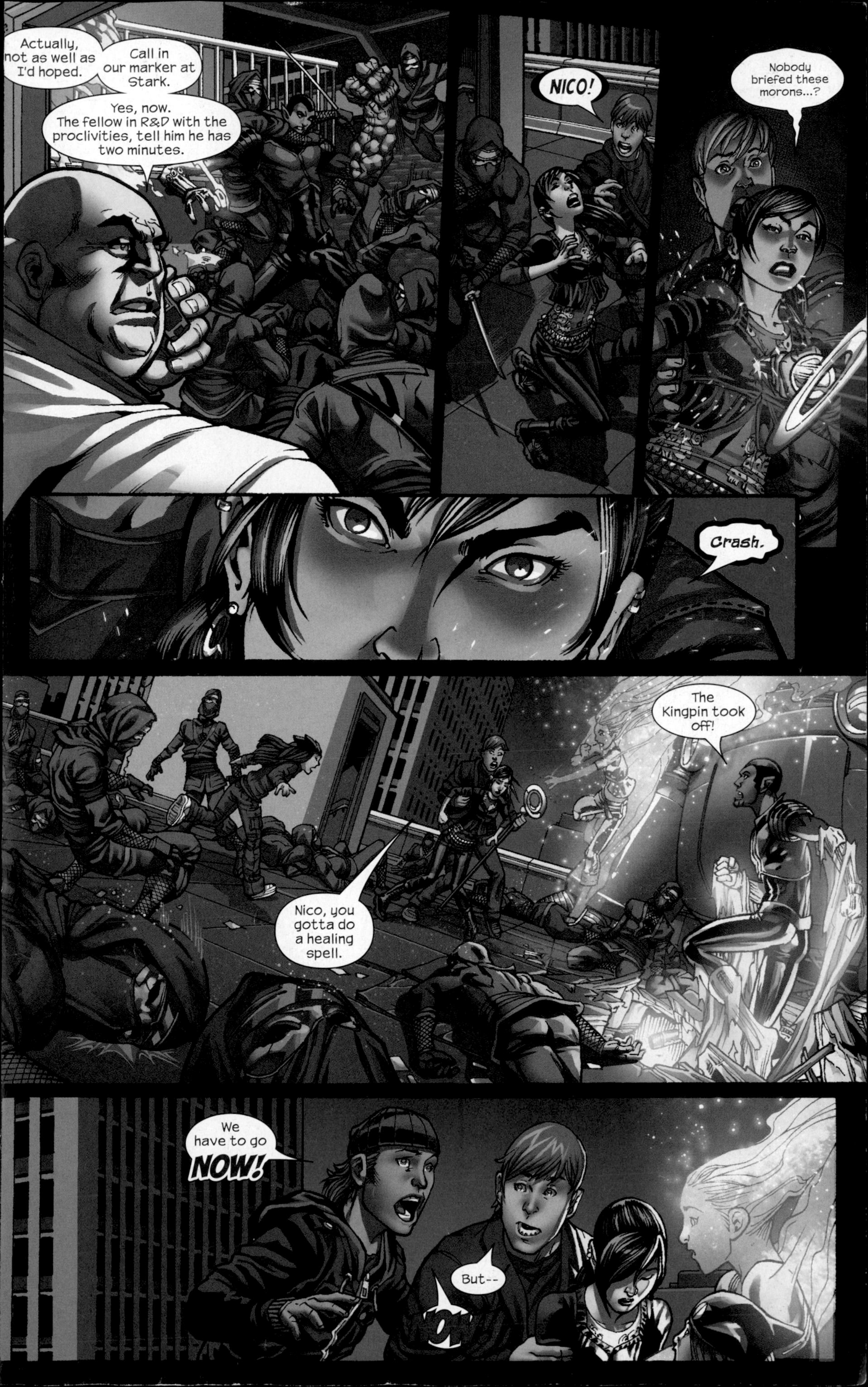

Actually, not as well as I'd hoped.
Call in our marker at Stark.
Yes, now. The fellow in R&D with the proclivities, tell him he has two minutes.
NICO!
Nobody briefed these morons...?
Crash.
The Kingpin took off!
Nico, you gotta do a healing spell.
We have to go NOW!
But--

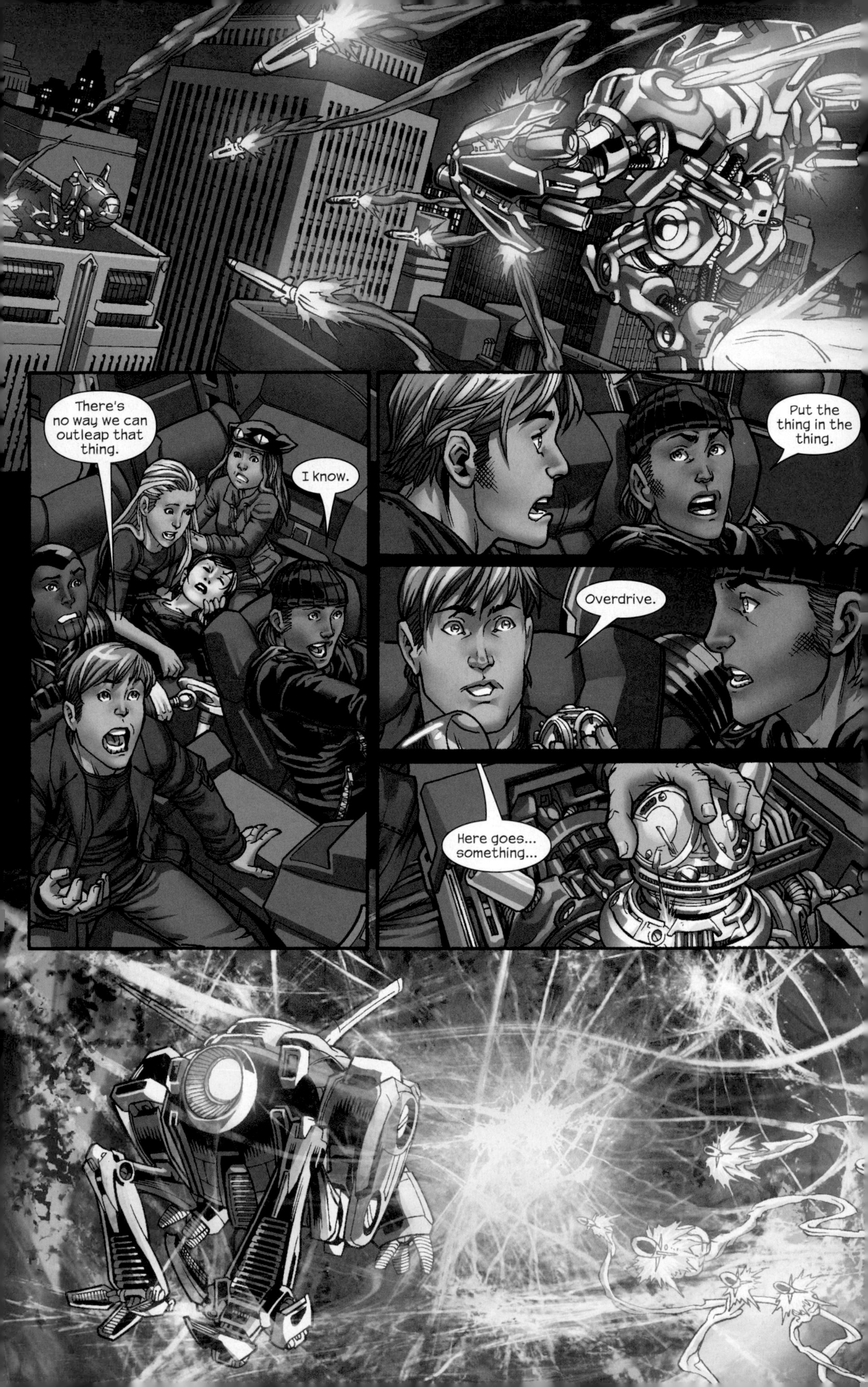
There's no way we can outleap that thing.
I know.
Put the thing in the thing.
Overdrive.
Here goes... something...

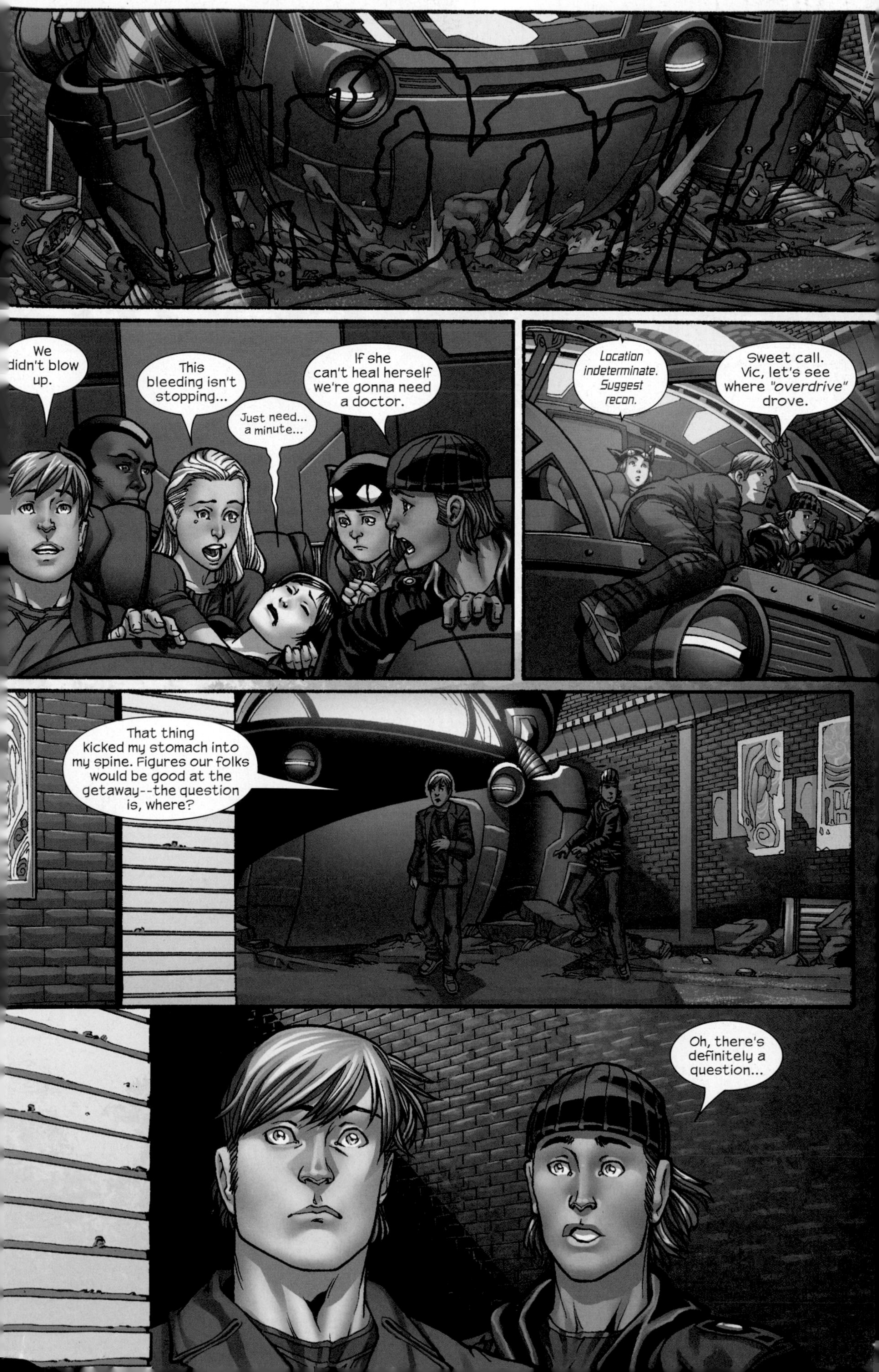

We didn't blow up.
This bleeding isn't stopping...
Just need... a minute...
If she can't heal herself we're gonna need a doctor.
Location indeterminate. Suggest recon.
Sweet call. Vic, let's see where "overdrive" drove.
That thing kicked my stomach into my spine. Figures our folks would be good at the getaway--the question is, where?
Oh, there's definitely a question...

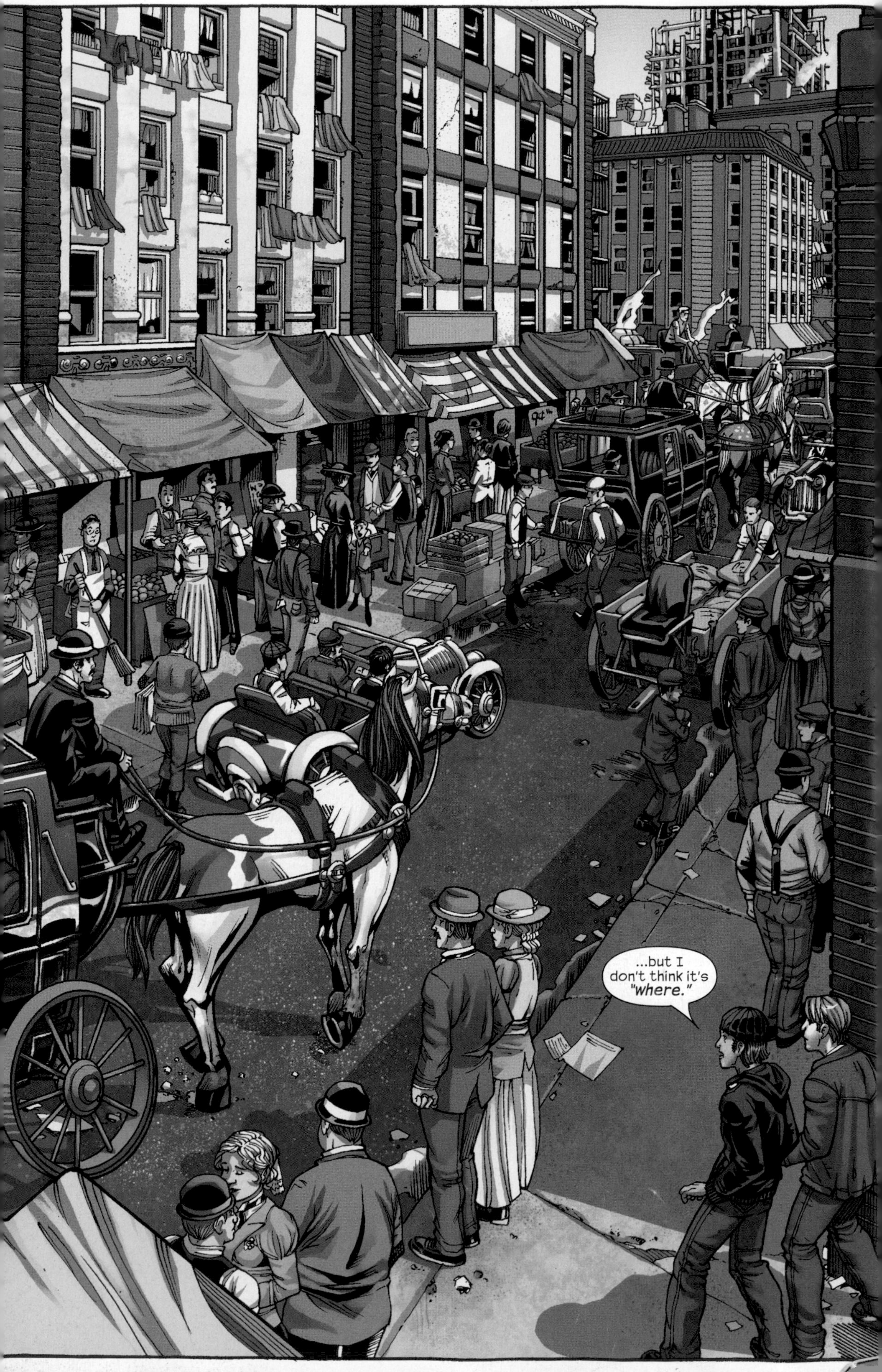
...but I don't think it's "where."

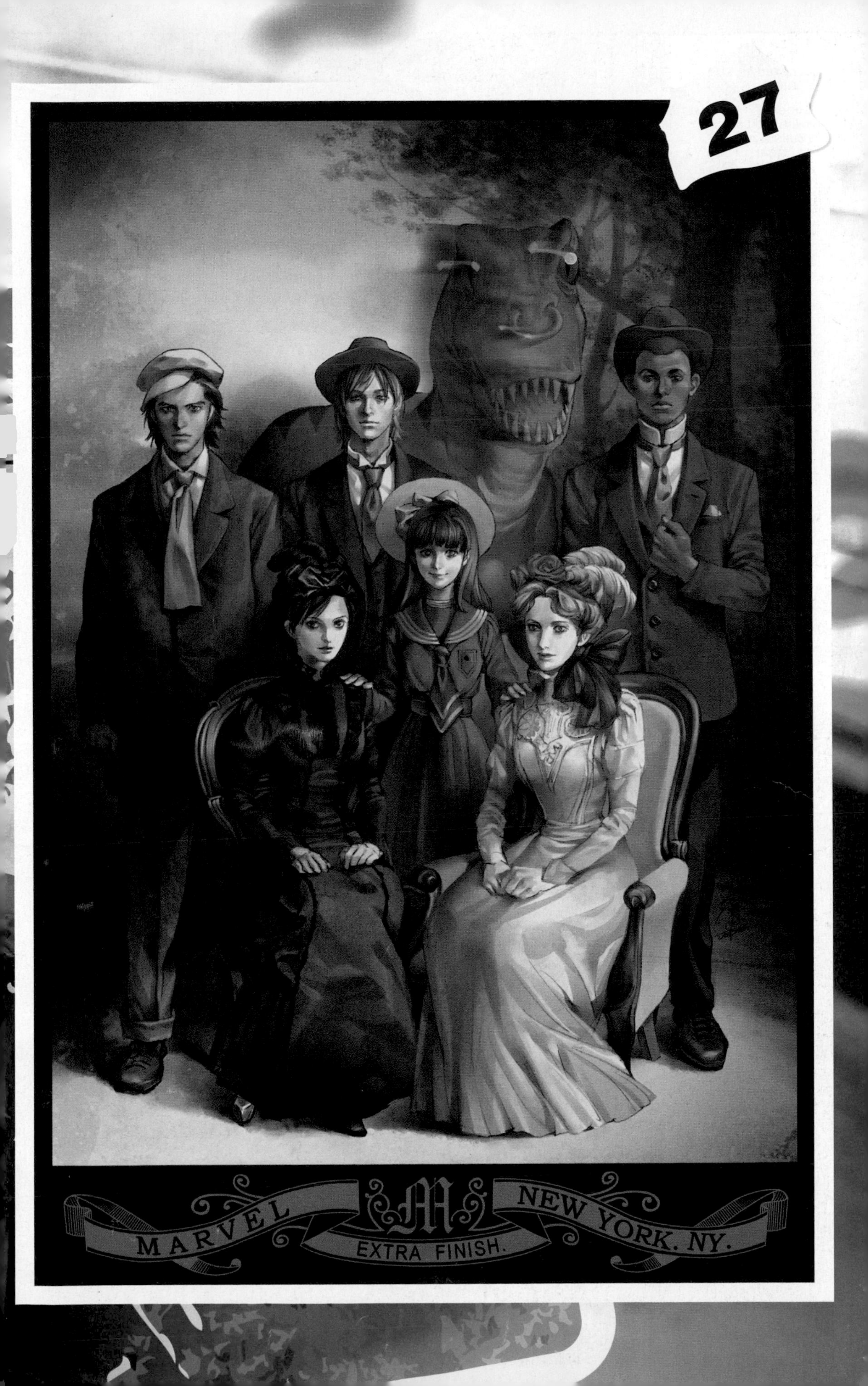
27
MARVEL
EXTRA FINISH.
NEW YORK. NY.

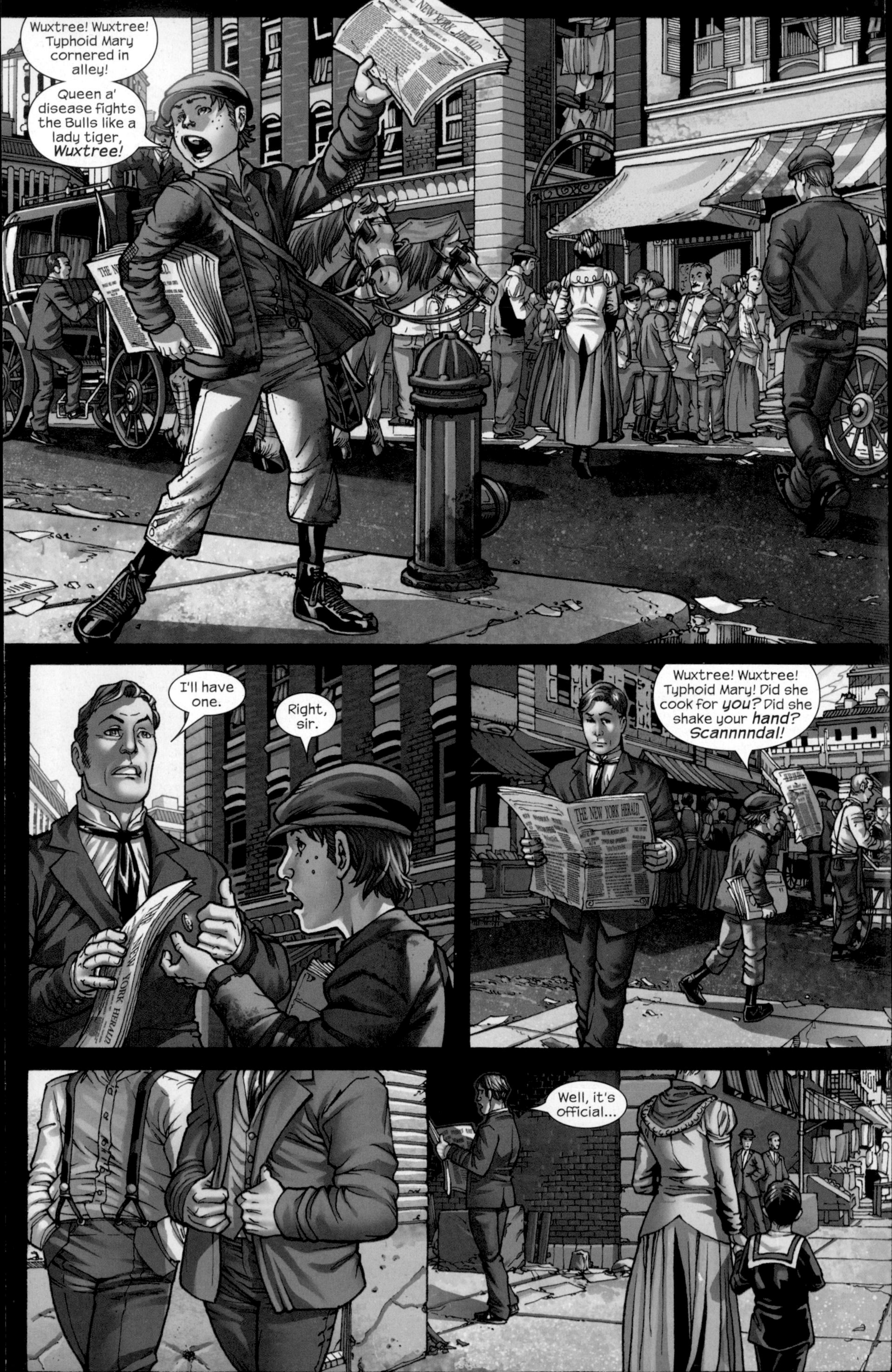
Wuxtree! Wuxtree! Typhoid Mary cornered in alley!
Queen a' disease fights the Bulls like a lady tiger, *Wuxtree!*
I'll have one.
Right, sir.
Wuxtree! Wuxtree! Typhoid Mary! Did she cook for *you?* Did she shake your *hand? Scannnndal!*
Well, it's official...

We're a hundred years from home.

THE NEW YORK HERALD.
WHOLE NO. 24601   NEW YORK, WEDNESDAY, JUNE 27, 1907   PRICE, FOUR CENTS
TYPHOID MARY APPREHENDED
Typhus Terror At An End.

Wow. This is *amazingly* bad.

Should you be sitting? That healing spell--

--worked great. I'm fine, except for the amazingly bad.

"Typhoid Mary." Didn't she fight Daredevil?

We have to get back to our time as soon as possible.

Our time where men are attacking us with missiles and ninjas?

Yeah, we were like three seconds from being blown to bits, which I've sort of had enough of.

As usual, you're missing the bigger issue. What you should be worried about is the Butterfly Effect.

Dude, I'm totally on top of the Butterfly Effect!

What were they, like, bigger?

I don't think it'll be a problem--which is the good news, since we're going nowhere.

But if we mess with the time stream, don't we end up never being born, or Hitler won, or something?

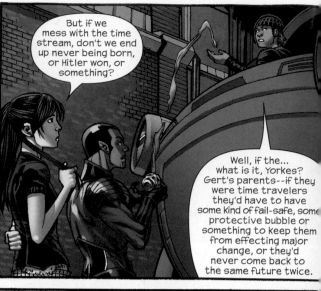

Well, if the... what is it, Yorkes? Gert's parents--if they were time travelers they'd have to have some kind of fail-safe, some protective bubble or something to keep them from effecting major change, or they'd never come back to the same future twice.

They'd also have to have a power source good for a round trip. We can't assume anything is working in our favor.

We also can't hide in an alley and do nothing.

You're not even pretending to contain your excitement.

How often do we get this chance? A world we've never seen!

You've seen many worlds--

But this is our planet. Our history. We're living in history.

Right. We're living in something I flunked. How do we make it go away?

Inky.

I vote spell.

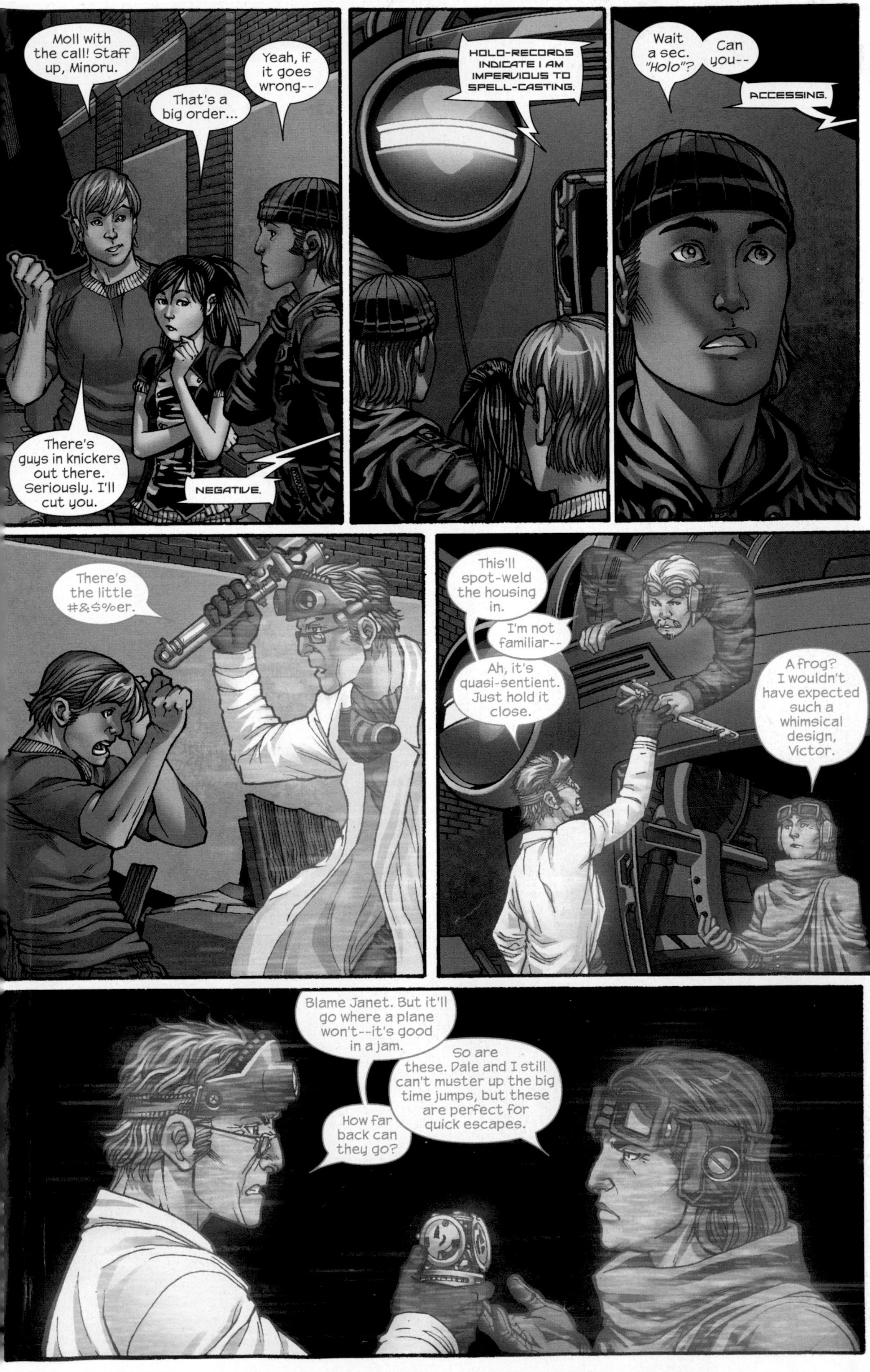
Moll with the call! Staff up, Minoru.
That's a big order...
Yeah, if it goes wrong--
There's guys in knickers out there. Seriously. I'll cut you.
NEGATIVE.
HOLO-RECORDS INDICATE I AM IMPERVIOUS TO SPELL-CASTING.
Wait a sec. "Holo"?
Can you--
ACCESSING.
There's the little #&$%er.
This'll spot-weld the housing in.
I'm not familiar--
Ah, it's quasi-sentient. Just hold it close.
A frog? I wouldn't have expected such a whimsical design, Victor.
Blame Janet. But it'll go where a plane won't--it's good in a jam.
So are these. Dale and I still can't muster up the big time jumps, but these are perfect for quick escapes.
How far back can they go?

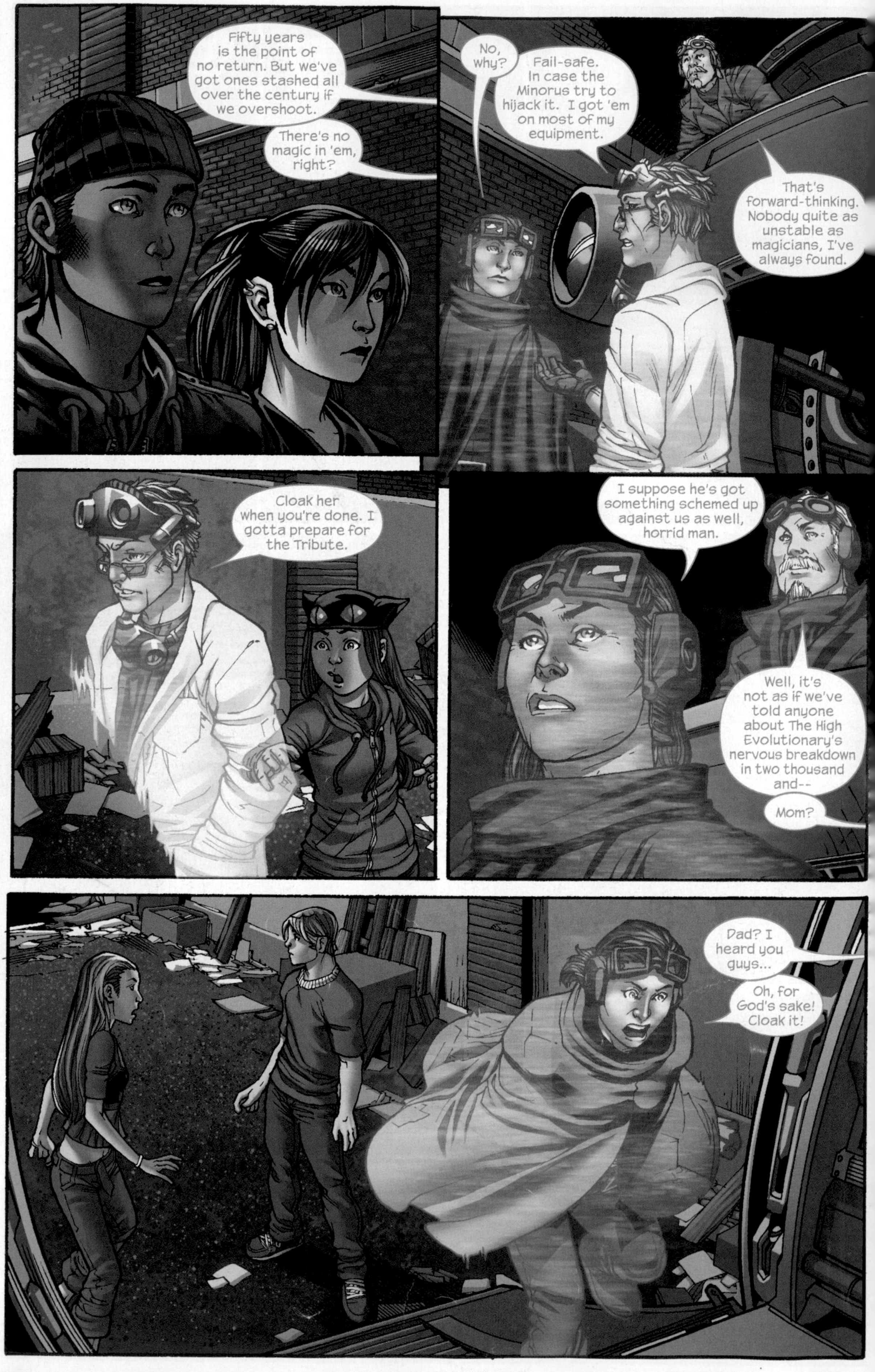
Fifty years is the point of no return. But we've got ones stashed all over the century if we overshoot.
There's no magic in 'em, right?
No, why?
Fail-safe. In case the Minorus try to hijack it. I got 'em on most of my equipment.
That's forward-thinking. Nobody quite as unstable as magicians, I've always found.
Cloak her when you're done. I gotta prepare for the Tribute.
I suppose he's got something schemed up against us as well, horrid man.
Well, it's not as if we've told anyone about The High Evolutionary's nervous breakdown in two thousand and--
Mom?
Dad? I heard you guys...
Oh, for God's sake! Cloak it!

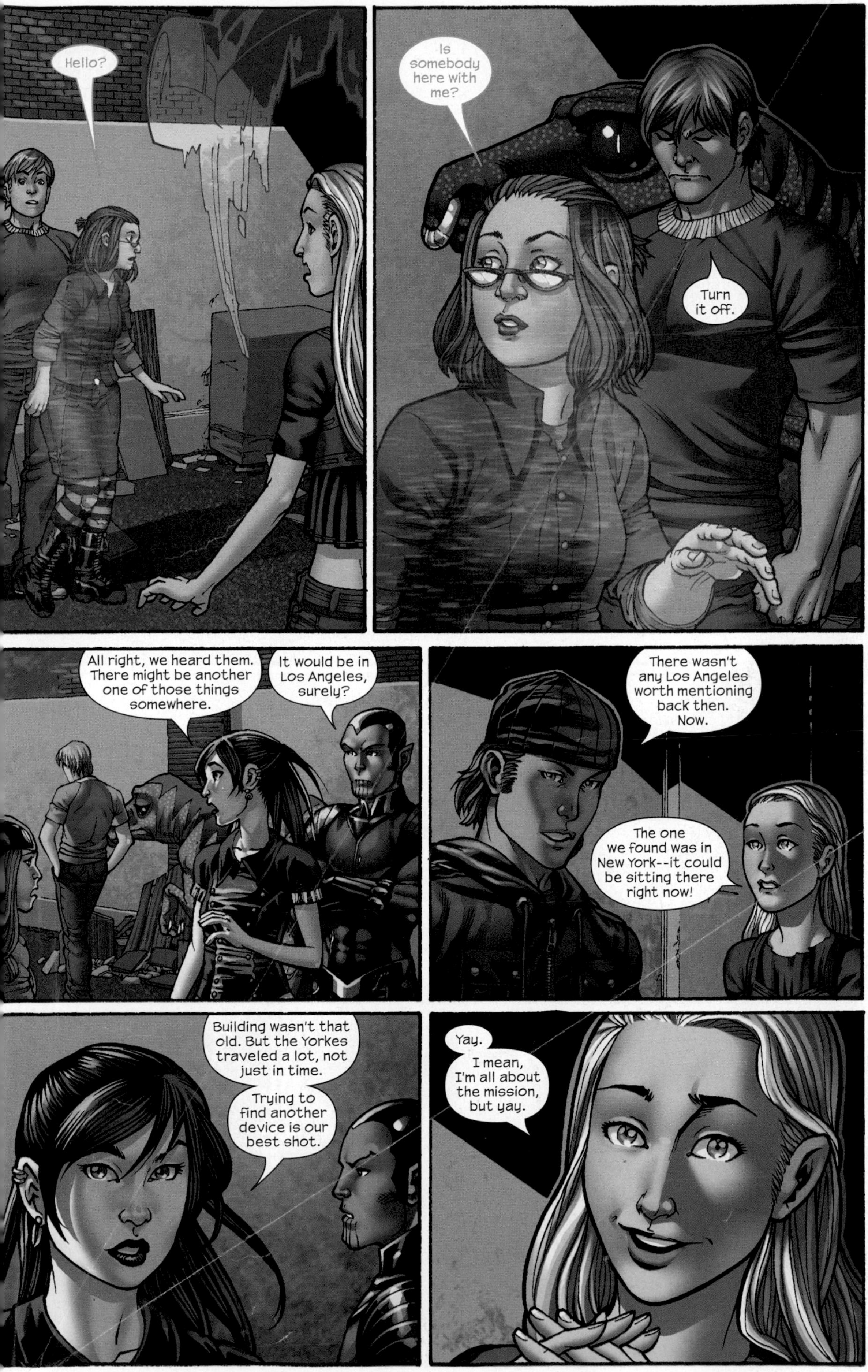
Hello?
Is somebody here with me?
Turn it off.
All right, we heard them. There might be another one of those things somewhere.
It would be in Los Angeles, surely?
There wasn't any Los Angeles worth mentioning back then. Now.
The one we found was in New York--it could be sitting there right now!
Building wasn't that old. But the Yorkes traveled a lot, not just in time.
Trying to find another device is our best shot.
Yay.
I mean, I'm all about the mission, but yay.

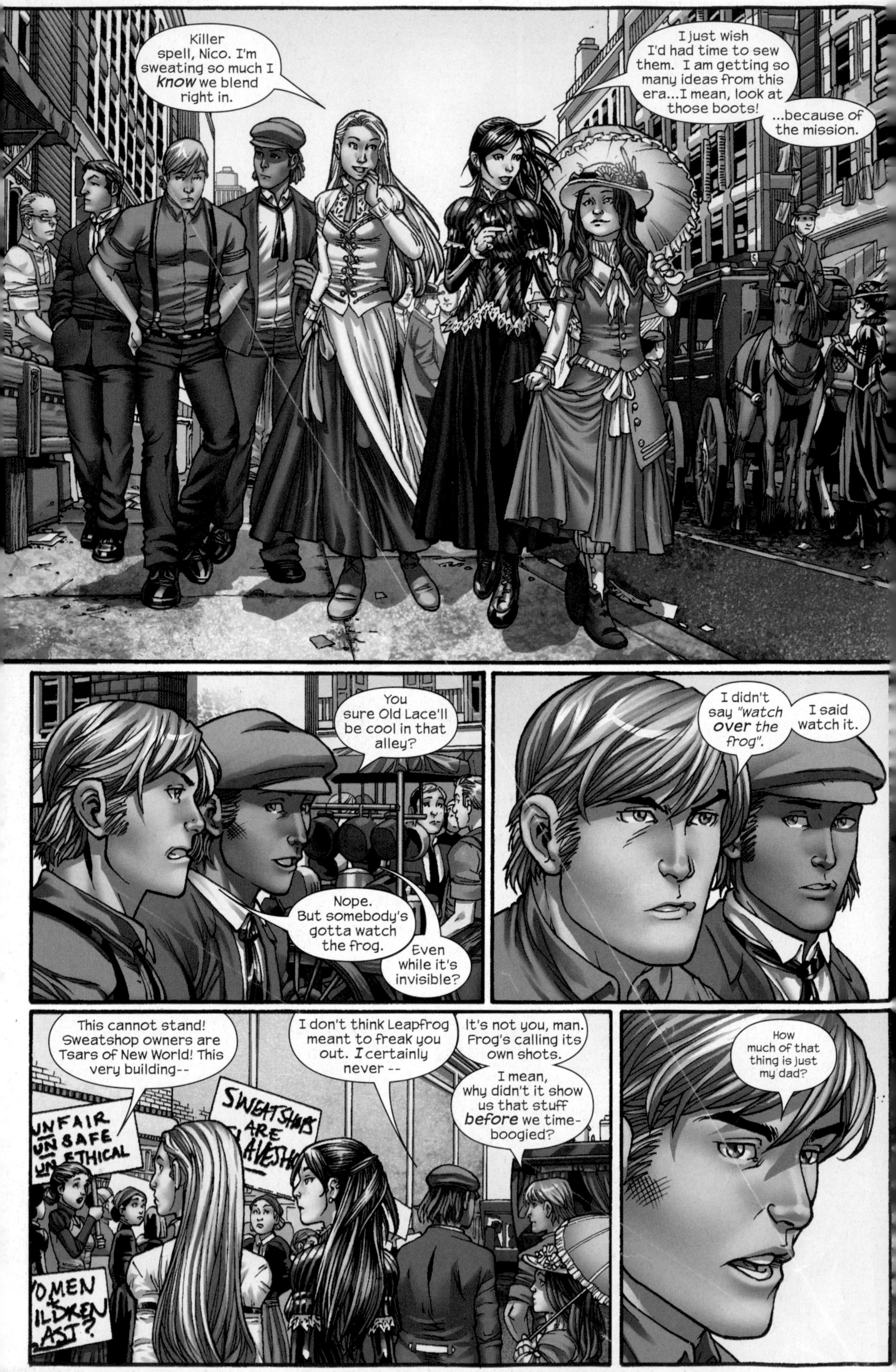
Killer spell, Nico. I'm sweating so much I *know* we blend right in.
I just wish I'd had time to sew them. I am getting so many ideas from this era...I mean, look at those boots!
...because of the mission.
You sure Old Lace'll be cool in that alley?
Nope. But somebody's gotta watch the frog.
Even while it's invisible?
I didn't say *"watch over the frog"*.
I said watch it.
This cannot stand! Sweatshop owners are Tsars of New World! This very building--
UNFAIR UNSAFE UNETHICAL
SWEATSHOPS ARE SLAVESHO
I don't think Leapfrog meant to freak you out. *I* certainly never --
It's not you, man. Frog's calling its own shots.
I mean, why didn't it show us that stuff *before* we time-boogied?
How much of that thing is just my dad?

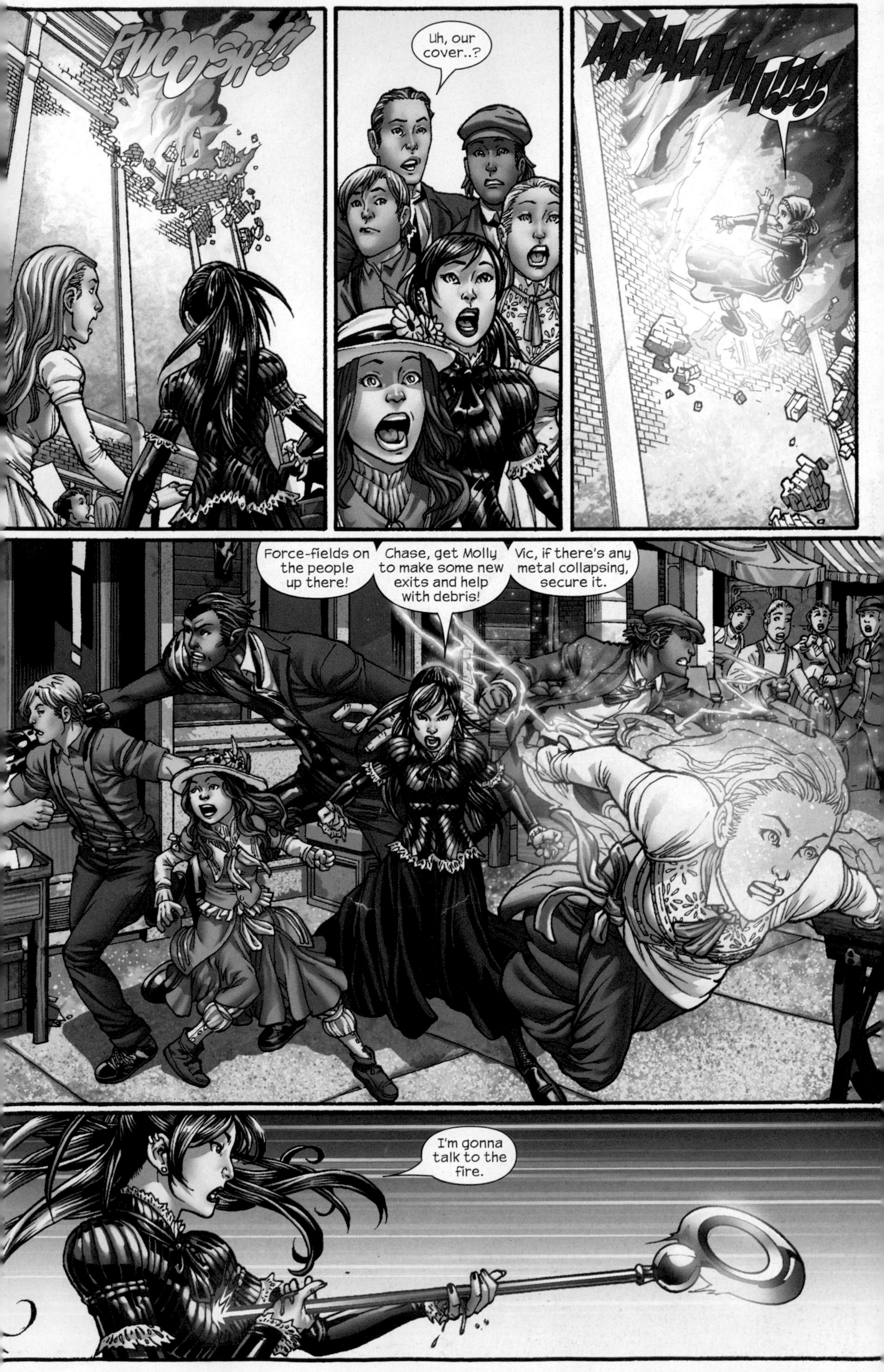
FWOOSH!!!
Uh, our cover..?
AAAAAAIIIII...!!
Force-fields on the people up there!
Chase, get Molly to make some new exits and help with debris!
Vic, if there's any metal collapsing, secure it.
I'm gonna talk to the fire.

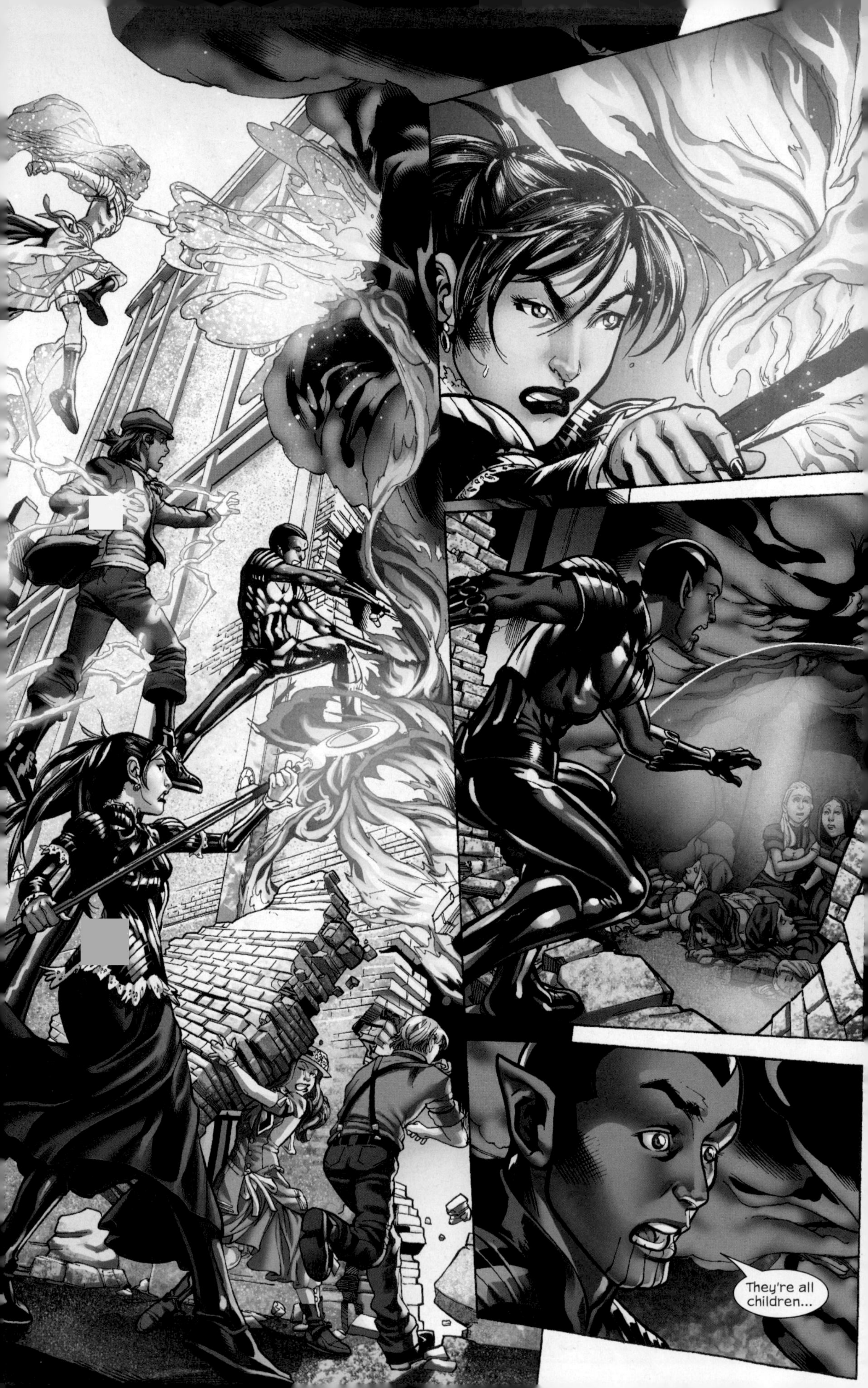
They're all children...

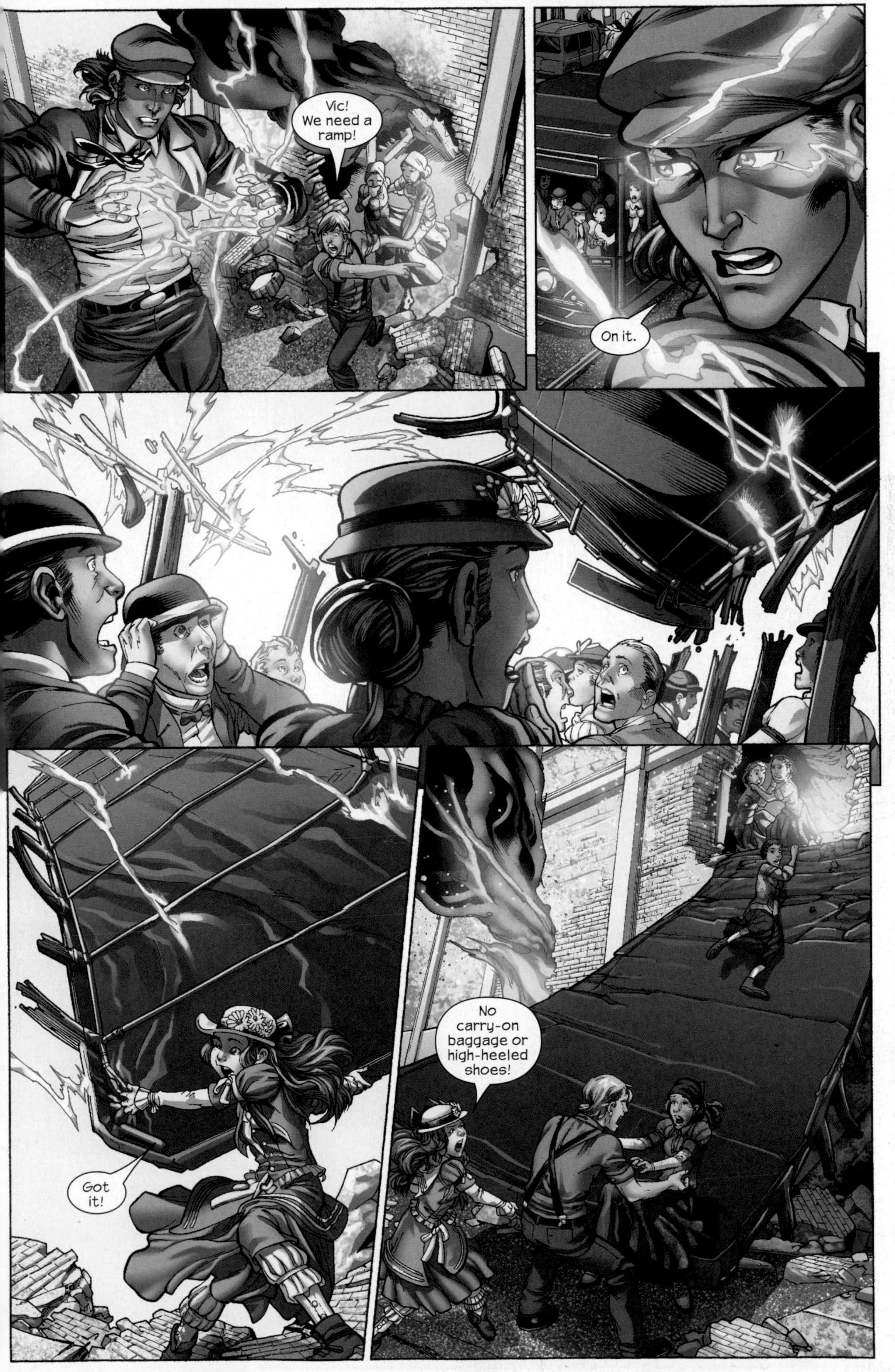
Vic! We need a ramp!
On it.
Got it!
No carry-on baggage or high-heeled shoes!

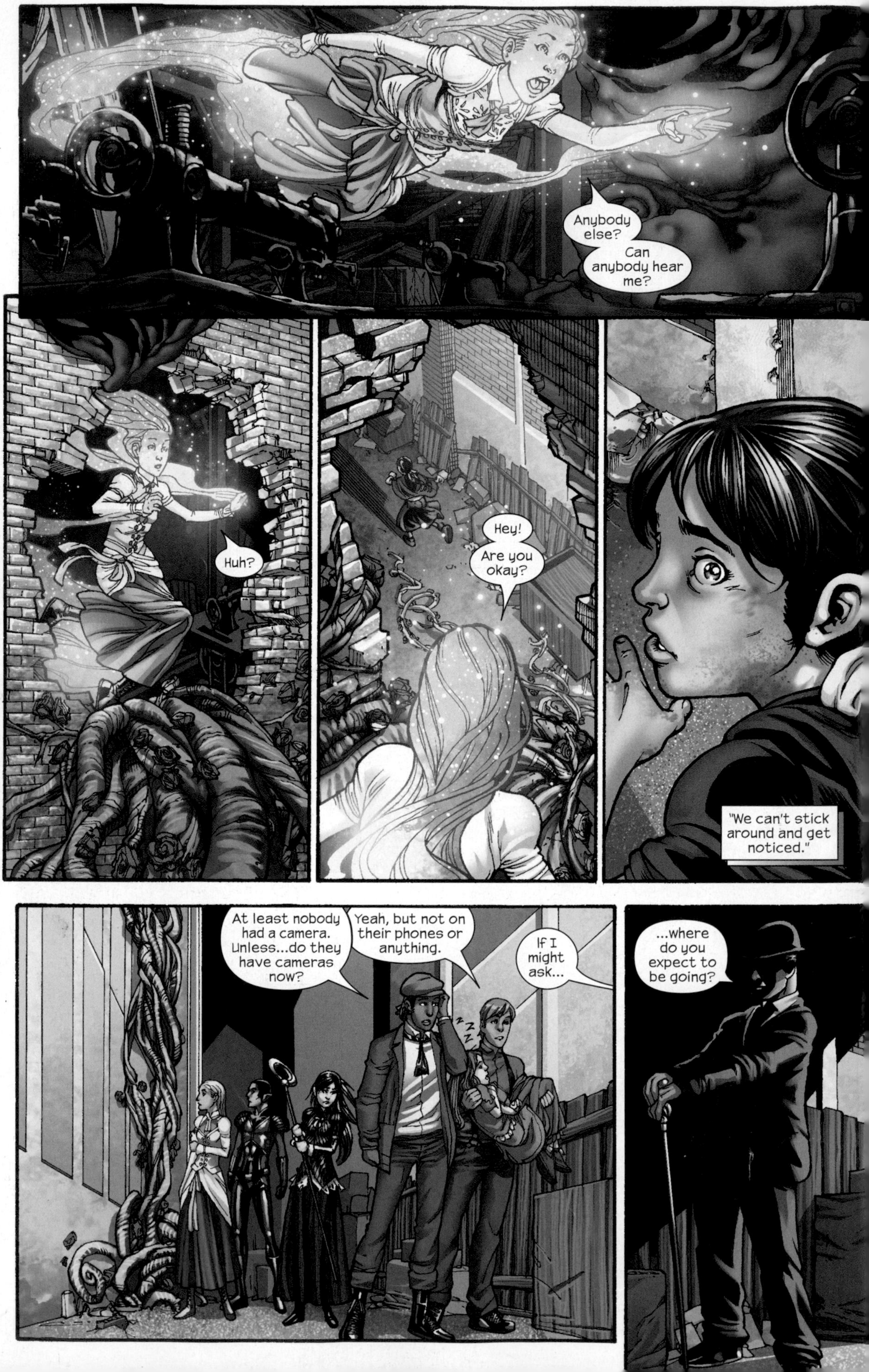
Anybody else?
Can anybody hear me?
Huh?
Hey!
Are you okay?
"We can't stick around and get noticed."
At least nobody had a camera. Unless...do they have cameras now?
Yeah, but not on their phones or anything.
If I might ask...
...where do you expect to be going?

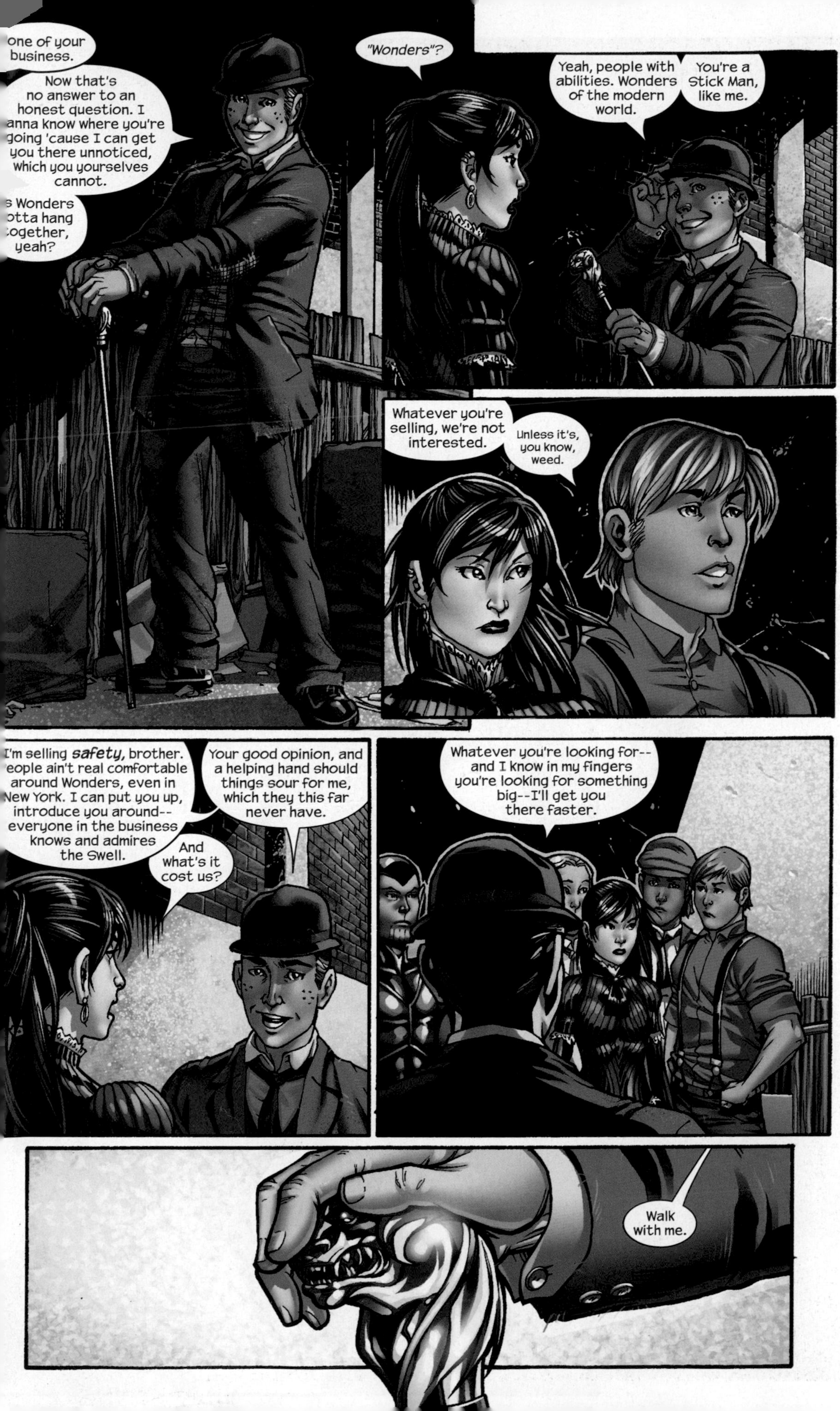

one of your business.
Now that's no answer to an honest question. I wanna know where you're going 'cause I can get you there unnoticed, which you yourselves cannot.
's Wonders gotta hang together, yeah?
"Wonders"?
Yeah, people with abilities. Wonders of the modern world.
You're a Stick Man, like me.
Whatever you're selling, we're not interested.
Unless it's, you know, weed.
I'm selling *safety*, brother. People ain't real comfortable around Wonders, even in New York. I can put you up, introduce you around-- everyone in the business knows and admires the Swell.
And what's it cost us?
Your good opinion, and a helping hand should things sour for me, which they this far never have.
Whatever you're looking for-- and I know in my fingers you're looking for something big--I'll get you there faster.
Walk with me.

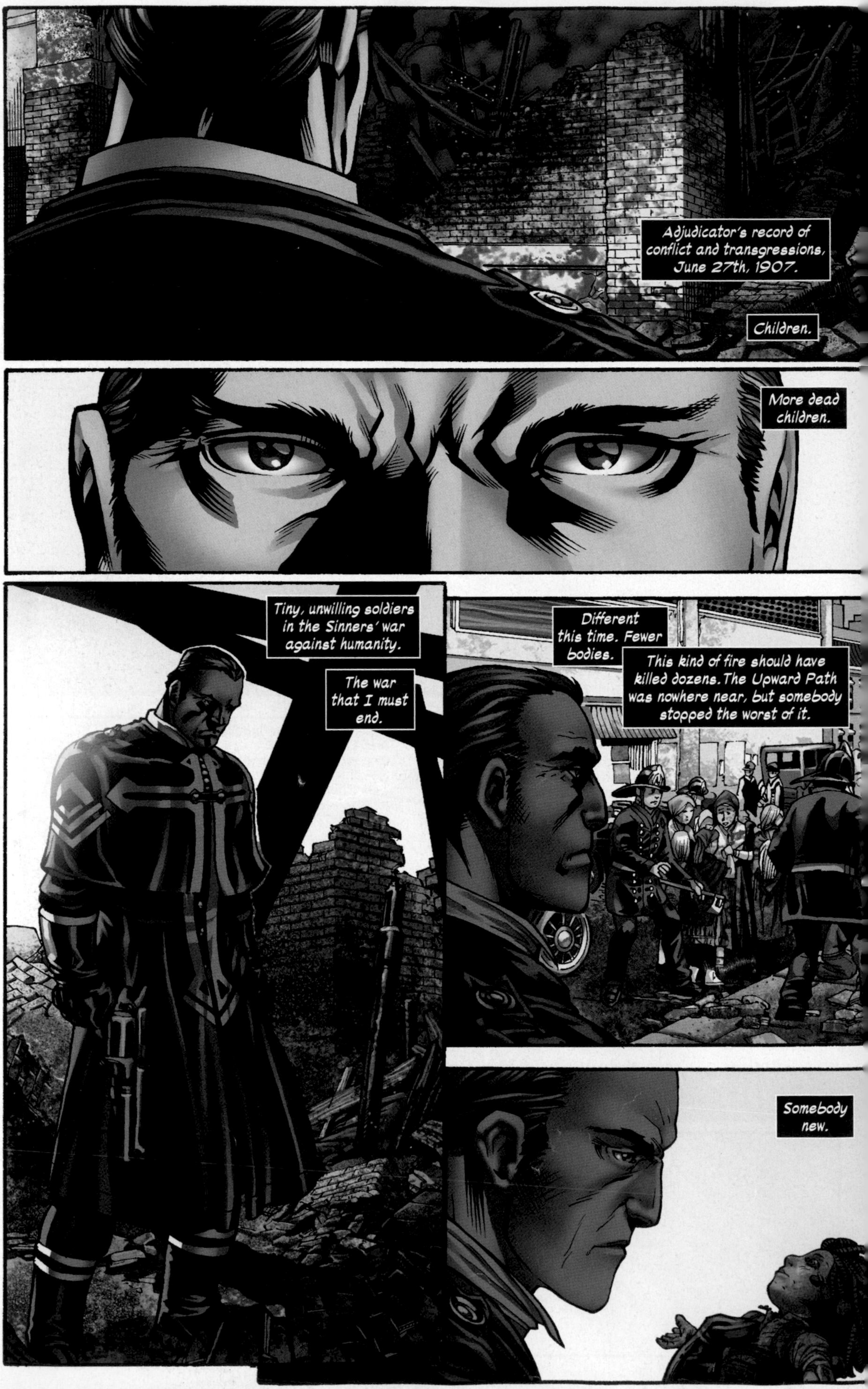
Adjudicator's record of conflict and transgressions, June 27th, 1907.
Children.
More dead children.
Tiny, unwilling soldiers in the Sinners' war against humanity.
The war that I must end.
Different this time. Fewer bodies.
This kind of fire should have killed dozens. The Upward Path was nowhere near, but somebody stopped the worst of it.
Somebody new.

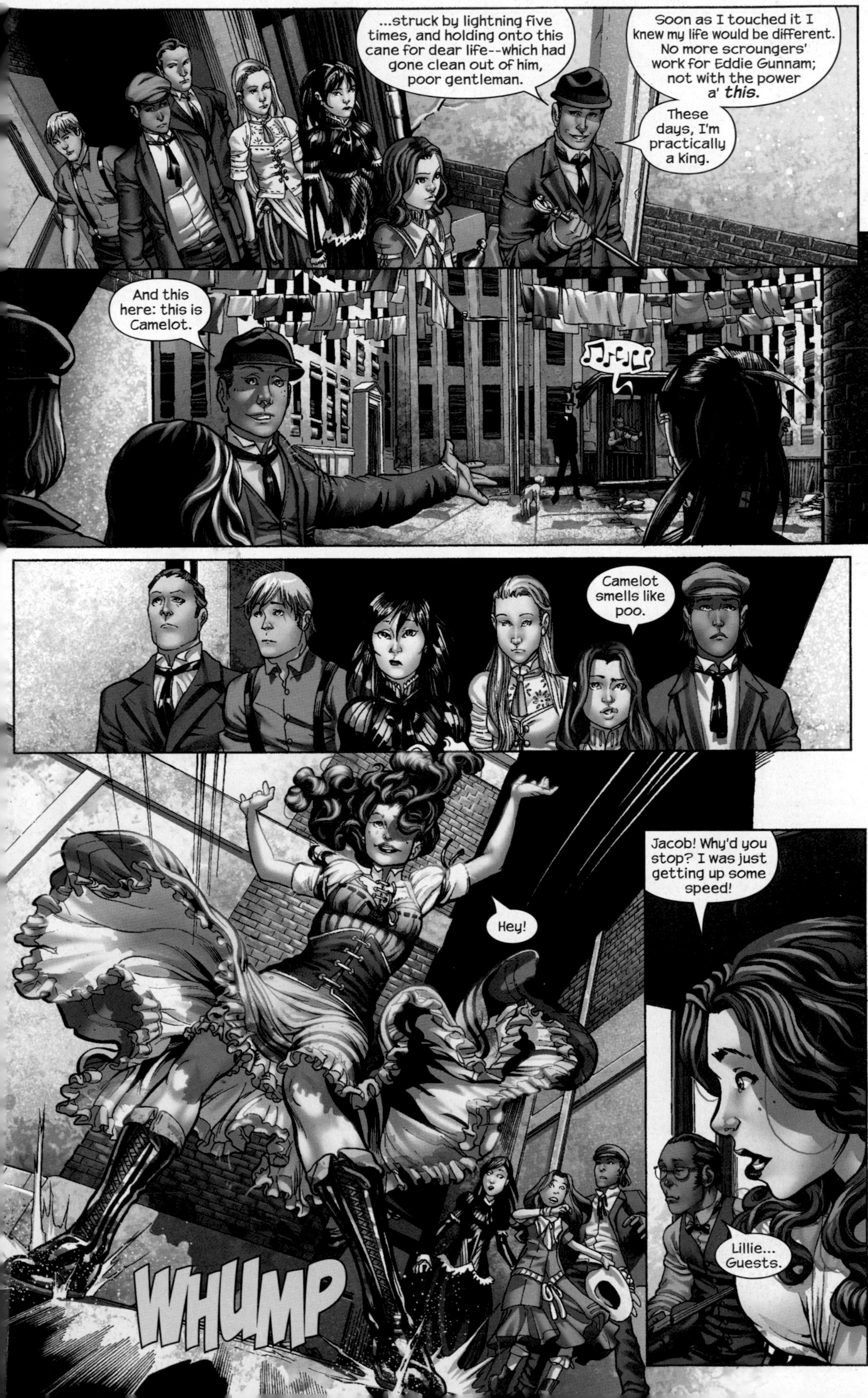
...struck by lightning five times, and holding onto this cane for dear life--which had gone clean out of him, poor gentleman.
Soon as I touched it I knew my life would be different. No more scroungers' work for Eddie Gunnam; not with the power a' *this.*
These days, I'm practically a king.
And this here: this is Camelot.
Camelot smells like poo.
Hey!
Jacob! Why'd you stop? I was just getting up some speed!
WHUMP
Lillie... Guests.

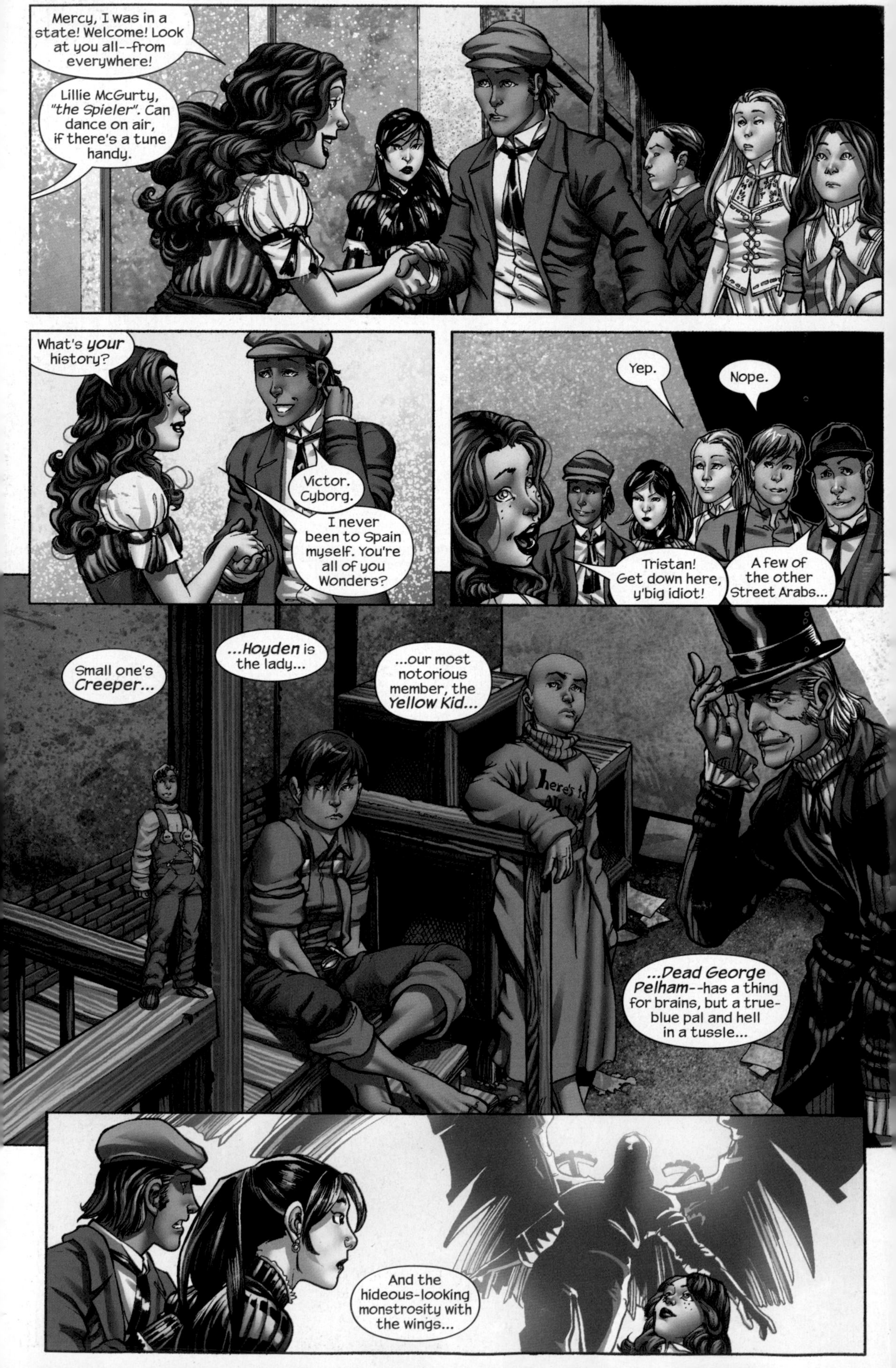

Mercy, I was in a state! Welcome! Look at you all--from everywhere!
Lillie McGurty, "the Spieler". Can dance on air, if there's a tune handy.
What's your history?
Victor. Cyborg.
I never been to Spain myself. You're all of you Wonders?
Yep.
Nope.
Tristan! Get down here, y'big idiot!
A few of the other Street Arabs...
Small one's Creeper...
...Hoyden is the lady...
...our most notorious member, the Yellow Kid...
...Dead George Pelham--has a thing for brains, but a true-blue pal and hell in a tussle...
And the hideous-looking monstrosity with the wings...

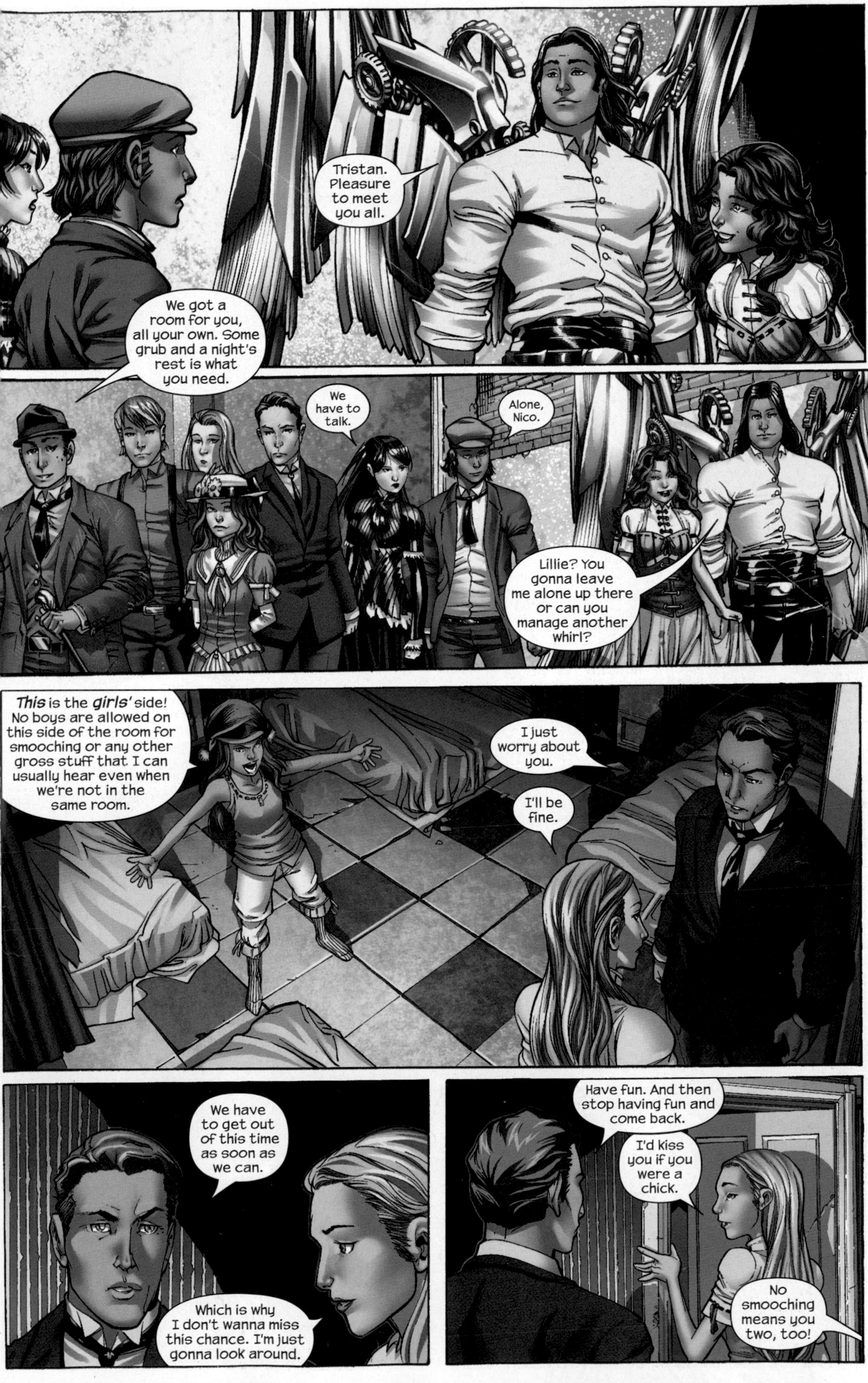
Tristan. Pleasure to meet you all.
We got a room for you, all your own. Some grub and a night's rest is what you need.
We have to talk.
Alone, Nico.
Lillie? You gonna leave me alone up there or can you manage another whirl?
This is the *girls'* side! No boys are allowed on this side of the room for smooching or any other gross stuff that I can usually hear even when we're not in the same room.
I just worry about you.
I'll be fine.
We have to get out of this time as soon as we can.
Which is why I don't wanna miss this chance. I'm just gonna look around.
Have fun. And then stop having fun and come back.
I'd kiss you if you were a chick.
No smooching means you two, too!

That's all? He gave you that message and let you go?

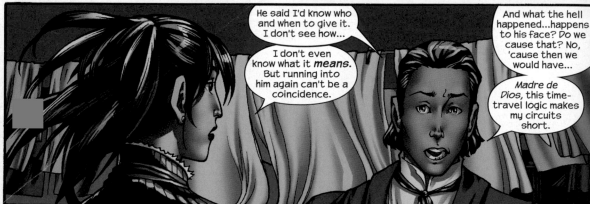

He said I'd know who and when to give it. I don't see how...

I don't even know what it *means*. But running into him again can't be a coincidence.

And what the hell happened...happens to his face? Do we cause that? No, 'cause then we would have...

Madre de Dios, this time-travel logic makes my circuits short.

Yeah, I smelled something burning when you met Miss Dance-On-Air, too.

What, Lillie? Please, she's clearly into Tristan.

That... wasn't the right response, was it?

Wow.

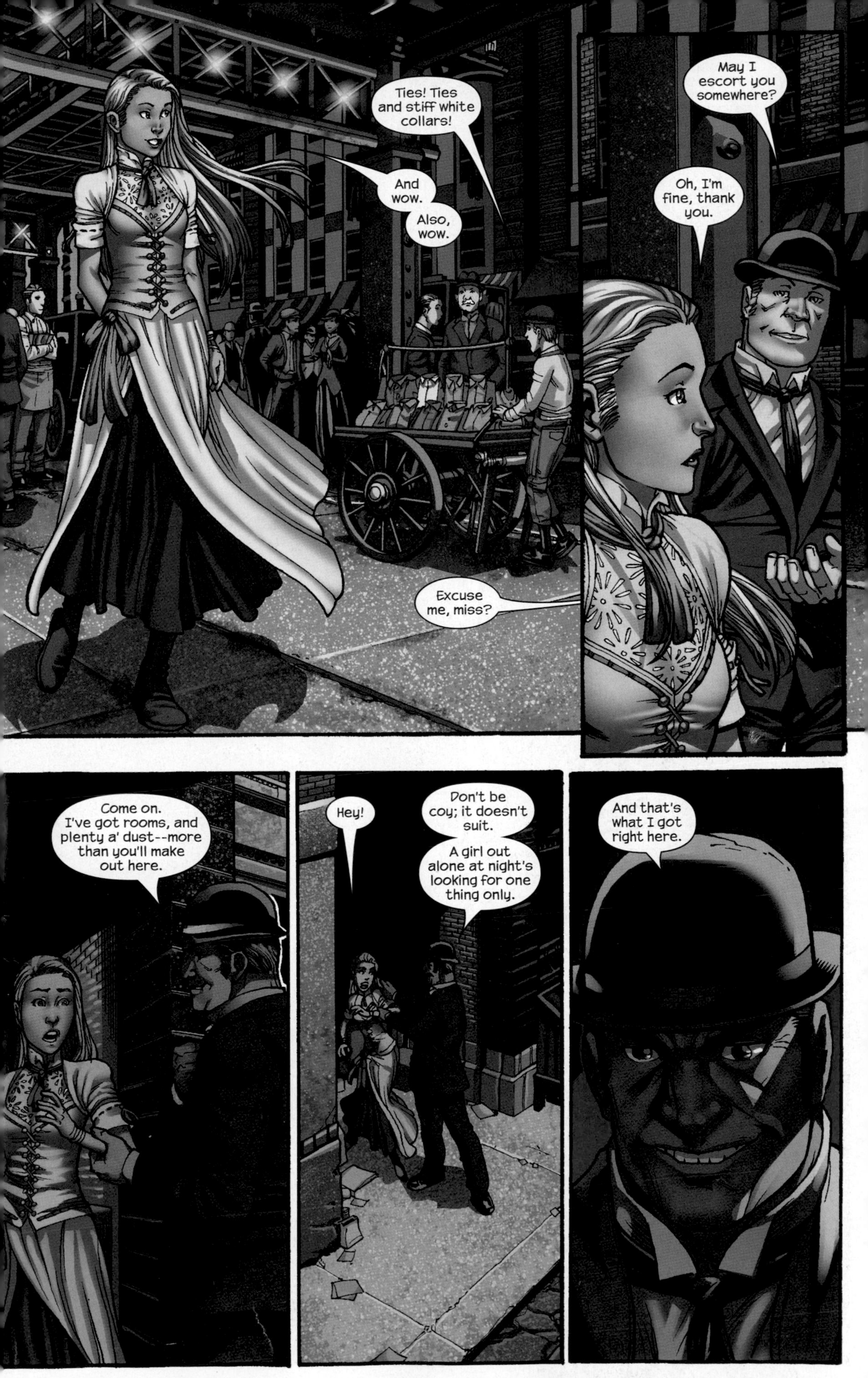
Ties! Ties and stiff white collars!
And wow.
Also, wow.
Excuse me, miss?
May I escort you somewhere?
Oh, I'm fine, thank you.
Come on. I've got rooms, and plenty a' dust--more than you'll make out here.
Hey!
Don't be coy; it doesn't suit.
A girl out alone at night's looking for one thing only.
And that's what I got right here.

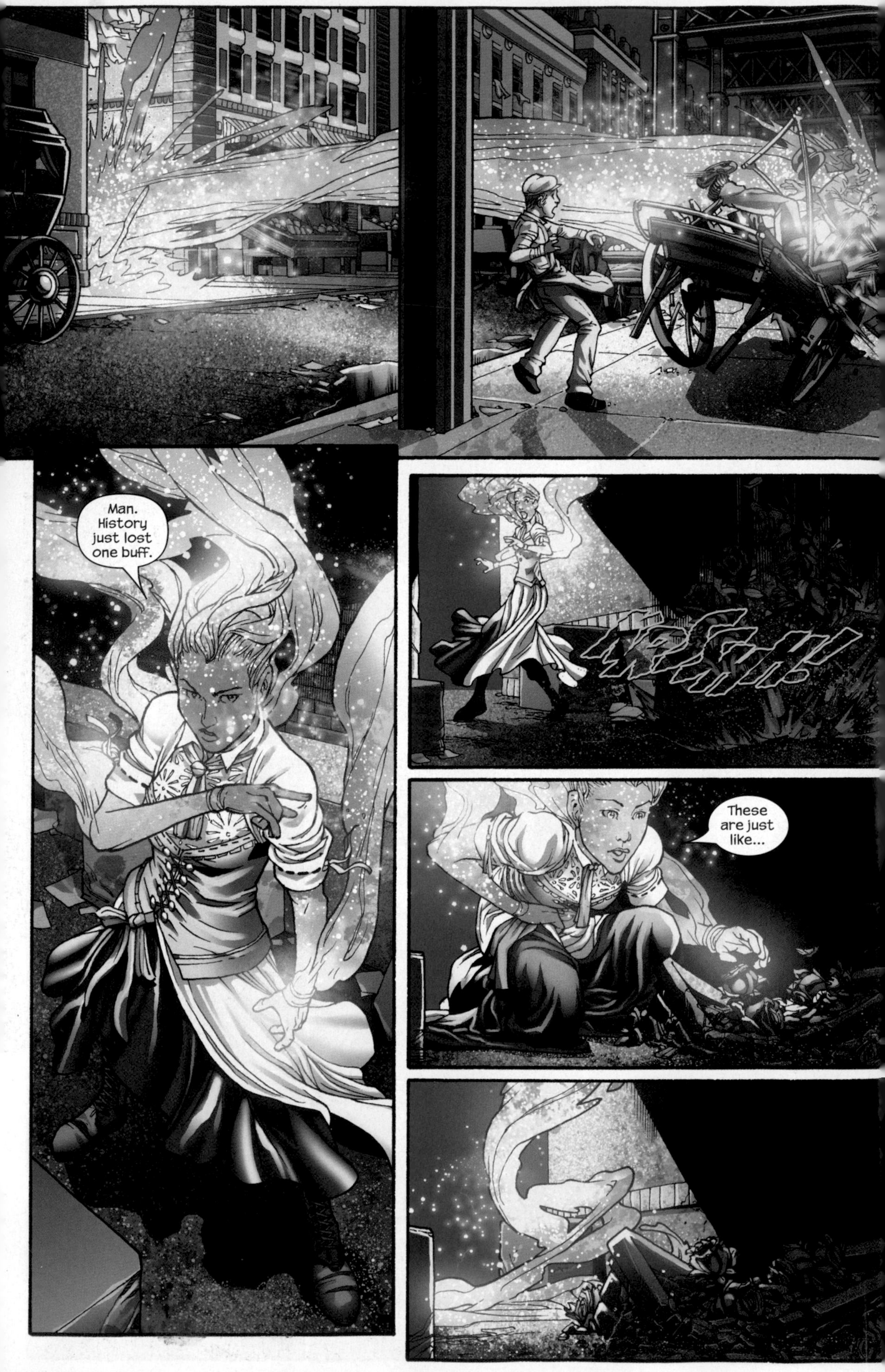
Man.
History
just lost
one buff.
These
are just
like...

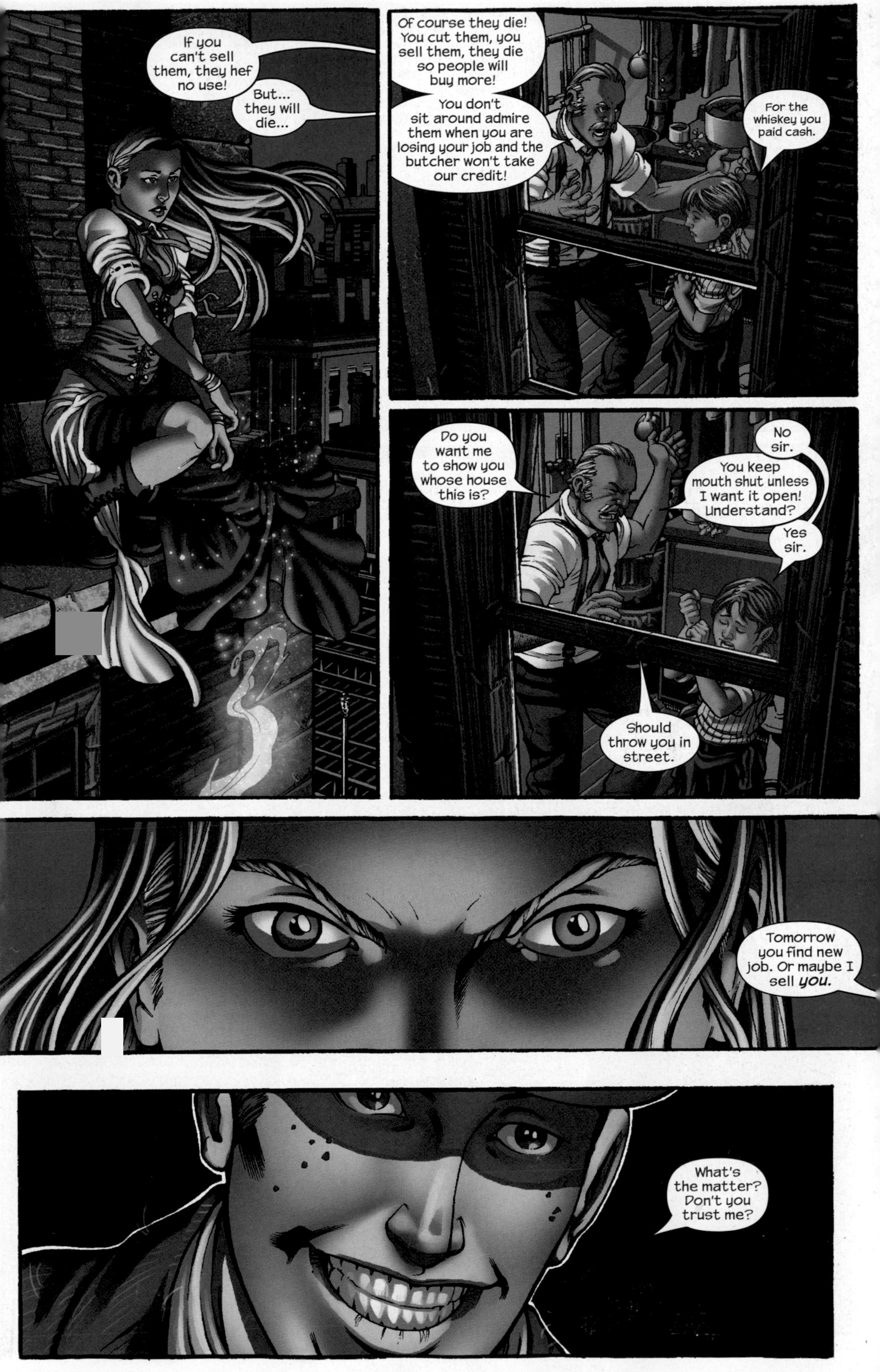
If you can't sell them, they hef no use!
But... they will die...
Of course they die! You cut them, you sell them, they die so people will buy more!
You don't sit around admire them when you are losing your job and the butcher won't take our credit!
For the whiskey you paid cash.
Do you want me to show you whose house this is?
No sir.
You keep mouth shut unless I want it open! Understand?
Yes sir.
Should throw you in street.
Tomorrow you find new job. Or maybe I sell *you.*
What's the matter? Don't you trust me?

The only reason anyone trusts you is that stick.

So yes, I trust you. But it bothers me that I do.

I seen these kids in action and I'm telling you, they're the genuine article.

I coulda gone to the Upward Path, they're sniffin' for recruits but I sez "No, get to the Mineola, talk to Maneater; he'll treat you square."

And what's your idea of square?

Finder's fee, plus a remembrance for any job they pull...

...maybe a word in for me with...you know... the Others?

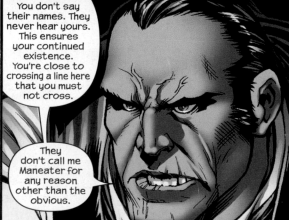

You don't say their names. They never hear yours. This ensures your continued existence. You're close to crossing a line here that you must not cross.

They don't call me Maneater for any reason other than the obvious.

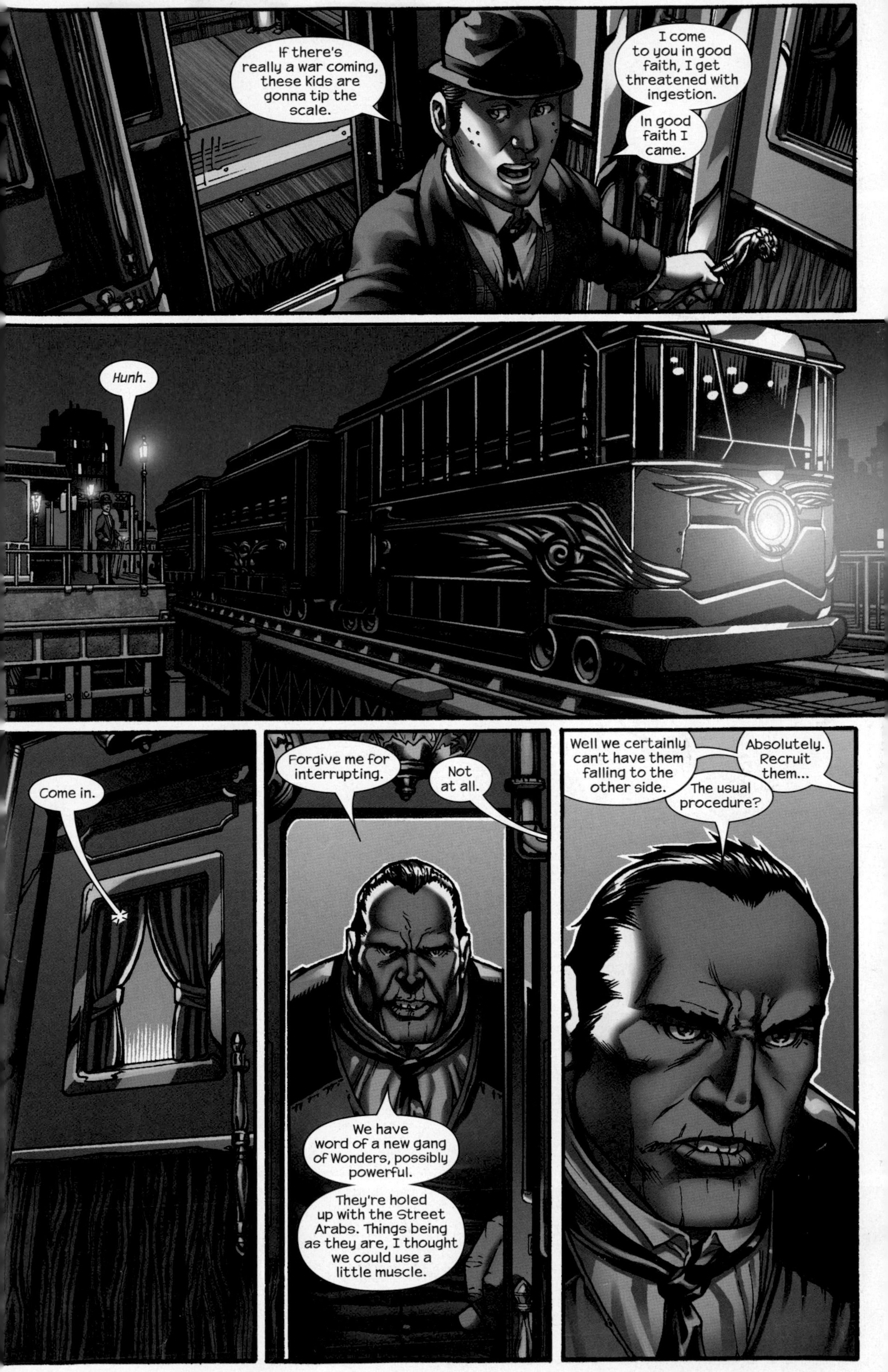
If there's really a war coming, these kids are gonna tip the scale.
I come to you in good faith, I get threatened with ingestion.
In good faith I came.
Hunh.
Come in.
Forgive me for interrupting.
Not at all.
We have word of a new gang of Wonders, possibly powerful.
They're holed up with the Street Arabs. Things being as they are, I thought we could use a little muscle.
Well we certainly can't have them falling to the other side.
Absolutely. Recruit them...
The usual procedure?

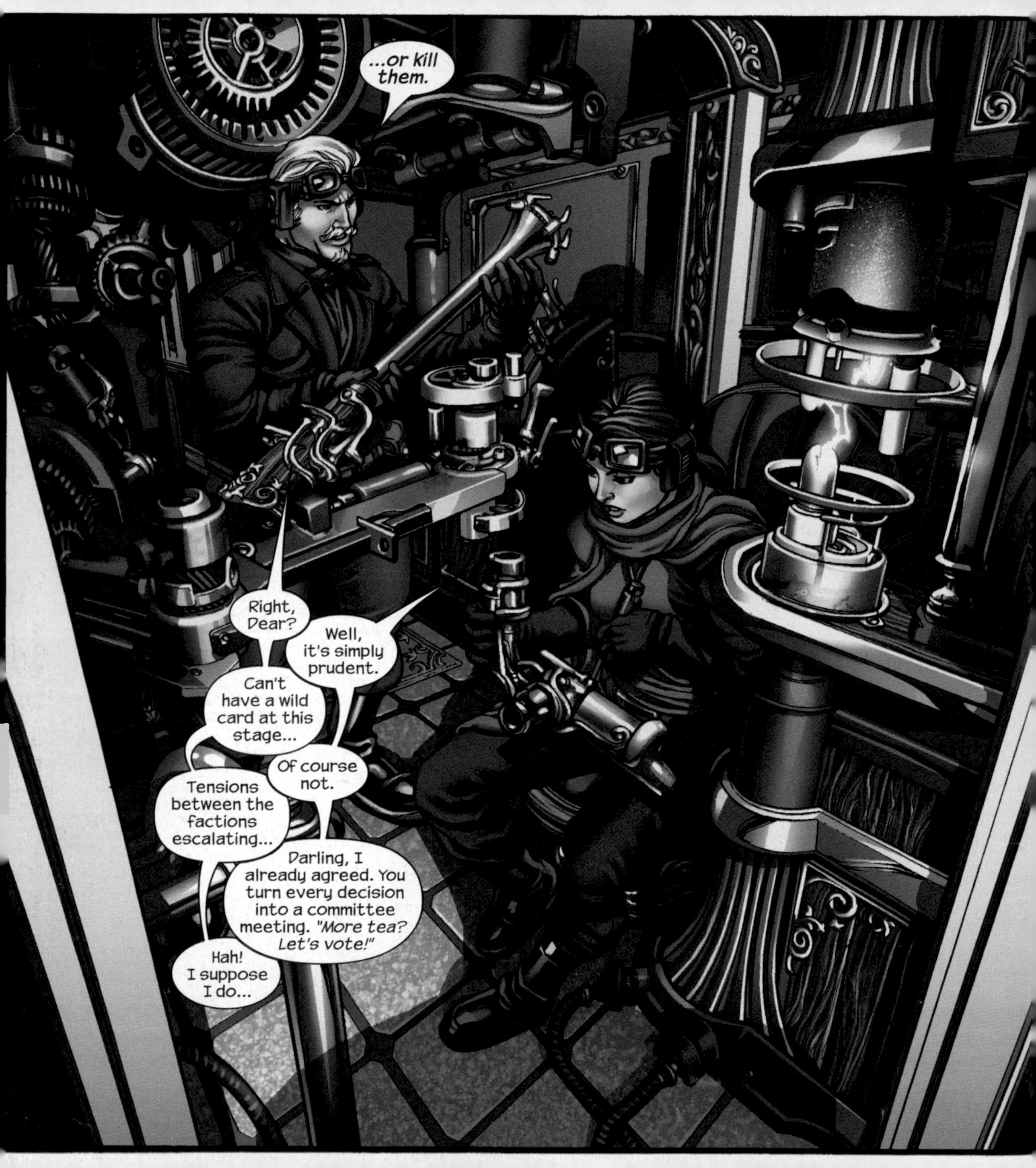
...or kill them.
Right, Dear?
Well, it's simply prudent.
Can't have a wild card at this stage...
Of course not.
Tensions between the factions escalating...
Darling, I already agreed. You turn every decision into a committee meeting. *"More tea? Let's vote!"*
Hah! I suppose I do...

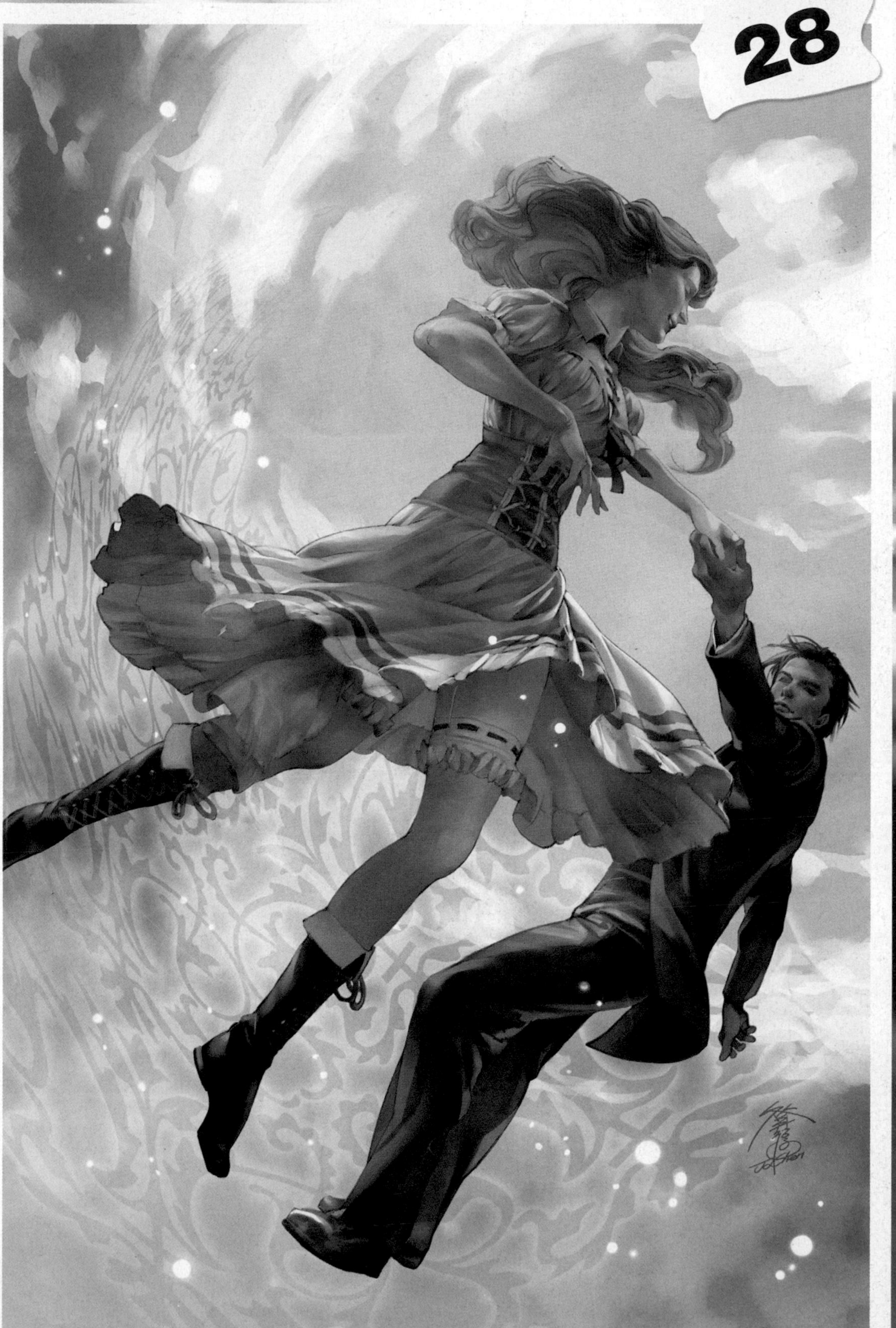
28

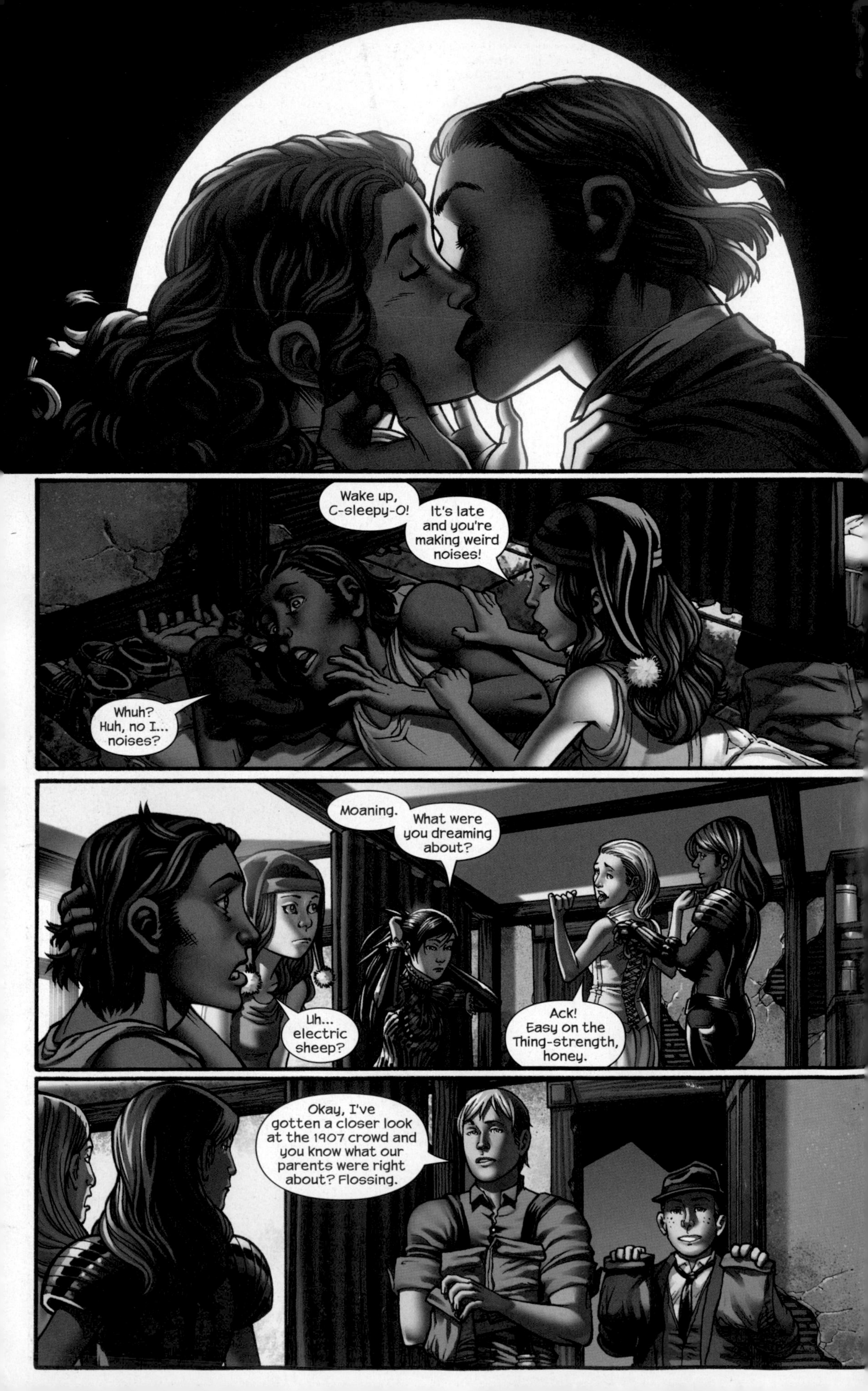
Wake up, C-sleepy-O!
It's late and you're making weird noises!
Whuh? Huh, no I... noises?
Moaning.
What were you dreaming about?
Uh... electric sheep?
Ack! Easy on the Thing-strength, honey.
Okay, I've gotten a closer look at the 1907 crowd and you know what our parents were right about? Flossing.

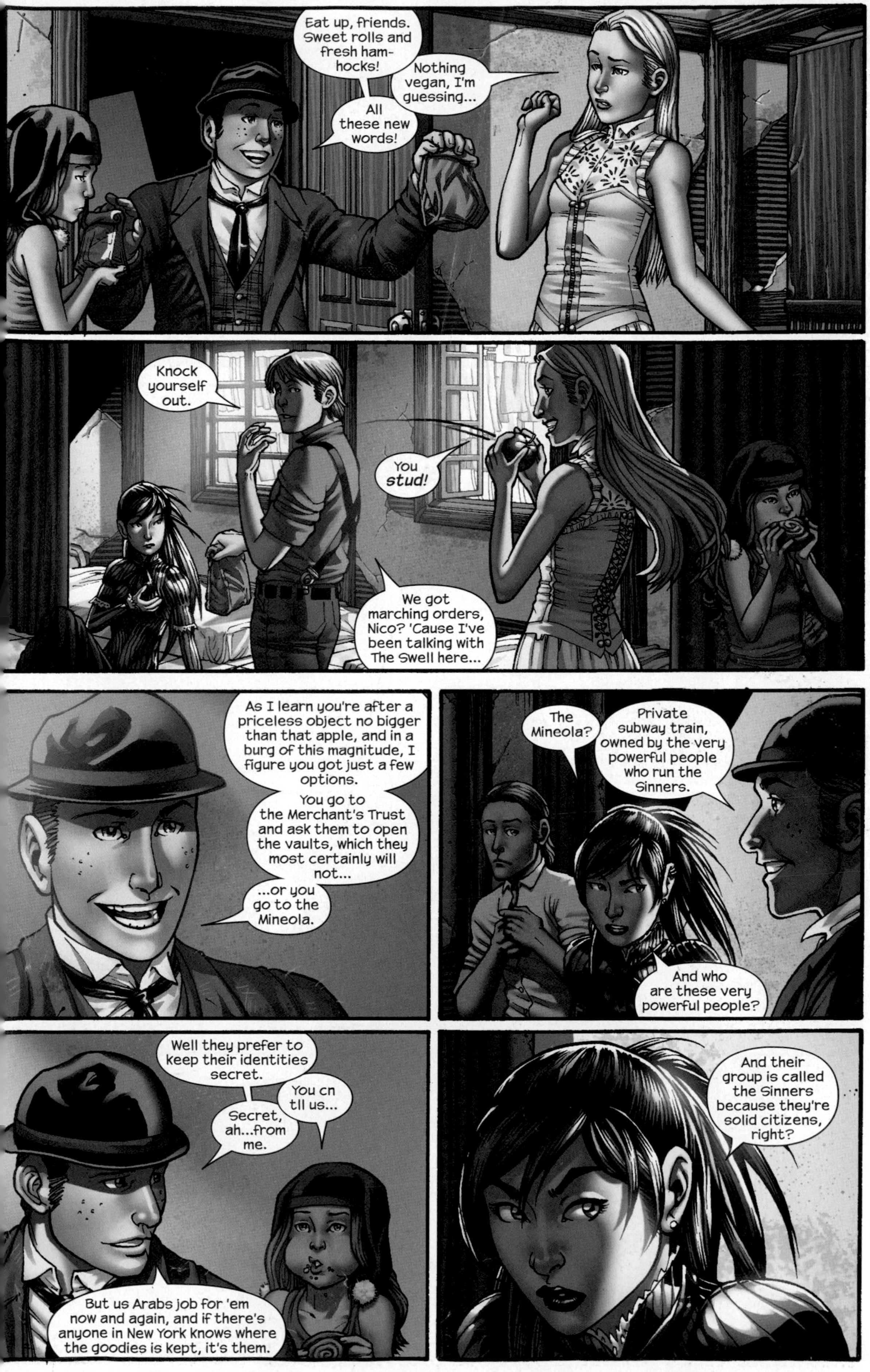

Eat up, friends. Sweet rolls and fresh ham-hocks!
All these new words!
Nothing vegan, I'm guessing...
Knock yourself out.
You *stud!*
We got marching orders, Nico? 'Cause I've been talking with The Swell here...
As I learn you're after a priceless object no bigger than that apple, and in a burg of this magnitude, I figure you got just a few options.
You go to the Merchant's Trust and ask them to open the vaults, which they most certainly will not...
...or you go to the Mineola.
The Mineola?
Private subway train, owned by the very powerful people who run the Sinners.
And who are these very powerful people?
Well they prefer to keep their identities secret.
Secret, ah...from me.
You cn tll us...
But us Arabs job for 'em now and again, and if there's anyone in New York knows where the goodies is kept, it's them.
And their group is called the Sinners because they're solid citizens, right?

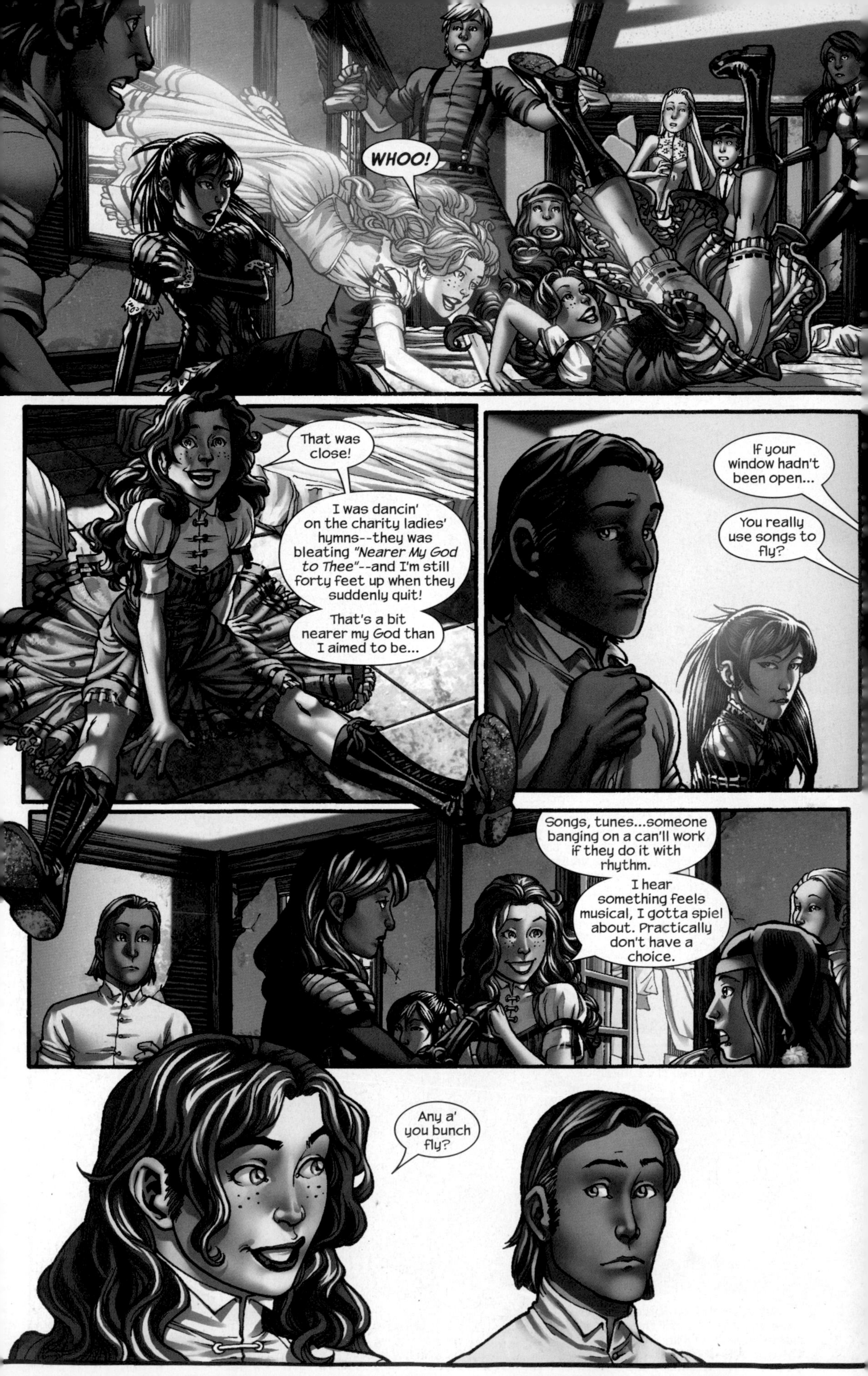
WHOO!
That was close!
I was dancin' on the charity ladies' hymns--they was bleating "Nearer My God to Thee"--and I'm still forty feet up when they suddenly quit!
That's a bit nearer my God than I aimed to be...
If your window hadn't been open...
You really use songs to fly?
Songs, tunes...someone banging on a can'll work if they do it with rhythm.
I hear something feels musical, I gotta spiel about. Practically don't have a choice.
Any a' you bunch fly?

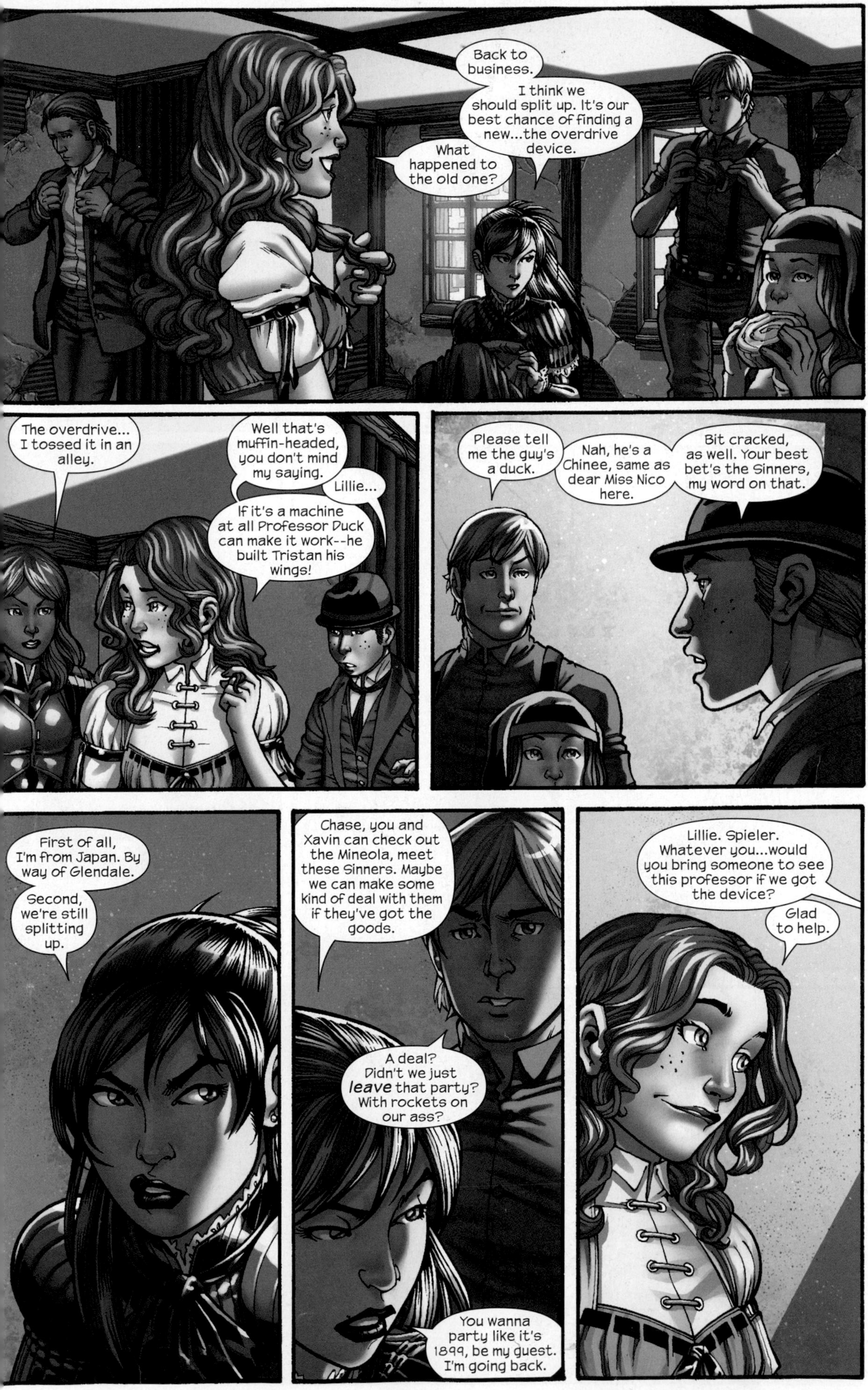
Back to business.
I think we should split up. It's our best chance of finding a new...the overdrive device.
What happened to the old one?
The overdrive... I tossed it in an alley.
Well that's muffin-headed, you don't mind my saying.
Lillie...
If it's a machine at all Professor Duck can make it work--he built Tristan his wings!
Please tell me the guy's a duck.
Nah, he's a Chinee, same as dear Miss Nico here.
Bit cracked, as well. Your best bet's the Sinners, my word on that.
First of all, I'm from Japan. By way of Glendale.
Second, we're still splitting up.
Chase, you and Xavin can check out the Mineola, meet these Sinners. Maybe we can make some kind of deal with them if they've got the goods.
A deal? Didn't we just *leave* that party? With rockets on our ass?
You wanna party like it's 1899, be my guest. I'm going back.
Lillie. Spieler. Whatever you...would you bring someone to see this professor if we got the device?
Glad to help.

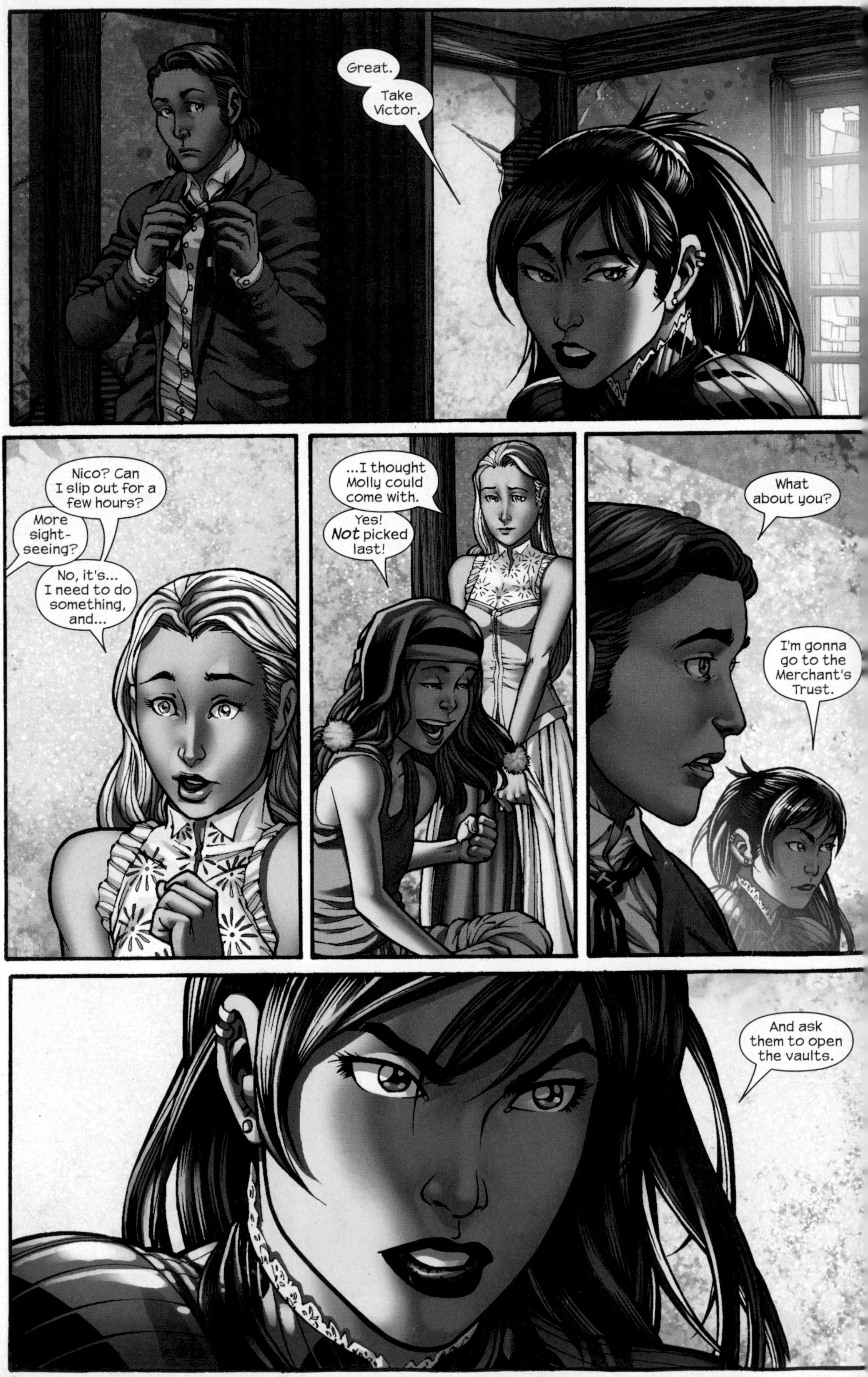
Great.
Take Victor.
Nico? Can I slip out for a few hours?
More sight-seeing?
No, it's... I need to do something, and...
...I thought Molly could come with.
Yes! **Not** picked last!
What about you?
I'm gonna go to the Merchant's Trust.
And ask them to open the vaults.

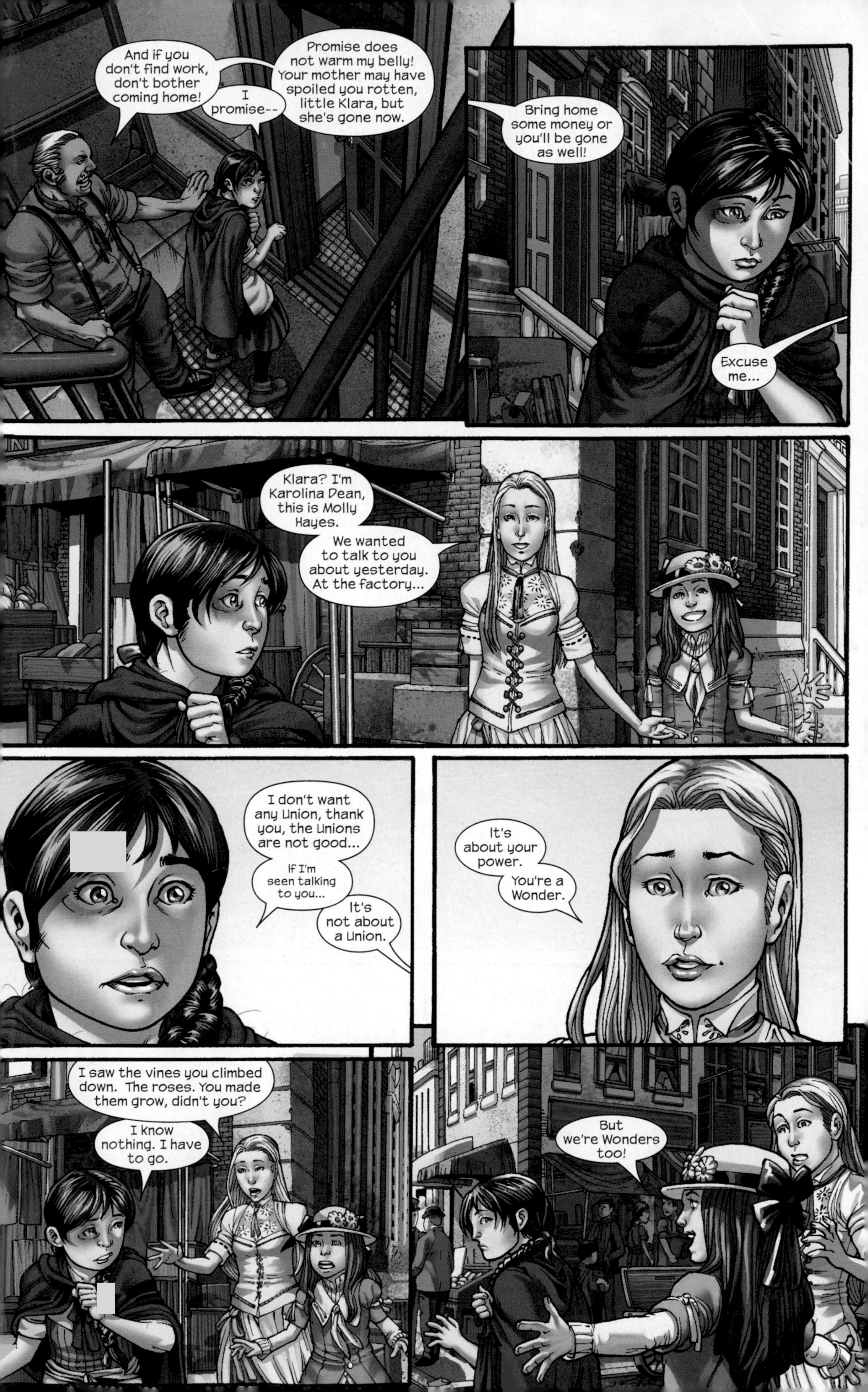
And if you don't find work, don't bother coming home!
I promise--
Promise does not warm my belly! Your mother may have spoiled you rotten, little Klara, but she's gone now.
Bring home some money or you'll be gone as well!
Excuse me...
Klara? I'm Karolina Dean, this is Molly Hayes.
We wanted to talk to you about yesterday. At the factory...
I don't want any Union, thank you, the Unions are not good...
If I'm seen talking to you...
It's not about a Union.
It's about your power.
You're a Wonder.
I saw the vines you climbed down. The roses. You made them grow, didn't you?
I know nothing. I have to go.
But we're Wonders too!

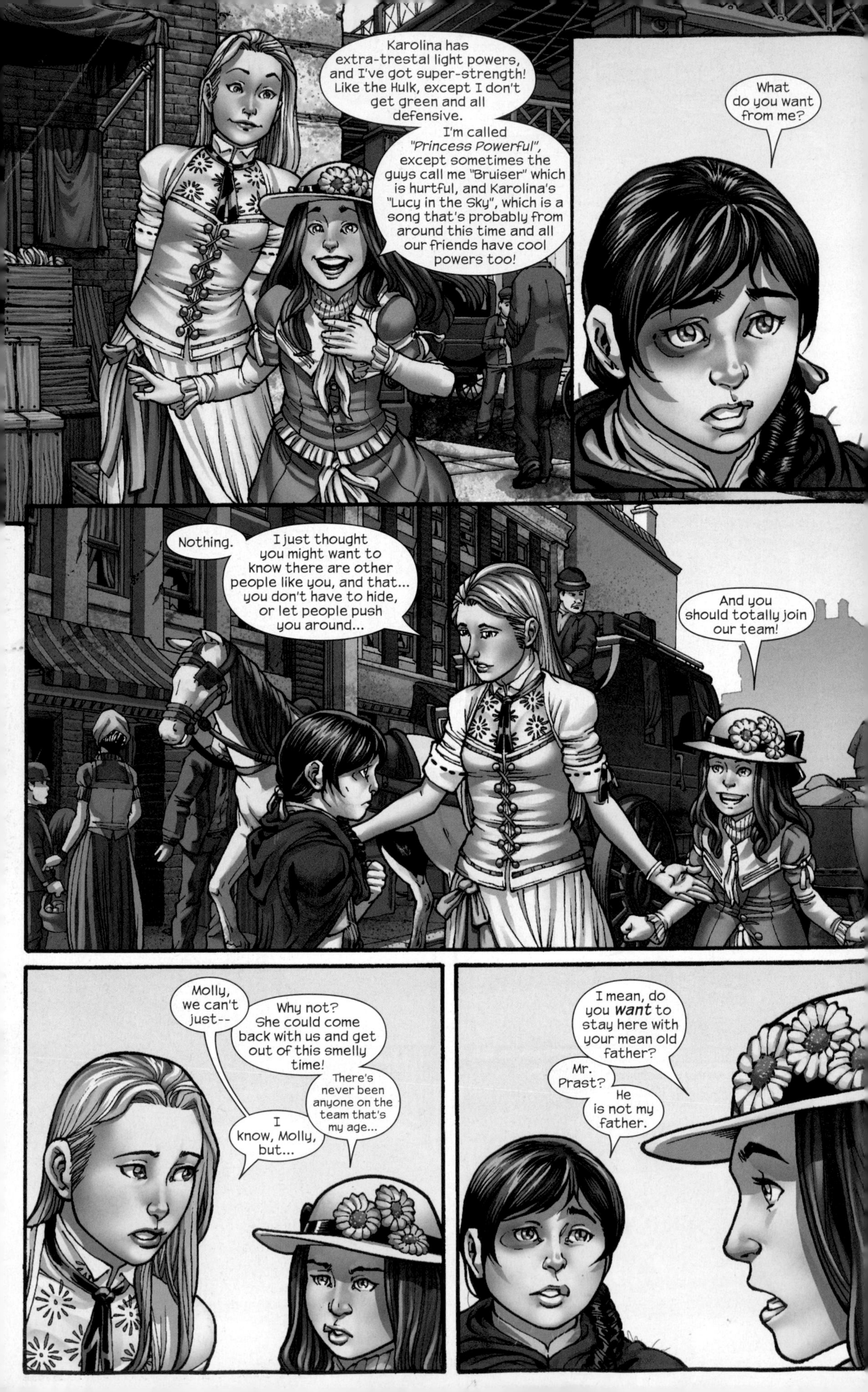
Karolina has extra-trestal light powers, and I've got super-strength! Like the Hulk, except I don't get green and all defensive.
I'm called "Princess Powerful", except sometimes the guys call me "Bruiser" which is hurtful, and Karolina's "Lucy in the Sky", which is a song that's probably from around this time and all our friends have cool powers too!
What do you want from me?
Nothing.
I just thought you might want to know there are other people like you, and that... you don't have to hide, or let people push you around...
And you should totally join our team!
Molly, we can't just--
Why not? She could come back with us and get out of this smelly time!
There's never been anyone on the team that's my age...
I know, Molly, but...
I mean, do you *want* to stay here with your mean old father?
Mr. Prast?
He is not my father.

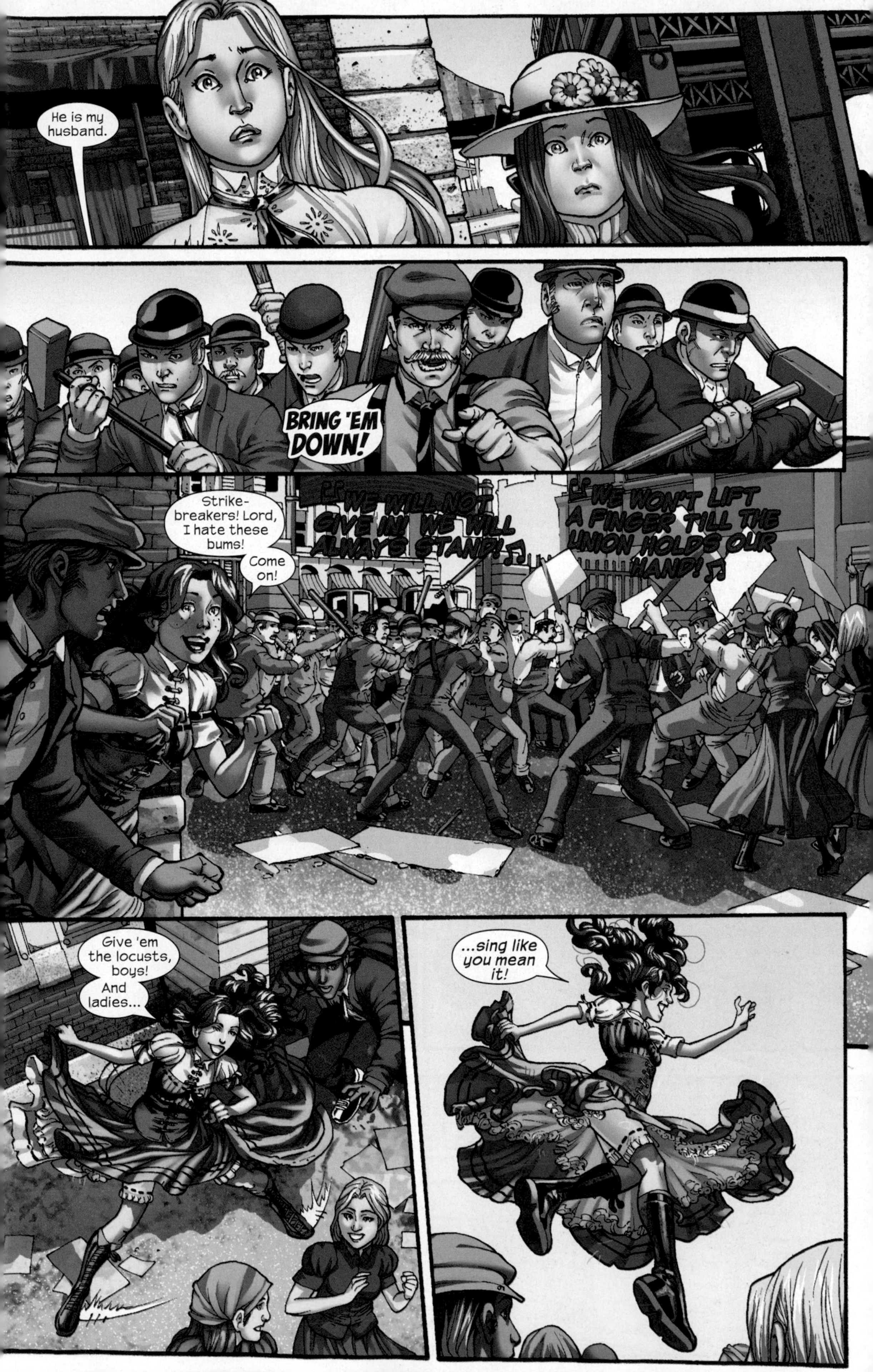

He is my husband.
BRING 'EM DOWN!
Strike-breakers! Lord, I hate these bums!
Come on!
WE WILL NOT GIVE IN! WE WILL ALWAYS STAND!
WE WON'T LIFT A FINGER TILL THE UNION HOLDS OUR HAND!
Give 'em the locusts, boys!
And ladies...
...sing like you mean it!

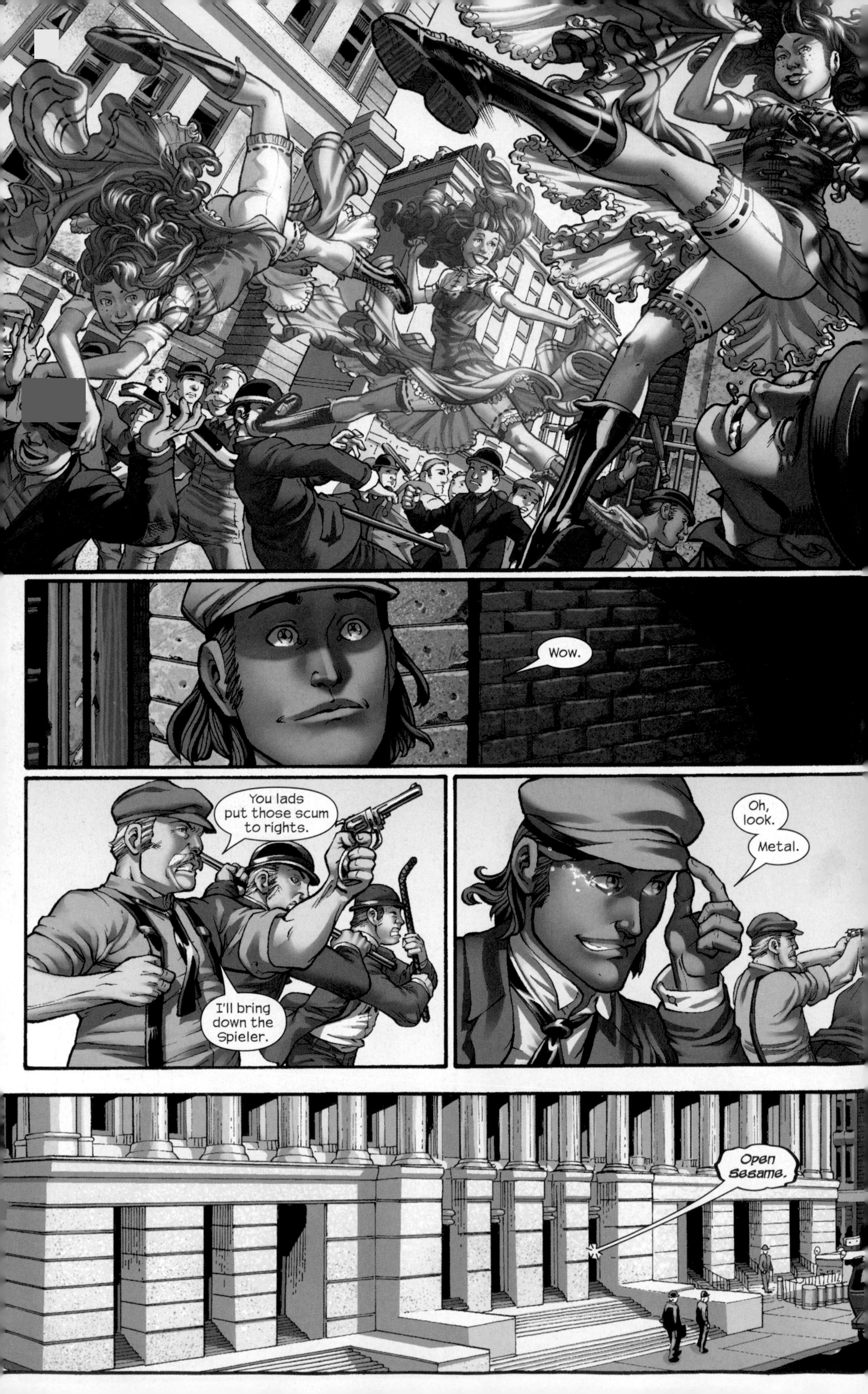
Wow.
You lads put those scum to rights.
I'll bring down the Spieler.
Oh, look.
Metal.
Open Sesame.

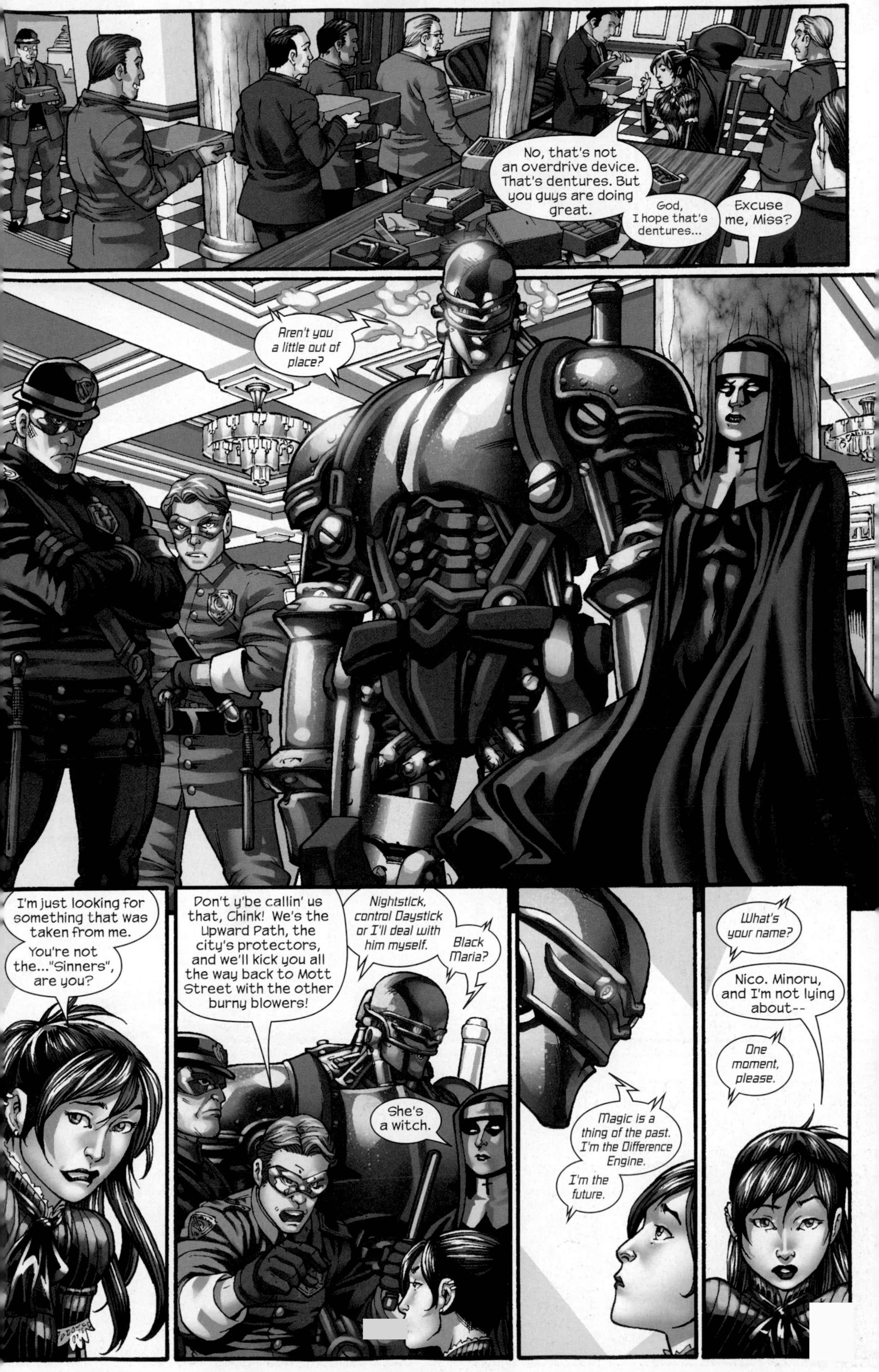
No, that's not an overdrive device. That's dentures. But you guys are doing great.
God, I hope that's dentures...
Excuse me, Miss?
Aren't you a little out of place?
I'm just looking for something that was taken from me.
You're not the..."Sinners", are you?
Don't y'be callin' us that, Chink! We's the Upward Path, the city's protectors, and we'll kick you all the way back to Mott Street with the other burny blowers!
Nightstick, control Daystick or I'll deal with him myself.
Black Maria?
She's a witch.
Magic is a thing of the past. I'm the Difference Engine.
I'm the future.
What's your name?
Nico. Minoru, and I'm not lying about--
One moment, please.

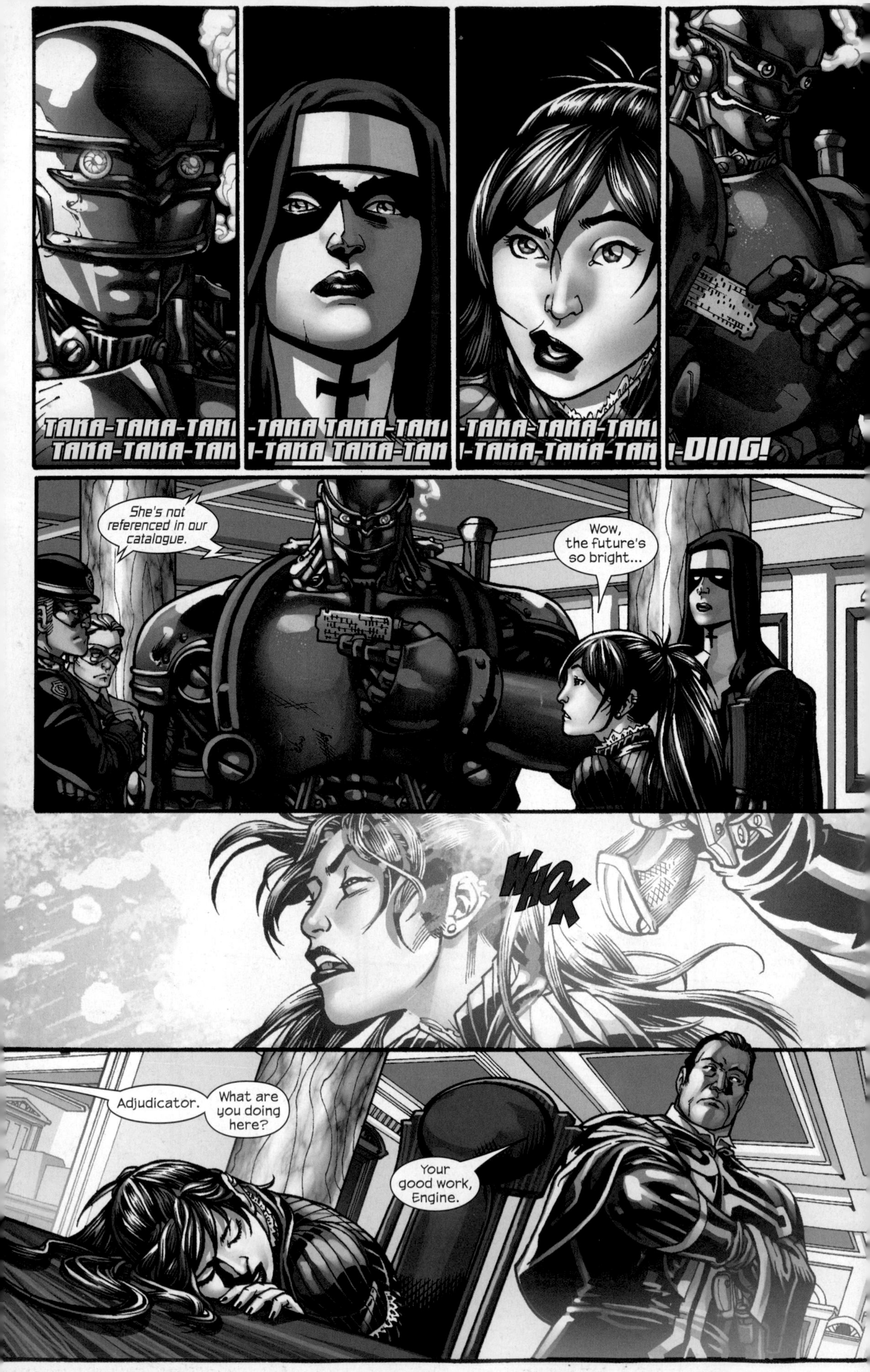
TAKA-TAKA-TAK
TAKA-TAKA-TAK
-TAKA TAKA-TAK
-TAKA TAKA-TAK
-TAKA-TAKA-TAK
-TAKA-TAKA-TAK
-DING!
She's not referenced in our catalogue.
Wow, the future's so bright...
WHOK
Adjudicator.
What are you doing here?
Your good work, Engine.

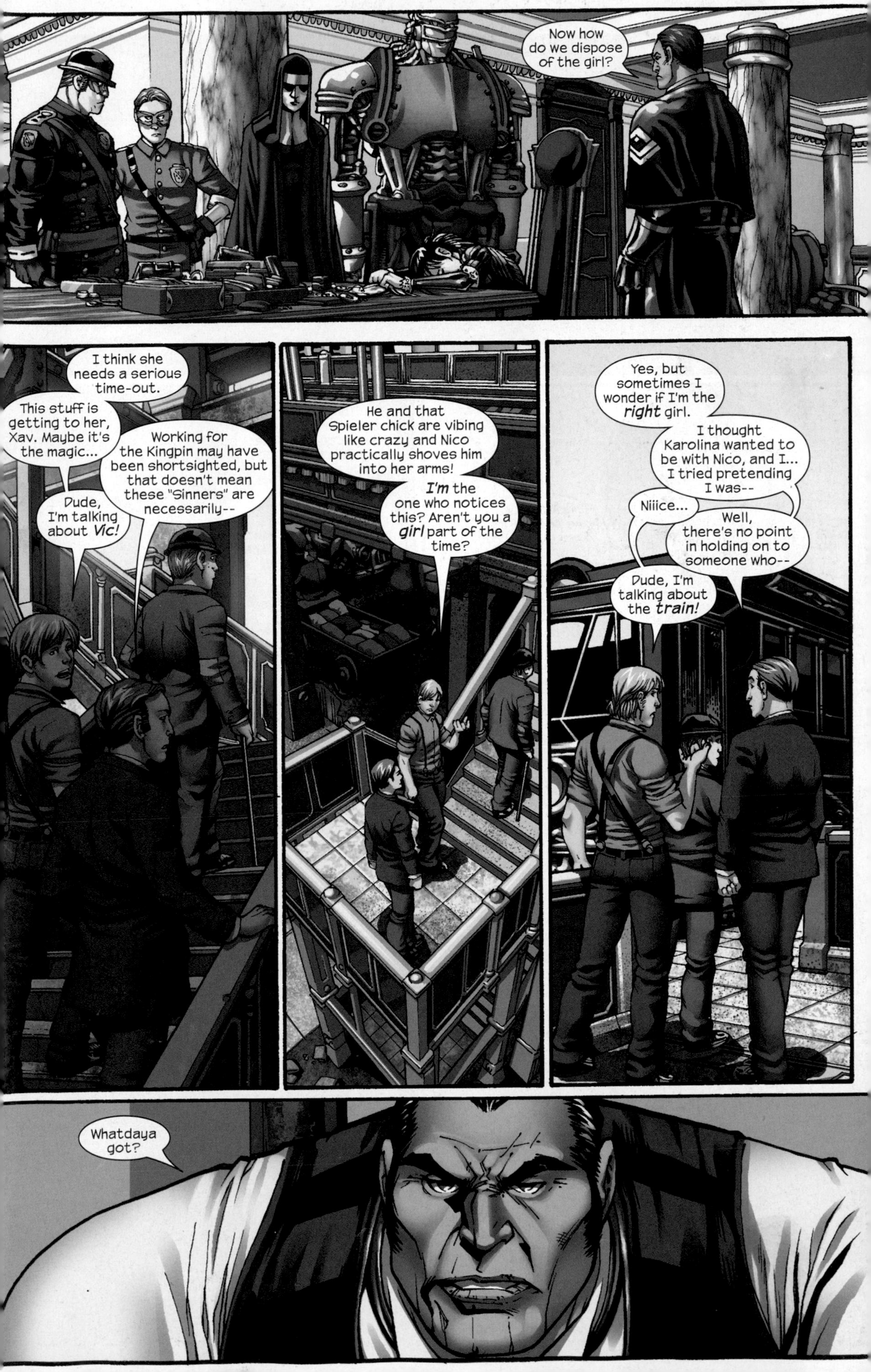
Now how do we dispose of the girl?
I think she needs a serious time-out.
This stuff is getting to her, Xav. Maybe it's the magic...
Working for the Kingpin may have been shortsighted, but that doesn't mean these "Sinners" are necessarily--
Dude, I'm talking about Vic!
He and that Spieler chick are vibing like crazy and Nico practically shoves him into her arms!
I'm the one who notices this? Aren't you a girl part of the time?
Yes, but sometimes I wonder if I'm the right girl.
I thought Karolina wanted to be with Nico, and I... I tried pretending I was--
Niiice...
Well, there's no point in holding on to someone who--
Dude, I'm talking about the train!
Whatdaya got?

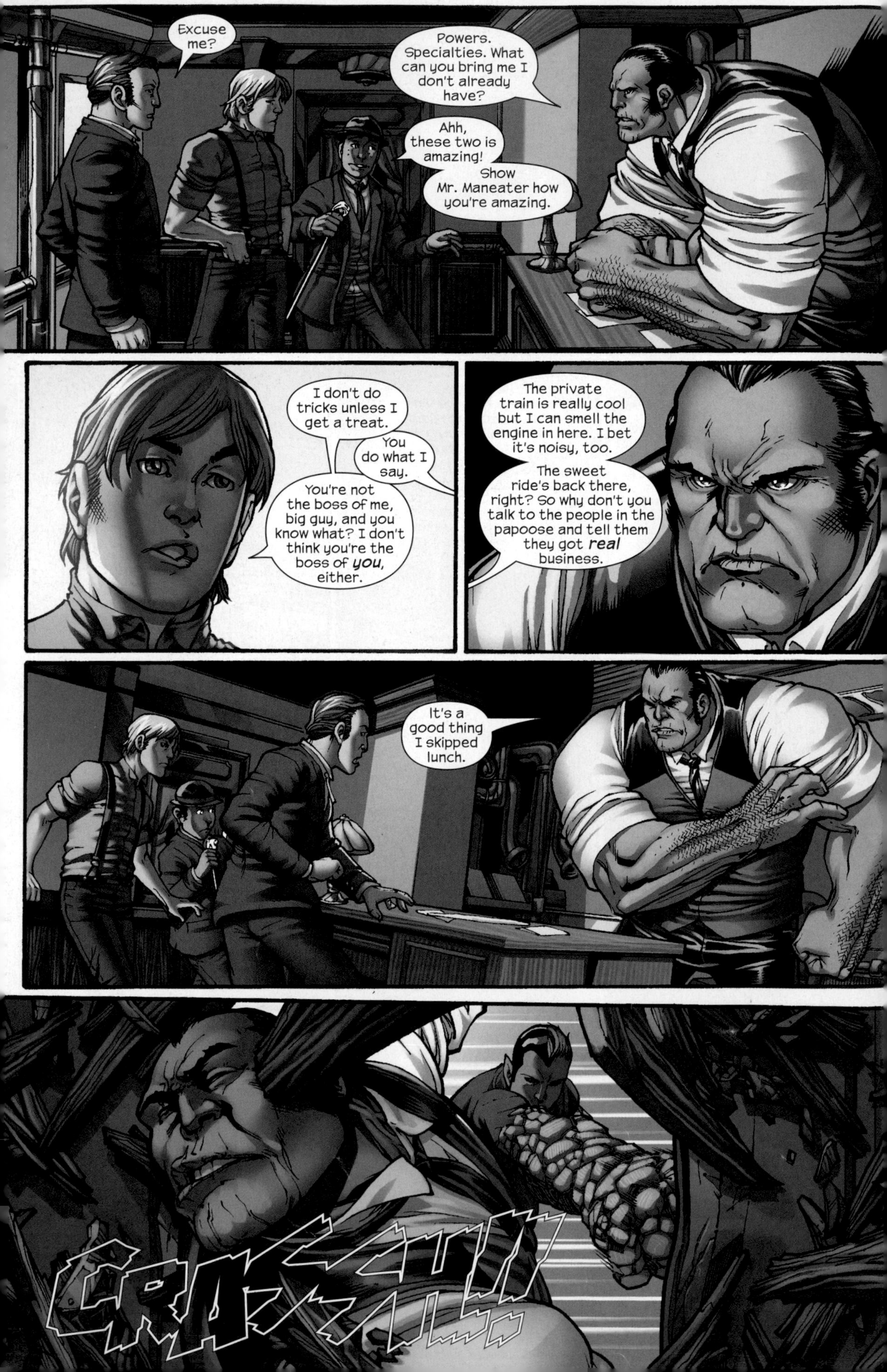
Excuse me?
Powers. Specialties. What can you bring me I don't already have?
Ahh, these two is amazing!
Show Mr. Maneater how you're amazing.
I don't do tricks unless I get a treat.
You do what I say.
You're not the boss of me, big guy, and you know what? I don't think you're the boss of *you*, either.
The private train is really cool but I can smell the engine in here. I bet it's noisy, too.
The sweet ride's back there, right? So why don't you talk to the people in the papoose and tell them they got *real* business.
It's a good thing I skipped lunch.
CRAKTHUD!

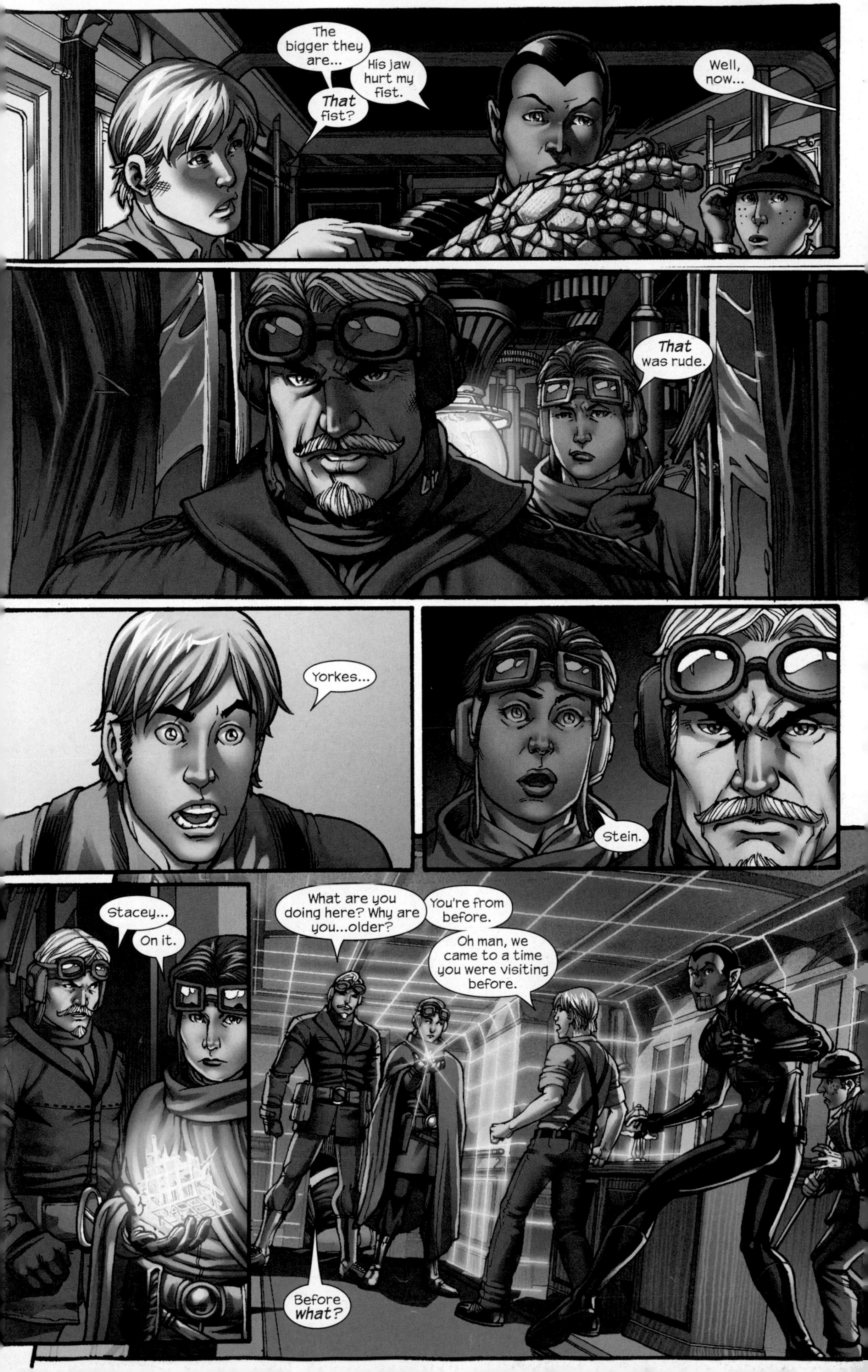
The bigger they are...
That fist?
His jaw hurt my fist.
Well, now...
That was rude.
Yorkes...
Stein.
Stacey...
On it.
What are you doing here? Why are you...older?
You're from before.
Oh man, we came to a time you were visiting before.
Before what?

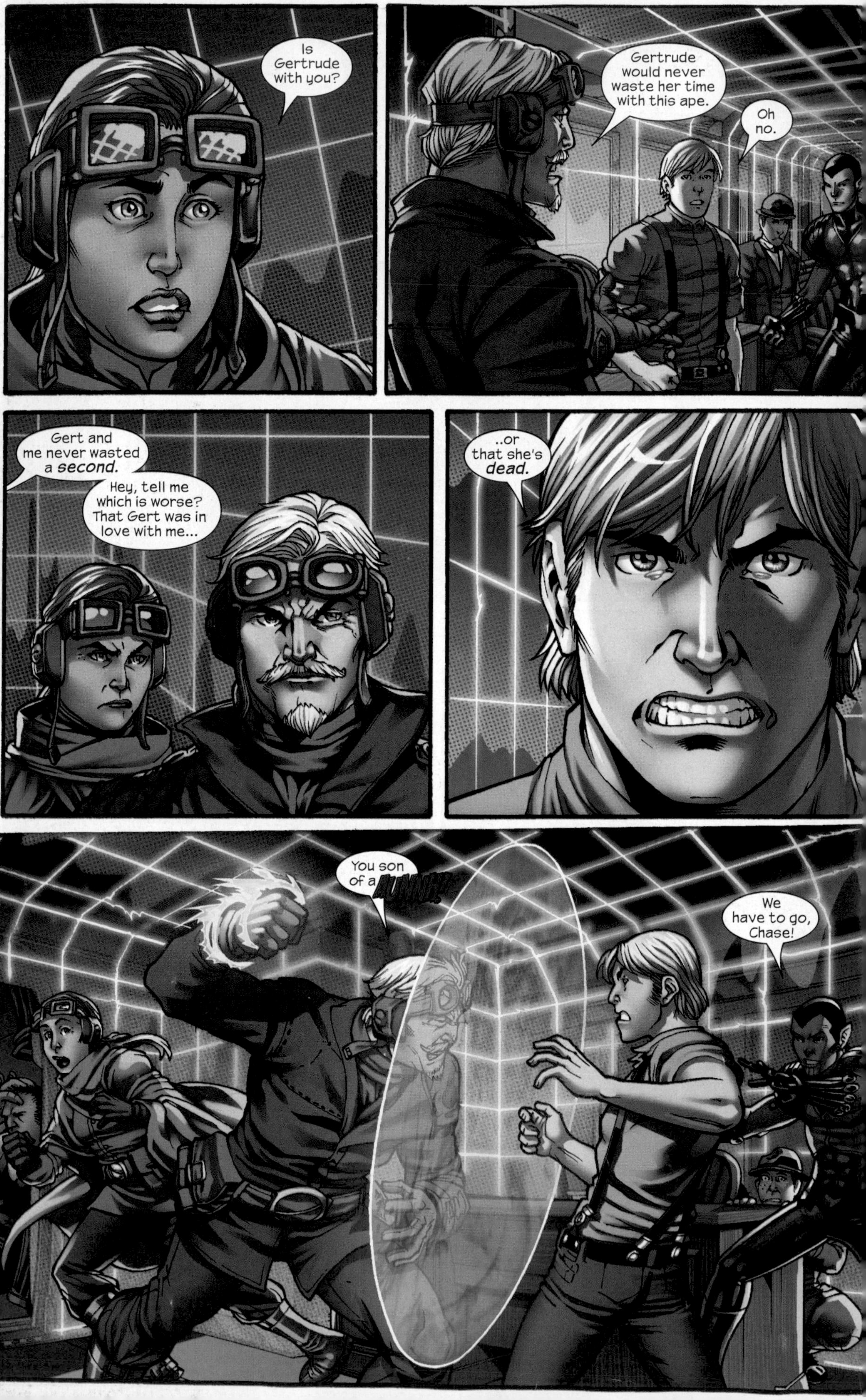
Is Gertrude with you?
Gertrude would never waste her time with this ape.
Oh no.
Gert and me never wasted a *second.*
Hey, tell me which is worse? That Gert was in love with me...
..or that she's *dead.*
You son of a
We have to go, Chase!

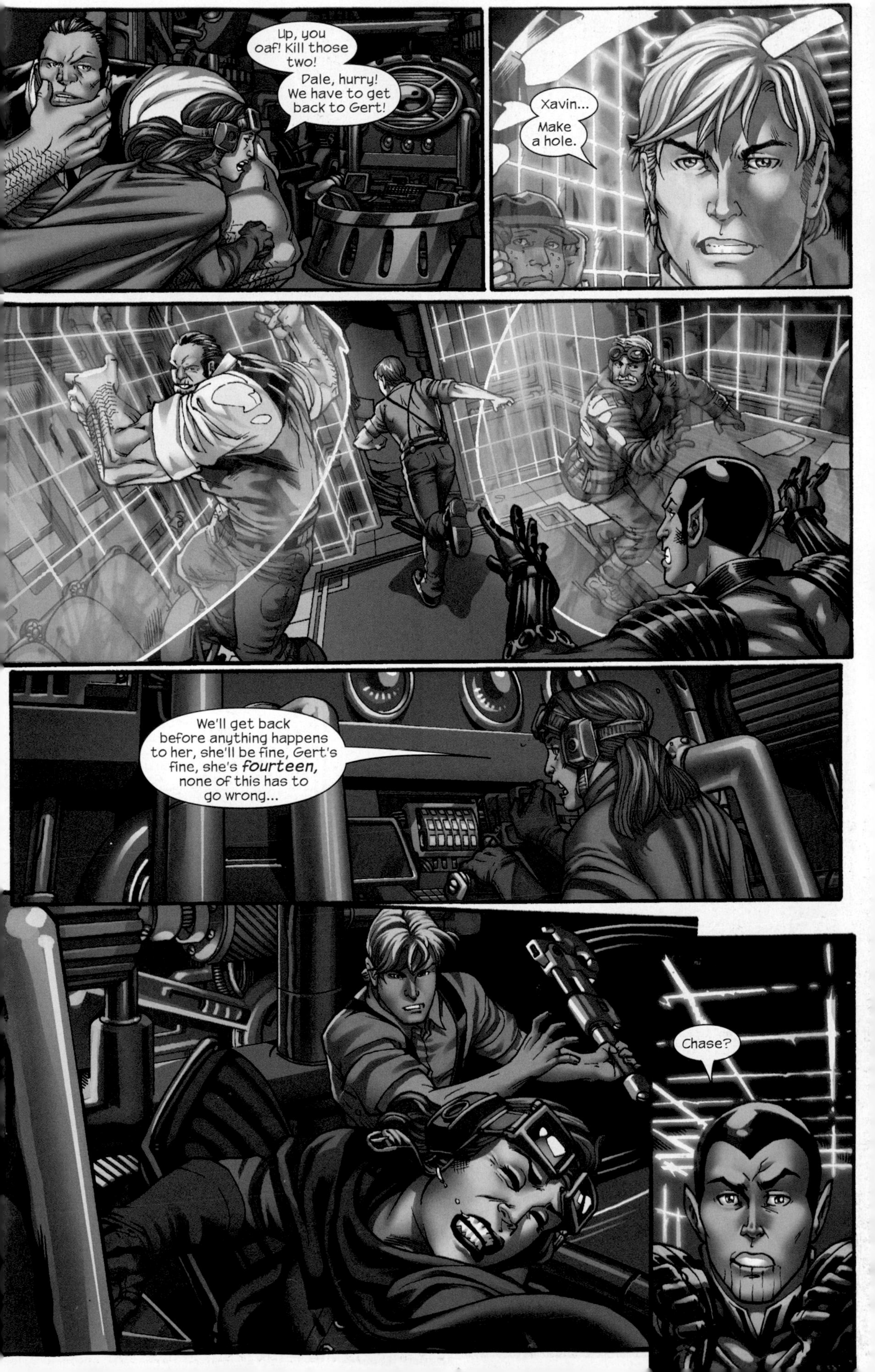

Up, you oaf! Kill those two!
Dale, hurry! We have to get back to Gert!
Xavin...
Make a hole.
We'll get back before anything happens to her, she'll be fine, Gert's fine, she's *fourteen,* none of this has to go wrong...
Chase?

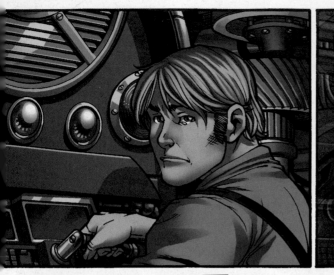
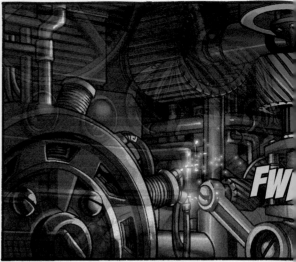

FWI

HHRRAAY!!

Ah, glory! What a rumpus!

Didjya see the pikers run?

You people don't kid around...

And you! Tossin' girders about...and did I see you *float*?

Well, you know, I'm a cyborg... I work well with electricity, microwaves...computers, which you won't have for a while...

C'mere.

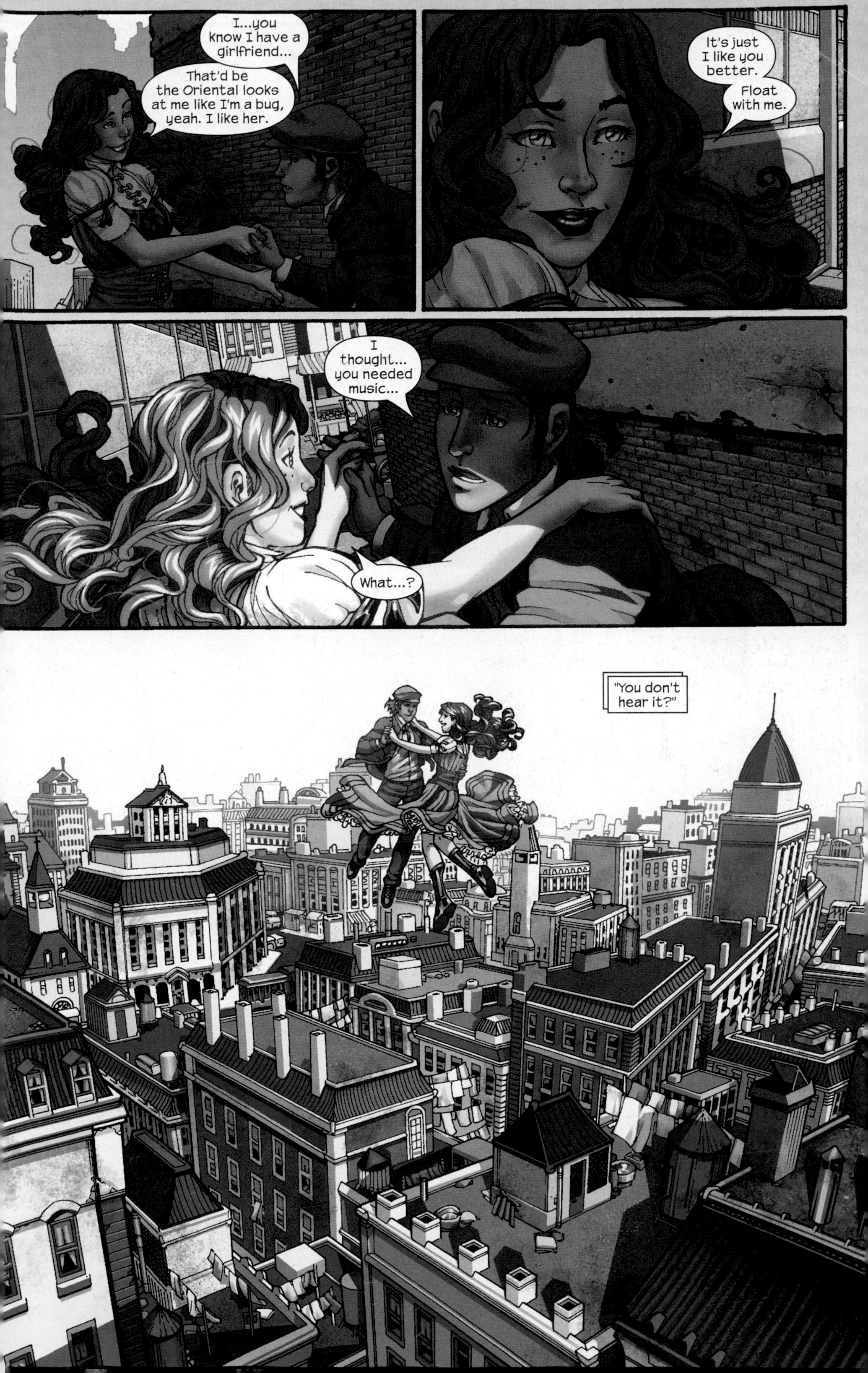

I...you know I have a girlfriend...
That'd be the Oriental looks at me like I'm a bug, yeah. I like her.
It's just I like you better.
Float with me.
I thought... you needed music...
What...?
"You don't hear it?"

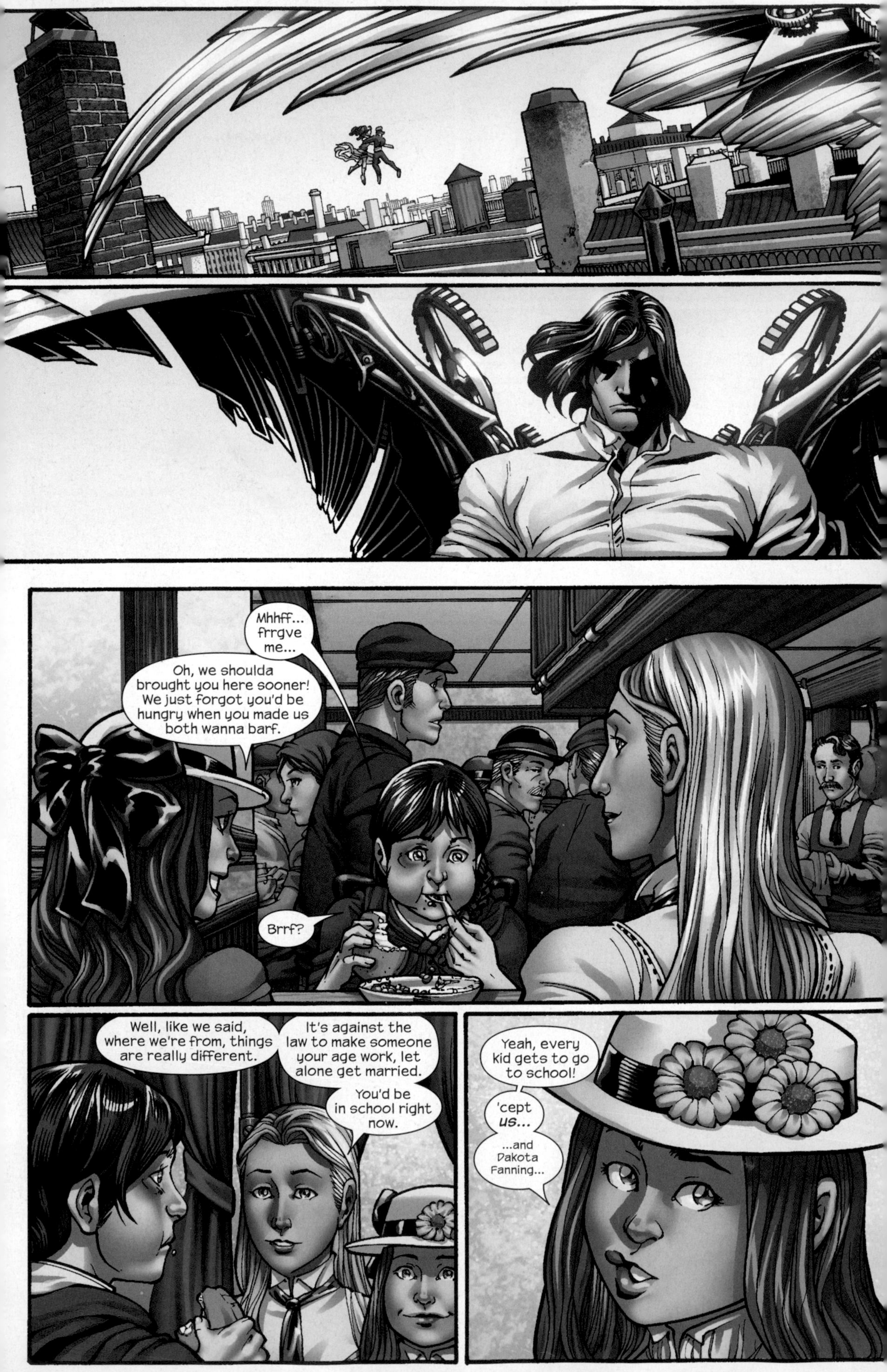
Mhhff... frrgve me...
Oh, we shoulda brought you here sooner! We just forgot you'd be hungry when you made us both wanna barf.
Brrf?
Well, like we said, where we're from, things are really different.
It's against the law to make someone your age work, let alone get married.
You'd be in school right now.
Yeah, every kid gets to go to school!
'cept *us...*
...and Dakota Fanning...

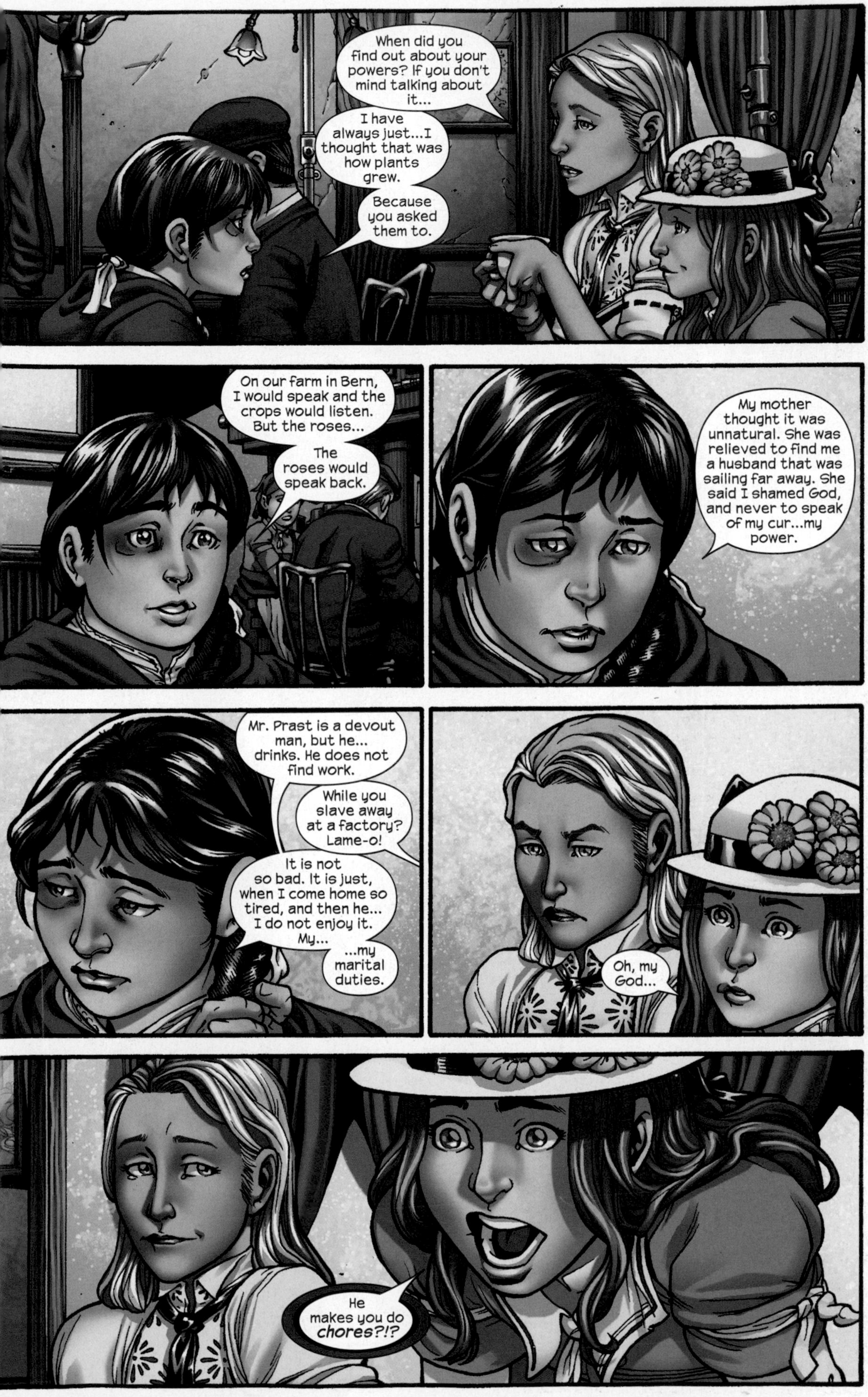
When did you find out about your powers? If you don't mind talking about it...
I have always just...I thought that was how plants grew.
Because you asked them to.
On our farm in Bern, I would speak and the crops would listen. But the roses...
The roses would speak back.
My mother thought it was unnatural. She was relieved to find me a husband that was sailing far away. She said I shamed God, and never to speak of my cur...my power.
Mr. Prast is a devout man, but he... drinks. He does not find work.
While you slave away at a factory? Lame-o!
It is not so bad. It is just, when I come home so tired, and then he... I do not enjoy it. My...
...my marital duties.
Oh, my God...
He makes you do chores?!?

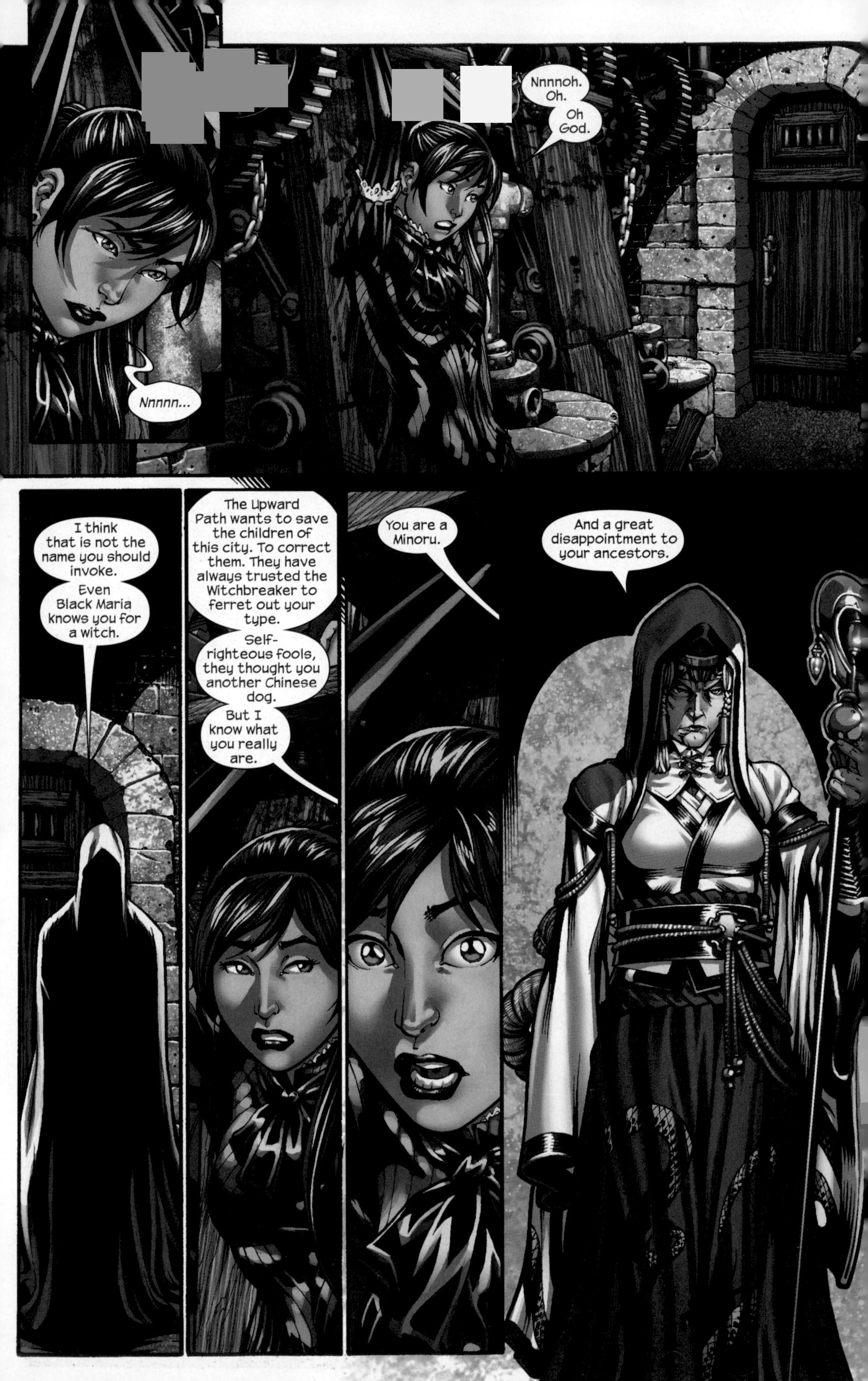
Nnnnn...
Nnnnoh. Oh.
Oh God.
I think that is not the name you should invoke.
Even Black Maria knows you for a witch.
The Upward Path wants to save the children of this city. To correct them. They have always trusted the Witchbreaker to ferret out your type.
Self-righteous fools, they thought you another Chinese dog.
But I know what you really are.
You are a Minoru.
And a great disappointment to your ancestors.

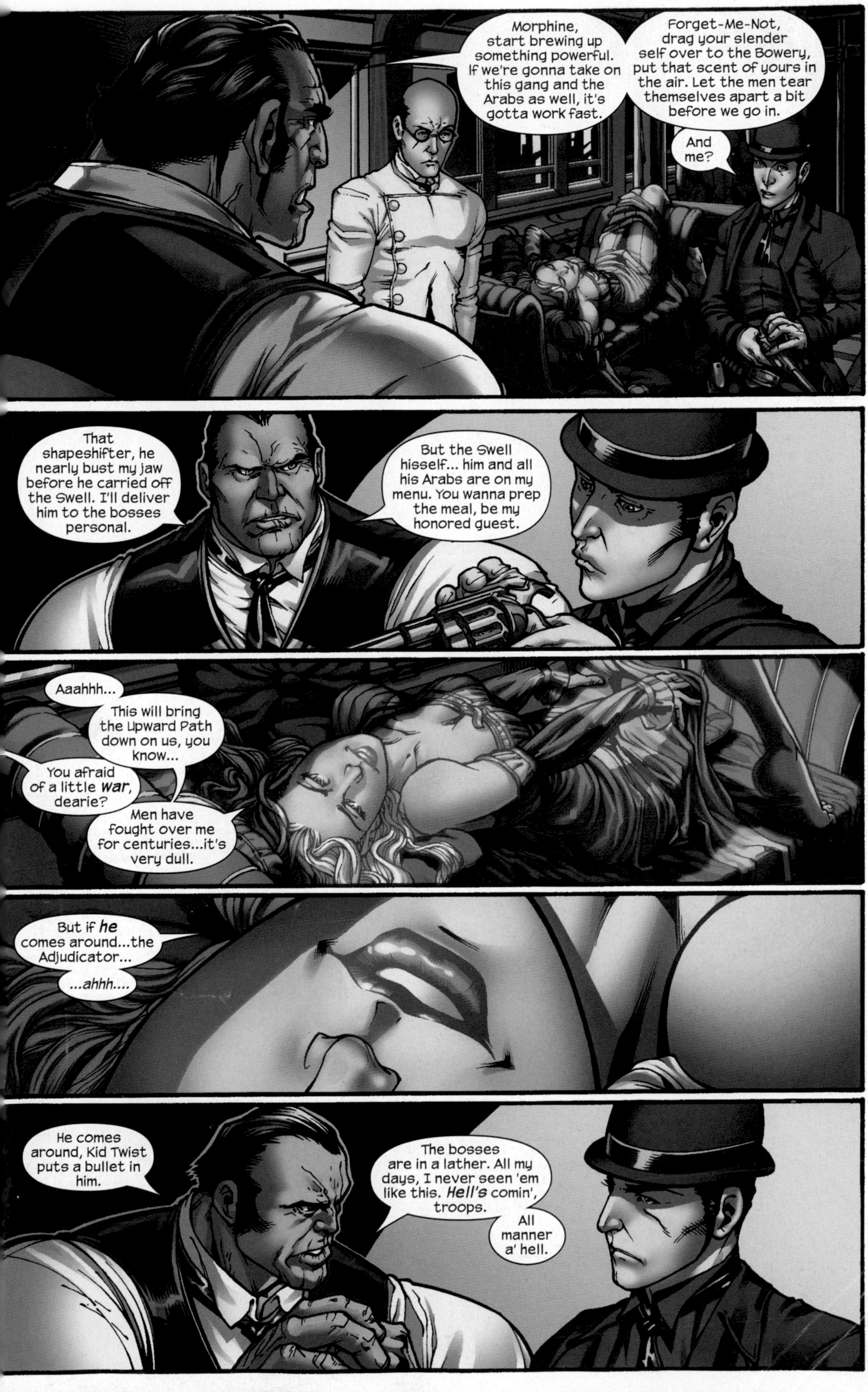
Morphine, start brewing up something powerful. If we're gonna take on this gang and the Arabs as well, it's gotta work fast.
Forget-Me-Not, drag your slender self over to the Bowery, put that scent of yours in the air. Let the men tear themselves apart a bit before we go in.
And me?
That shapeshifter, he nearly bust my jaw before he carried off the Swell. I'll deliver him to the bosses personal.
But the Swell hisself... him and all his Arabs are on my menu. You wanna prep the meal, be my honored guest.
Aaahhh...
This will bring the Upward Path down on us, you know...
You afraid of a little *war*, dearie?
Men have fought over me for centuries...it's very dull.
But if ***he*** comes around...the Adjudicator...
...ahhh....
He comes around, Kid Twist puts a bullet in him.
The bosses are in a lather. All my days, I never seen 'em like this. ***Hell's*** comin', troops.
All manner a' hell.

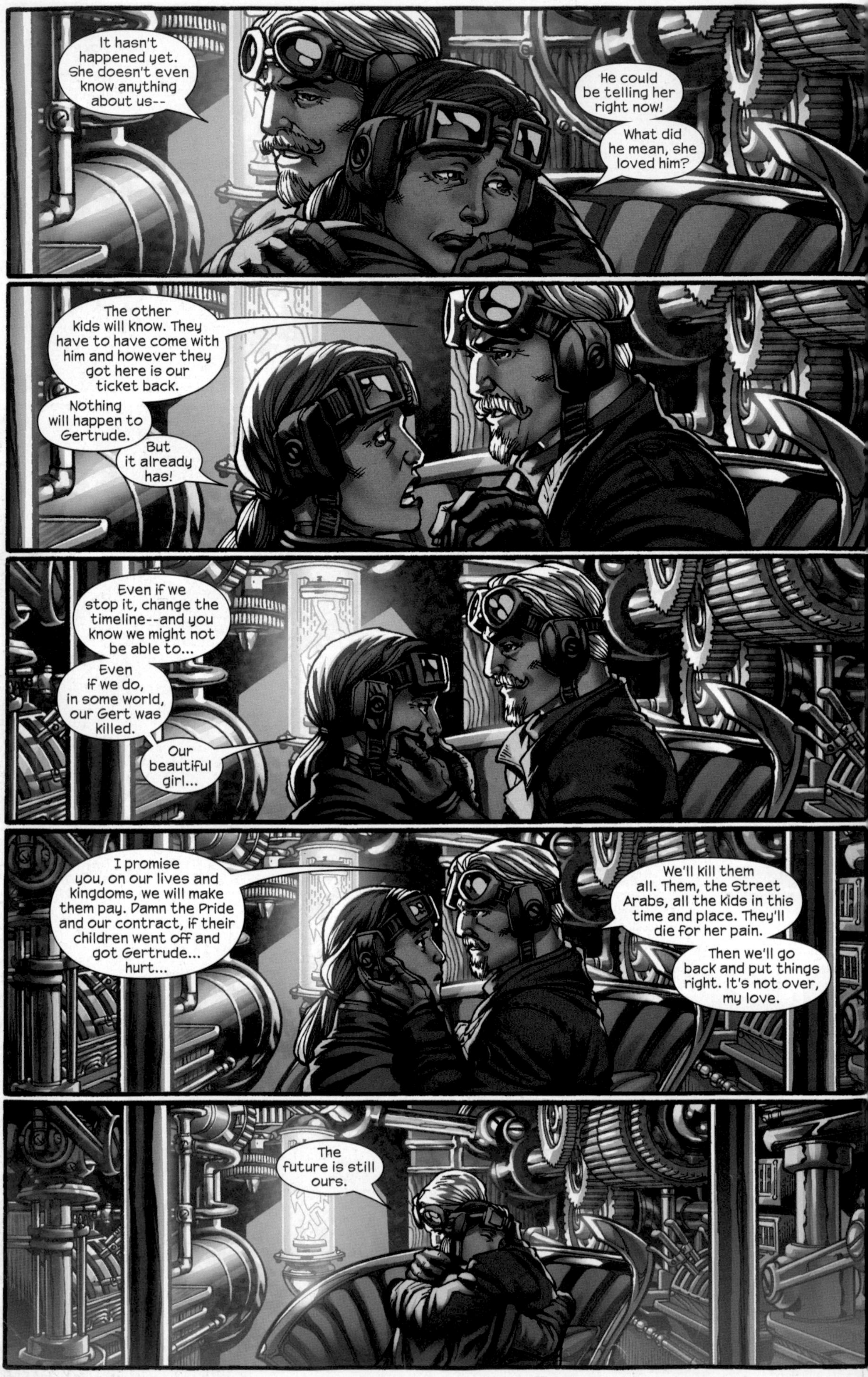
It hasn't happened yet. She doesn't even know anything about us--
He could be telling her right now!
What did he mean, she loved him?
The other kids will know. They have to have come with him and however they got here is our ticket back.
Nothing will happen to Gertrude.
But it already has!
Even if we stop it, change the timeline--and you know we might not be able to...
Even if we do, in some world, our Gert was killed.
Our beautiful girl...
I promise you, on our lives and kingdoms, we will make them pay. Damn the Pride and our contract, if their children went off and got Gertrude... hurt...
We'll kill them all. Them, the Street Arabs, all the kids in this time and place. They'll die for her pain.
Then we'll go back and put things right. It's not over, my love.
The future is still ours.

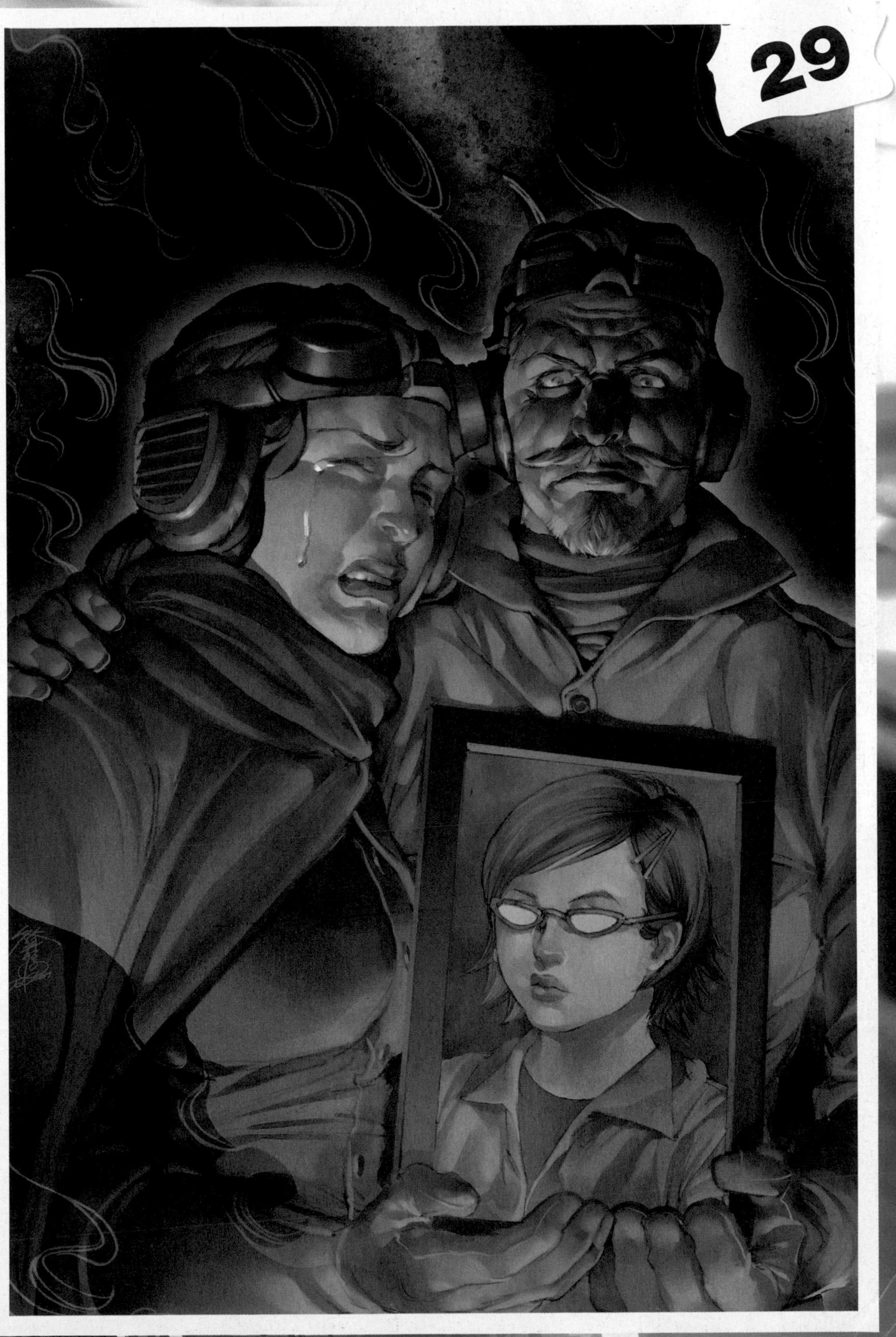
29

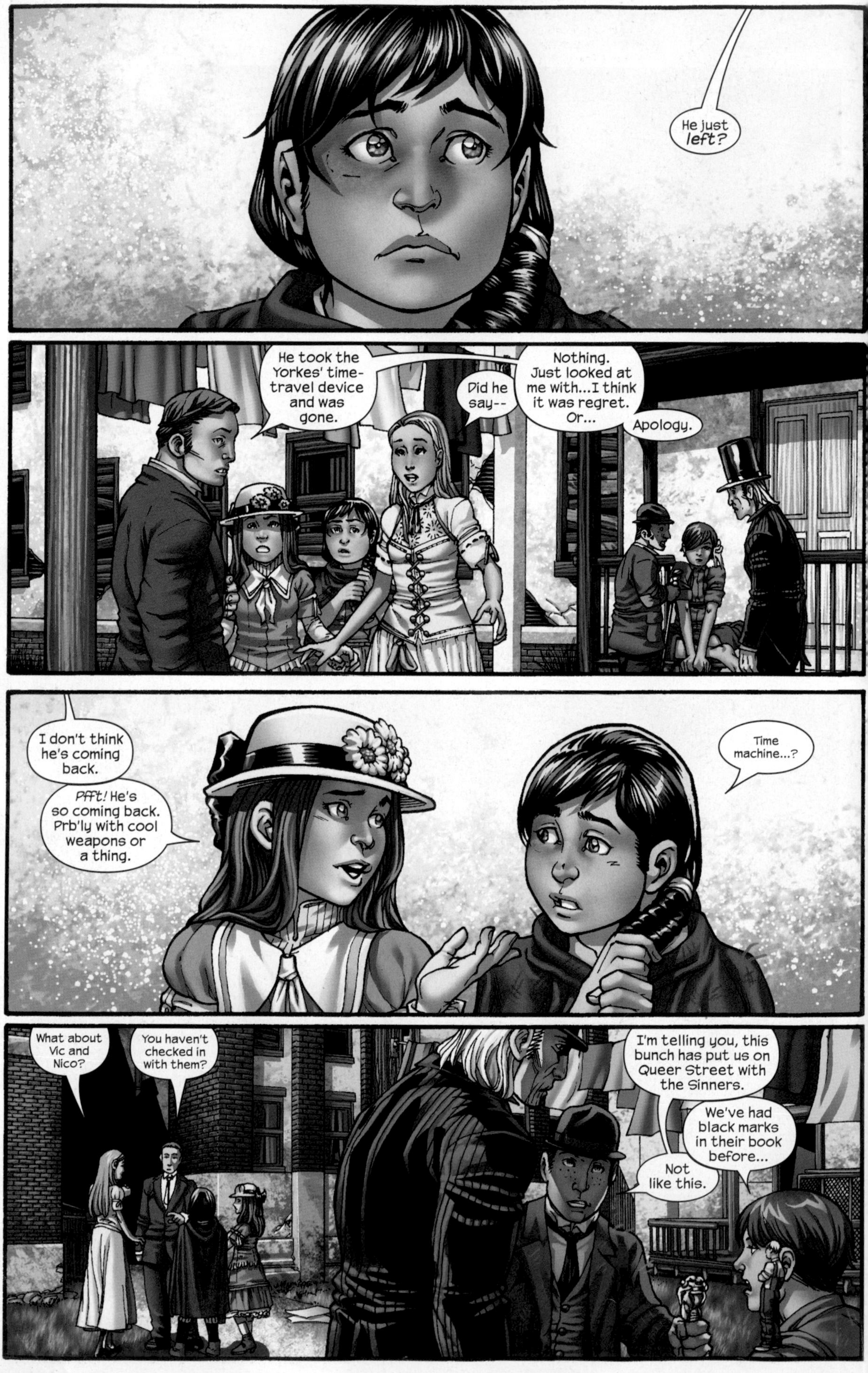
He just *left?*
He took the Yorkes' time-travel device and was gone.
Did he say--
Nothing. Just looked at me with...I think it was regret. Or...
Apology.
I don't think he's coming back.
Pfft! He's so coming back. Prb'ly with cool weapons or a thing.
Time machine...?
What about Vic and Nico?
You haven't checked in with them?
I'm telling you, this bunch has put us on Queer Street with the Sinners.
We've had black marks in their book before...
Not like this.

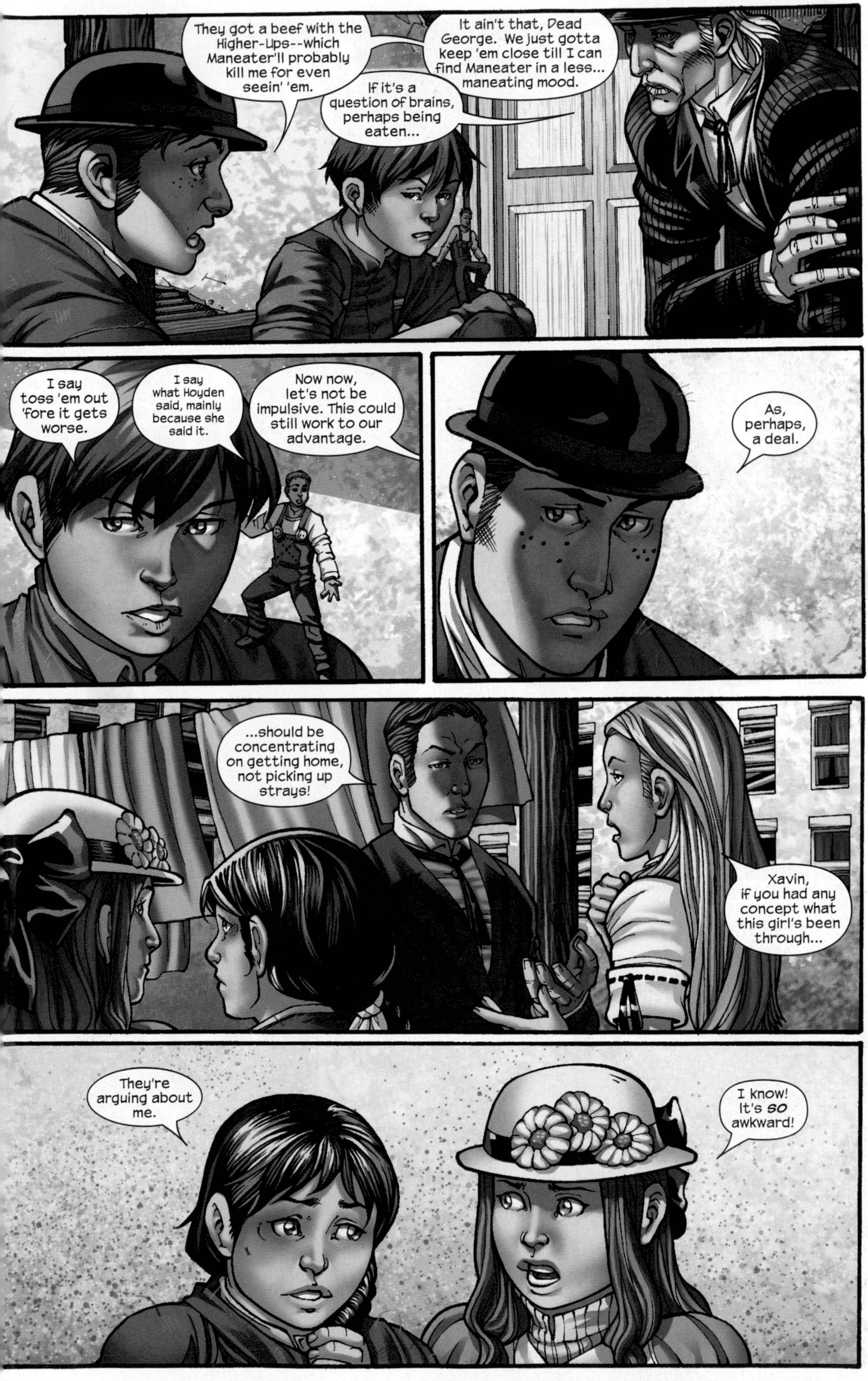
They got a beef with the Higher-Ups--which Maneater'll probably kill me for even seein' 'em.
It ain't that, Dead George. We just gotta keep 'em close till I can find Maneater in a less... maneating mood.
If it's a question of brains, perhaps being eaten...
I say toss 'em out 'fore it gets worse.
I say what Hoyden said, mainly because she said it.
Now now, let's not be impulsive. This could still work to our advantage.
As, perhaps, a deal.
...should be concentrating on getting home, not picking up strays!
Xavin, if you had any concept what this girl's been through...
They're arguing about me.
I know! It's *so* awkward!

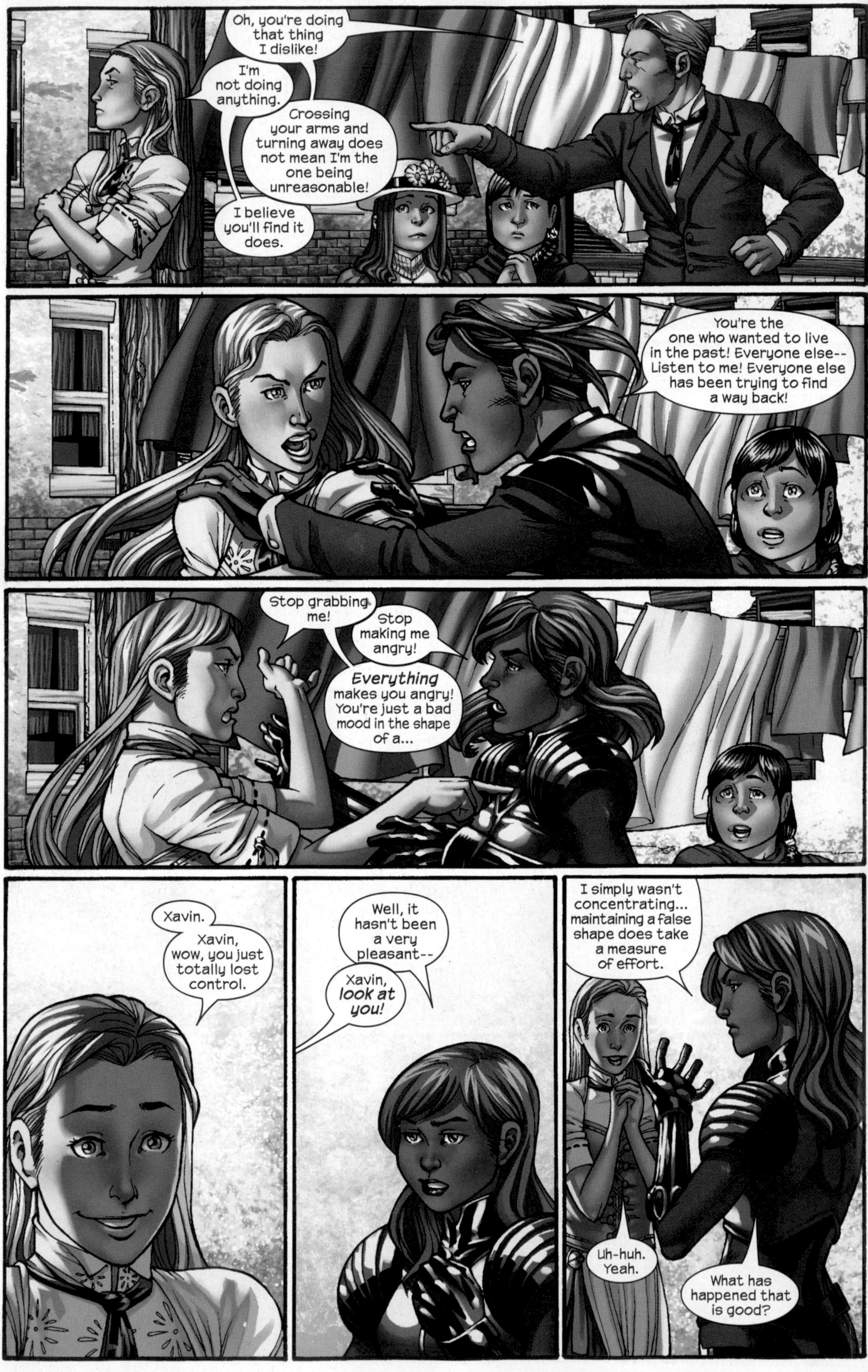
Oh, you're doing that thing I dislike!
I'm not doing anything.
Crossing your arms and turning away does not mean I'm the one being unreasonable!
I believe you'll find it does.
You're the one who wanted to live in the past! Everyone else-- Listen to me! Everyone else has been trying to find a way back!
Stop grabbing me!
Stop making me angry!
Everything makes you angry! You're just a bad mood in the shape of a...
Xavin.
Xavin, wow, you just totally lost control.
Well, it hasn't been a very pleasant--
Xavin, *look at you!*
I simply wasn't concentrating... maintaining a false shape does take a measure of effort.
Uh-huh. Yeah.
What has happened that is good?

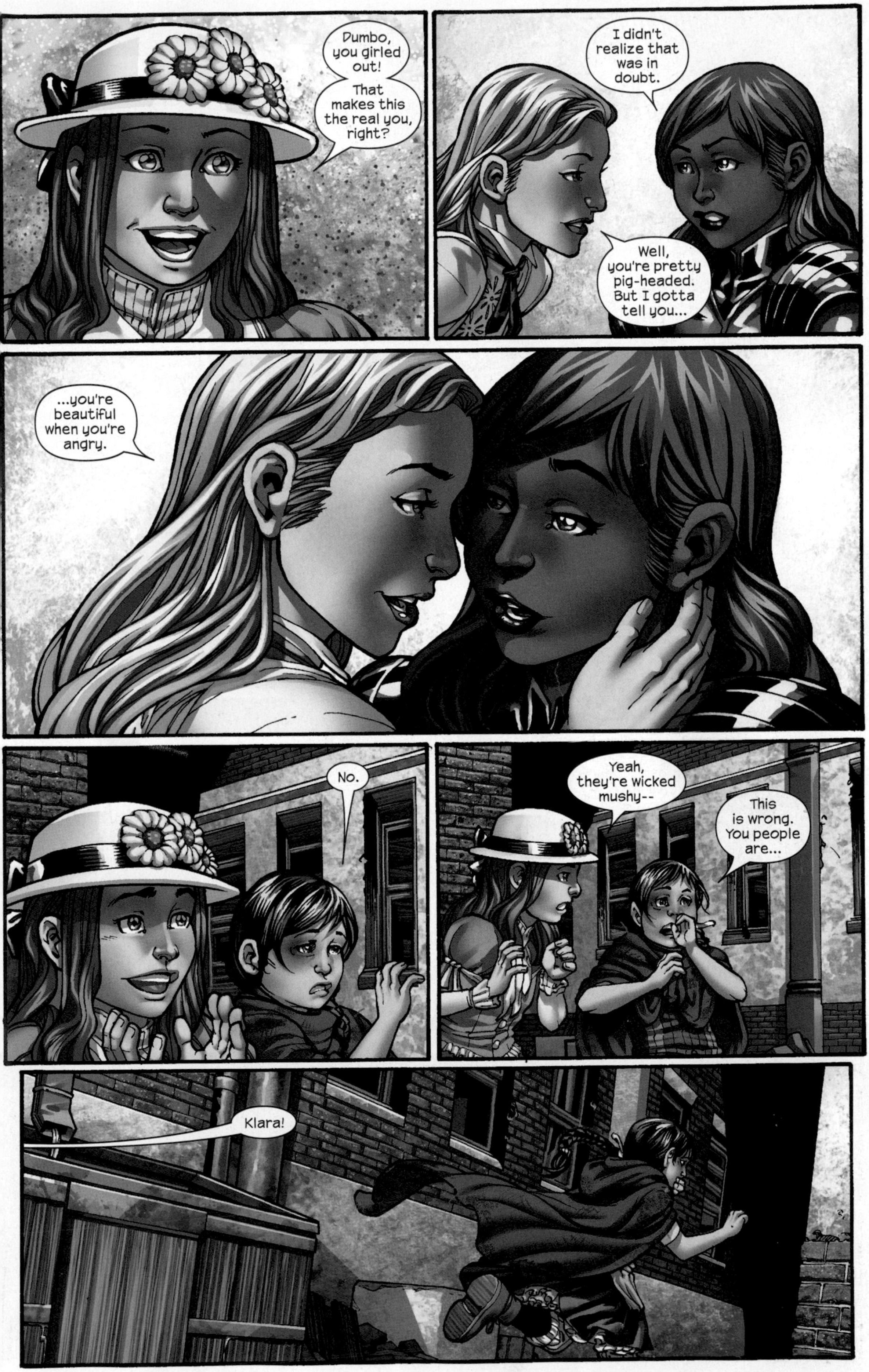
Dumbo, you girled out!
That makes this the real you, right?
I didn't realize that was in doubt.
Well, you're pretty pig-headed. But I gotta tell you...
...you're beautiful when you're angry.
No.
Yeah, they're wicked mushy--
This is wrong. You people are...
Klara!

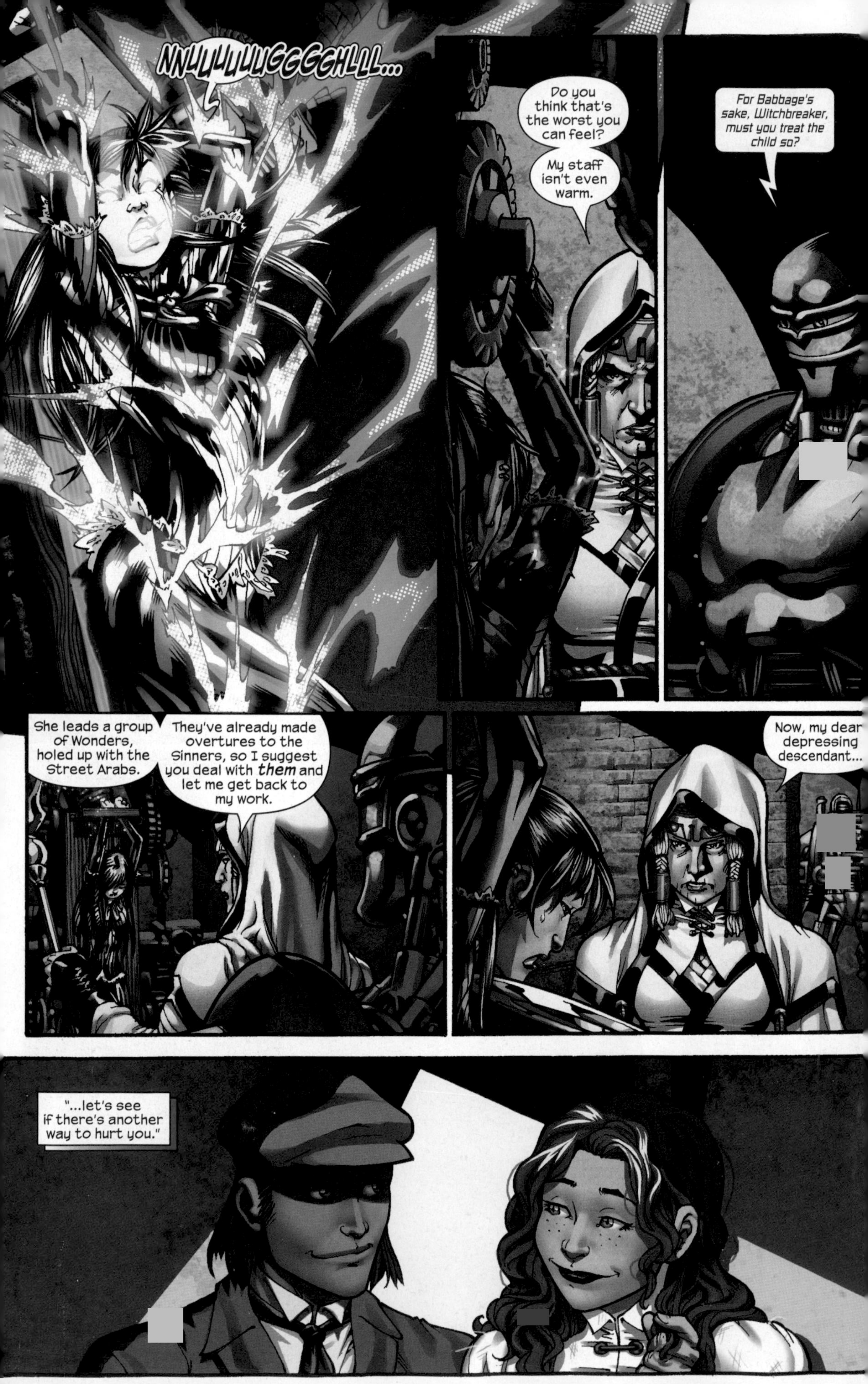
NNUUUUUUGGGGHLLL...
Do you think that's the worst you can feel?
My staff isn't even warm.
For Babbage's sake, Witchbreaker, must you treat the child so?
She leads a group of Wonders, holed up with the Street Arabs.
They've already made overtures to the Sinners, so I suggest you deal with *them* and let me get back to my work.
Now, my dear depressing descendant...
"...let's see if there's another way to hurt you."

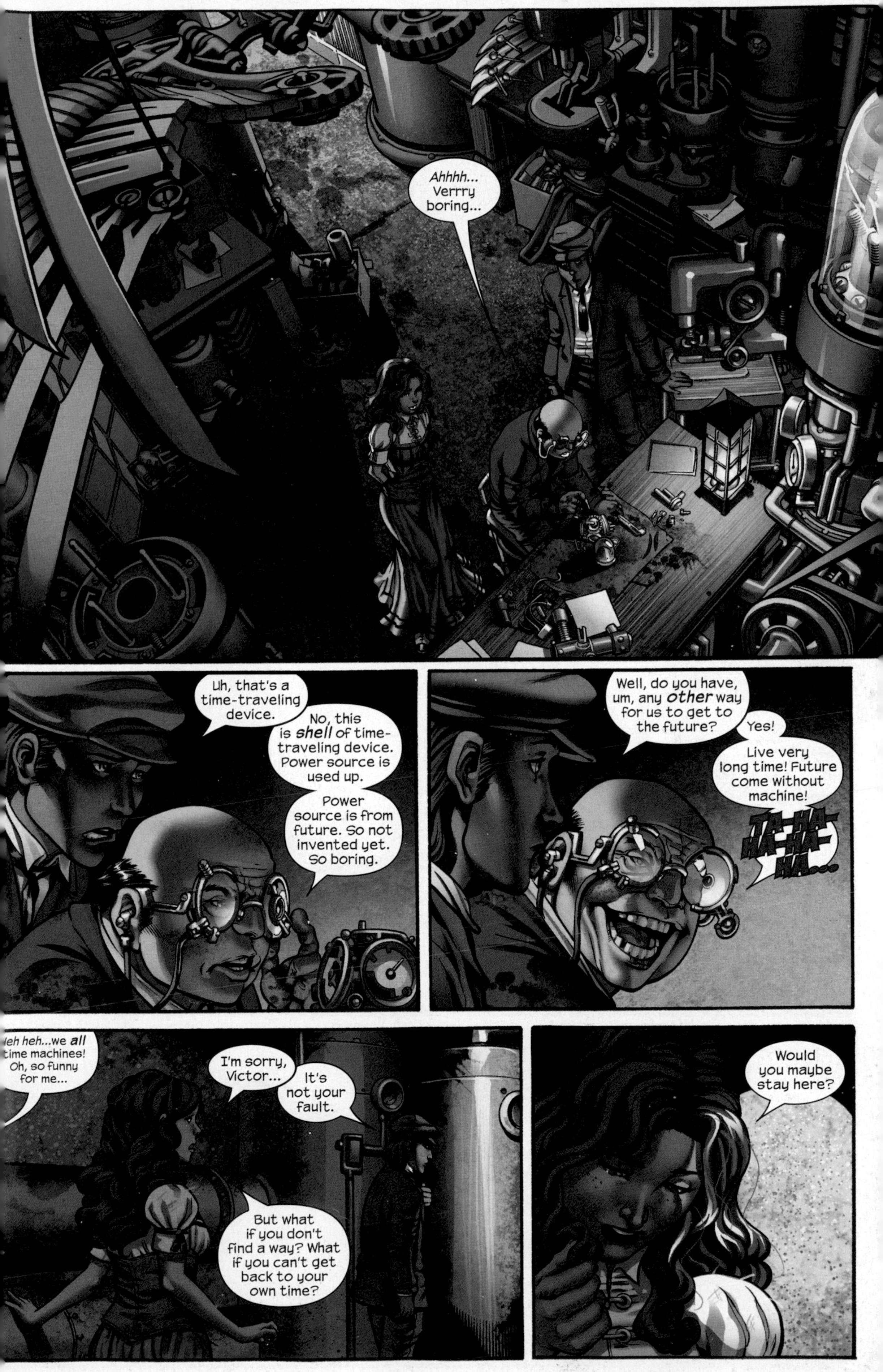
Ahhhh... Verrry boring...
Uh, that's a time-traveling device.
No, this is shell of time-traveling device. Power source is used up.
Power source is from future. So not invented yet. So boring.
Well, do you have, um, any other way for us to get to the future?
Yes!
Live very long time! Future come without machine!
HA-HA-HA-HA-HA...
Heh heh...we all time machines! Oh, so funny for me...
I'm sorry, Victor...
It's not your fault.
But what if you don't find a way? What if you can't get back to your own time?
Would you maybe stay here?

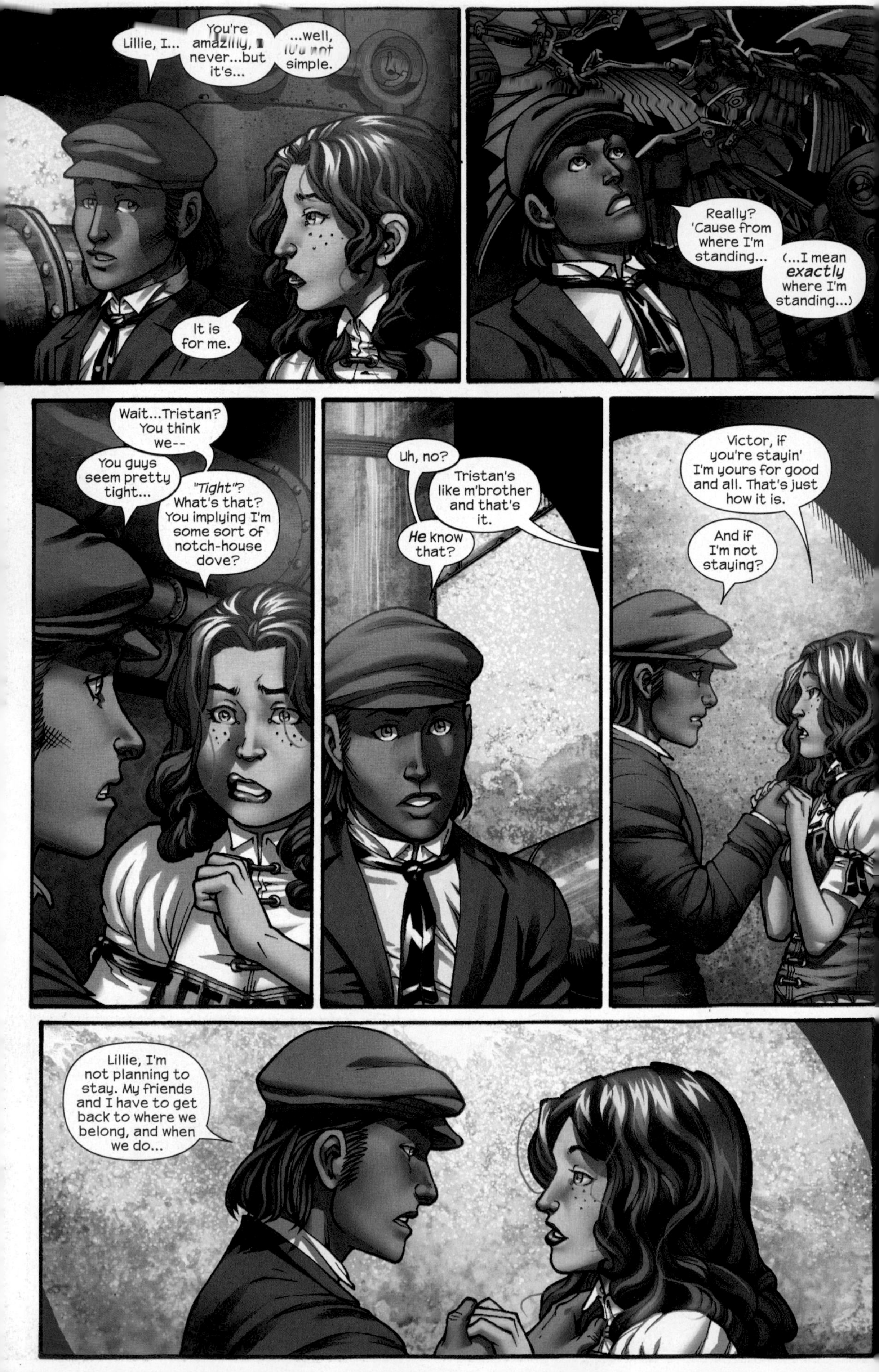
Lillie, I...
You're amazing, I never...but it's...
...well, it's not simple.
It is for me.
Really? 'Cause from where I'm standing...
(...I mean *exactly* where I'm standing...)
Wait...Tristan? You think we--
You guys seem pretty tight...
"Tight"? What's that? You implying I'm some sort of notch-house dove?
Uh, no?
Tristan's like m'brother and that's it.
He know that?
Victor, if you're stayin' I'm yours for good and all. That's just how it is.
And if I'm not staying?
Lillie, I'm not planning to stay. My friends and I have to get back to where we belong, and when we do...

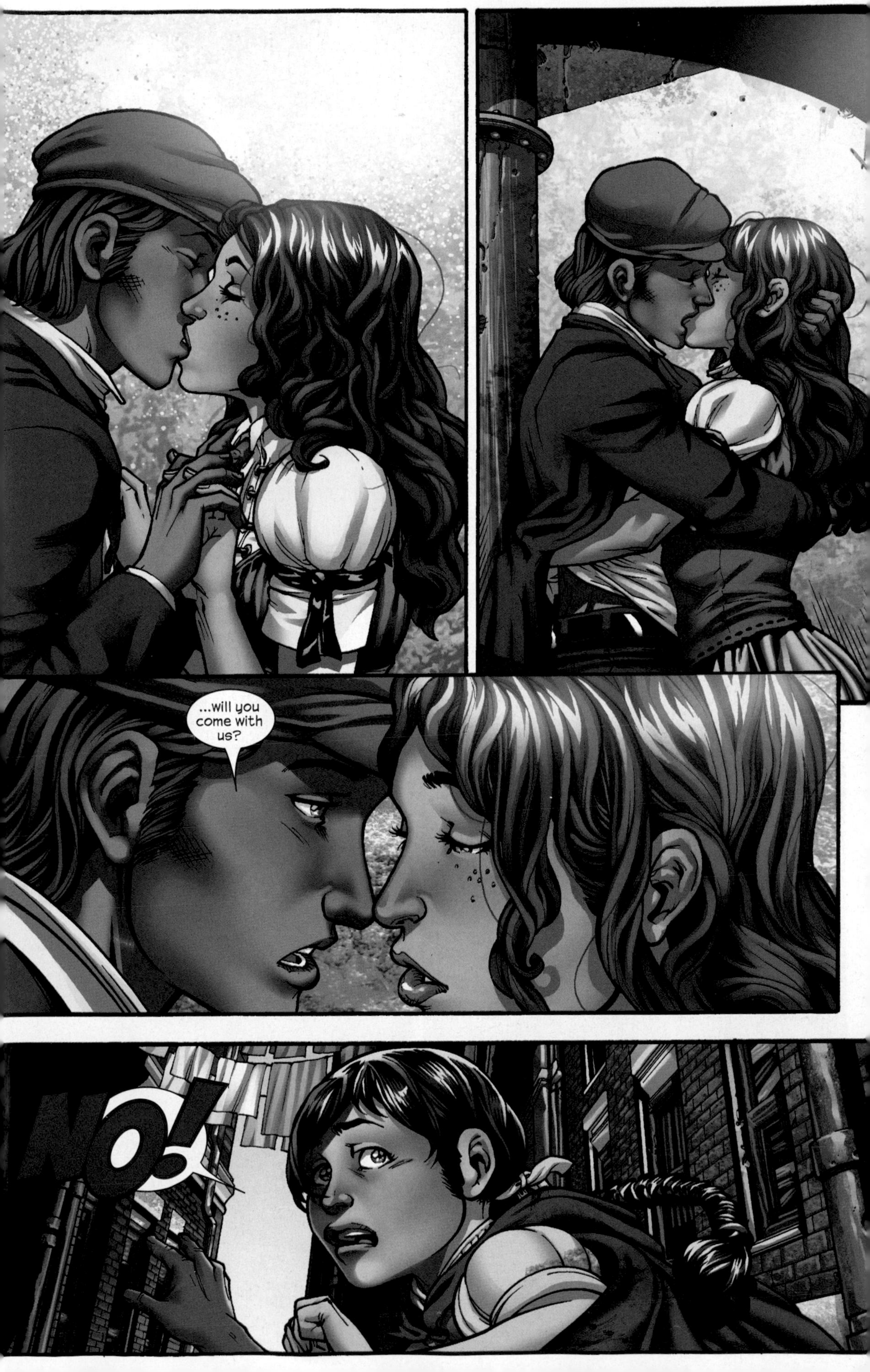
...will you come with us?
NO!

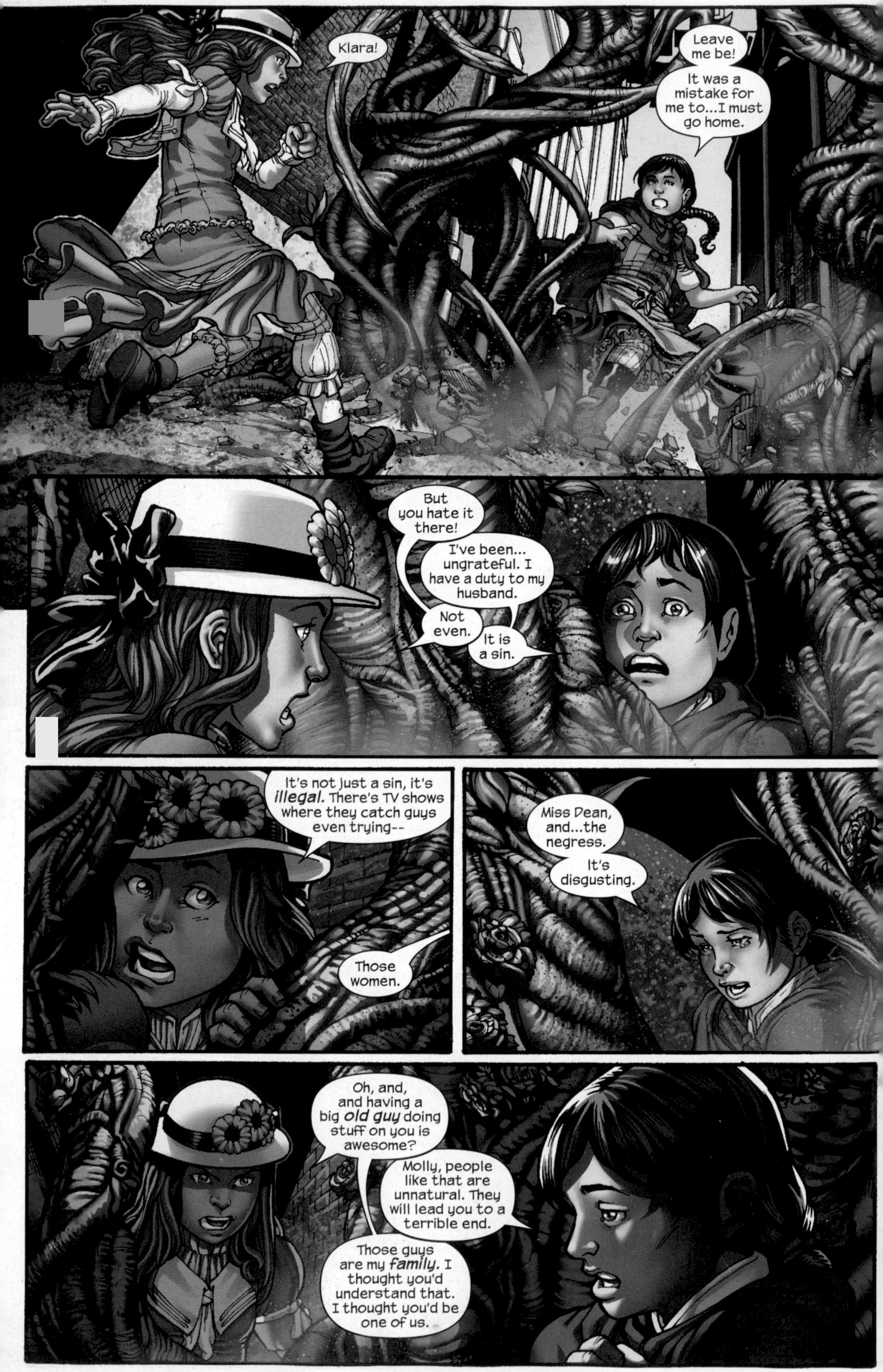
Klara!
Leave me be!
It was a mistake for me to...I must go home.
But you hate it there!
I've been... ungrateful. I have a duty to my husband.
Not even.
It is a sin.
It's not just a sin, it's *illegal.* There's TV shows where they catch guys even trying--
Those women.
Miss Dean, and...the negress.
It's disgusting.
Oh, and, and having a big *old guy* doing stuff on you is awesome?
Molly, people like that are unnatural. They will lead you to a terrible end.
Those guys are my *family.* I thought you'd understand that. I thought you'd be one of us.

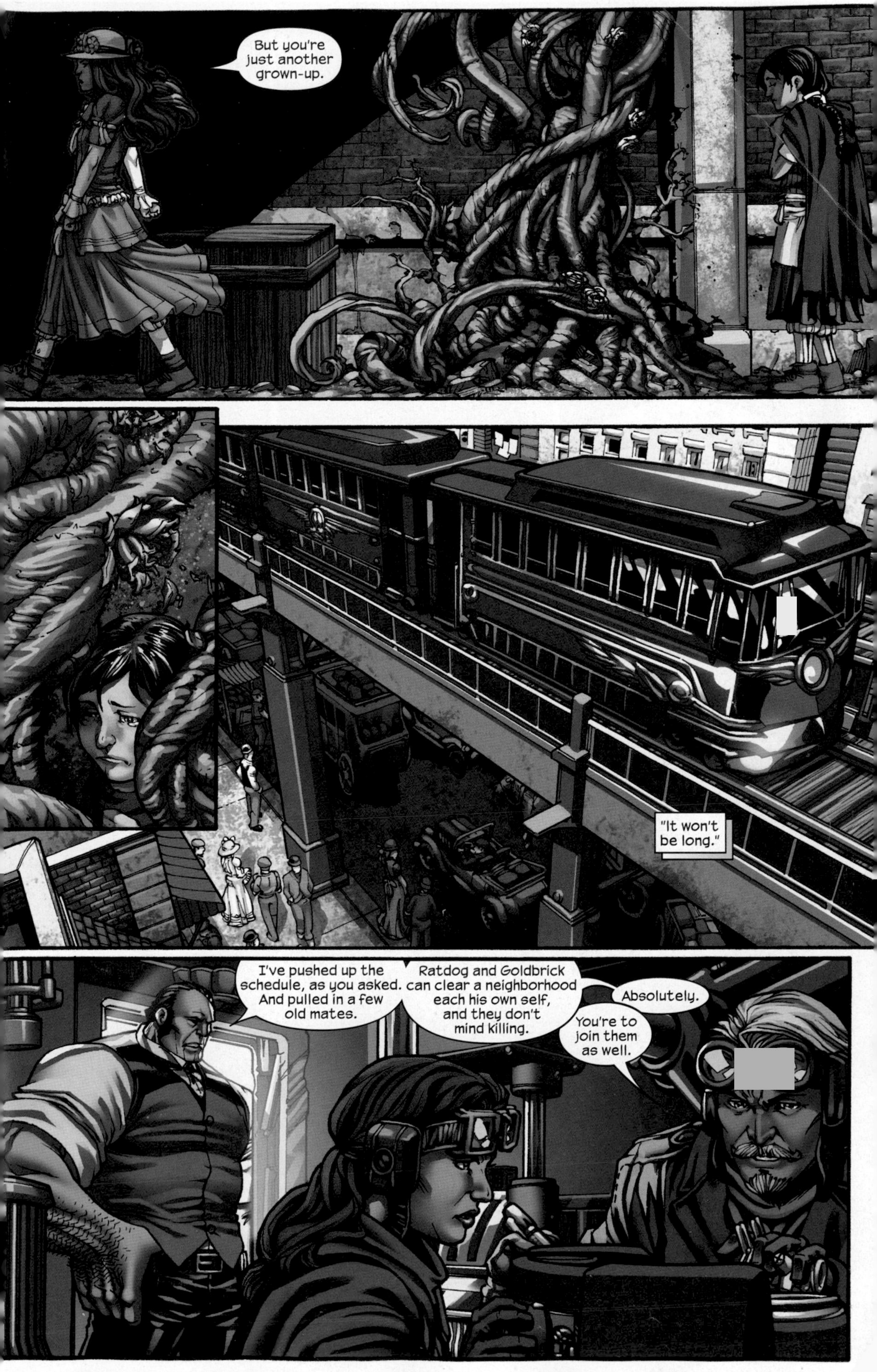

But you're just another grown-up.
"It won't be long."
I've pushed up the schedule, as you asked. And pulled in a few old mates.
Ratdog and Goldbrick can clear a neighborhood each his own self, and they don't mind killing.
Absolutely.
You're to join them as well.

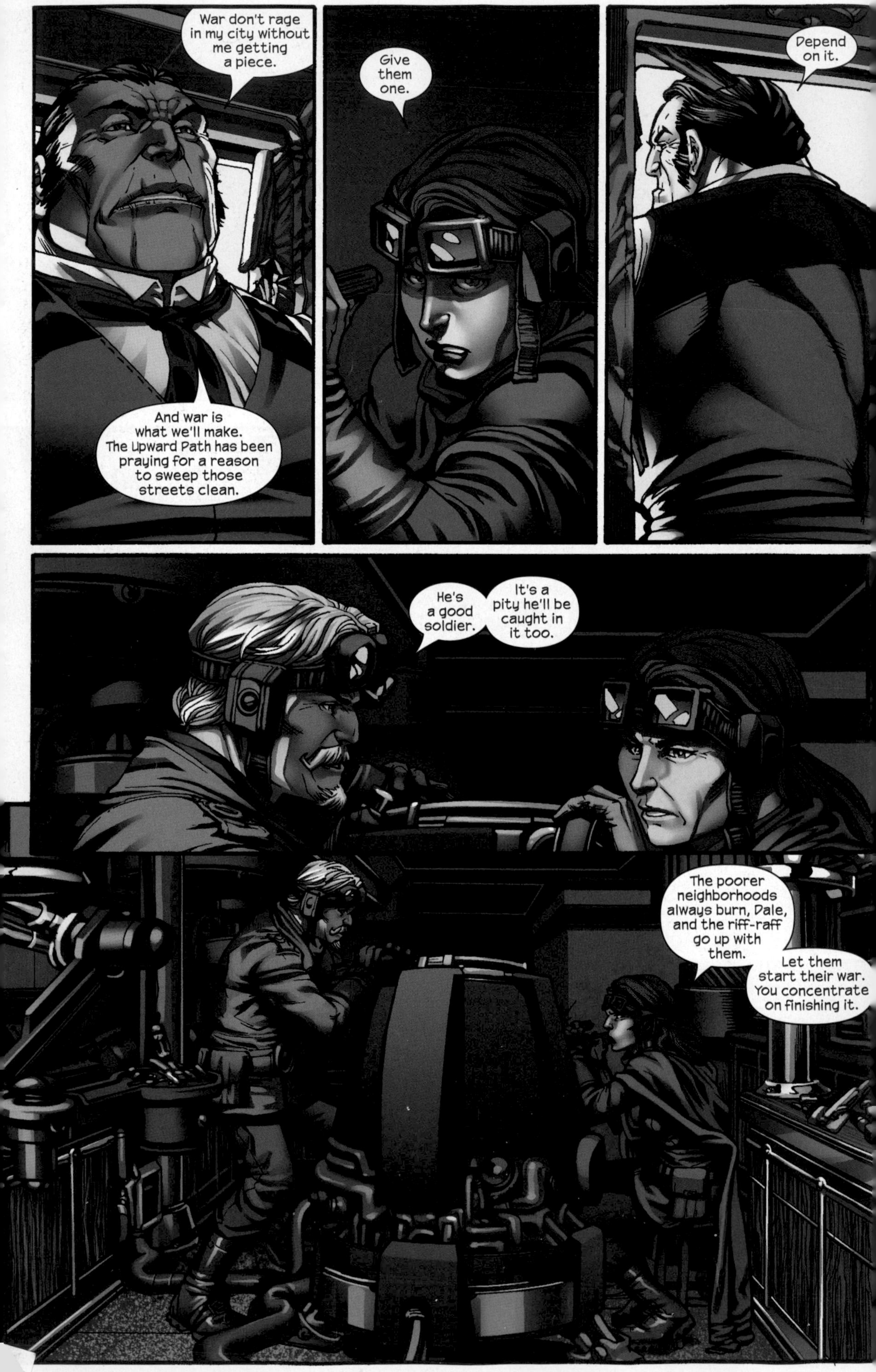
War don't rage in my city without me getting a piece.
And war is what we'll make. The Upward Path has been praying for a reason to sweep those streets clean.
Give them one.
Depend on it.
He's a good soldier.
It's a pity he'll be caught in it too.
The poorer neighborhoods always burn, Dale, and the riff-raff go up with them.
Let them start their war. You concentrate on finishing it.

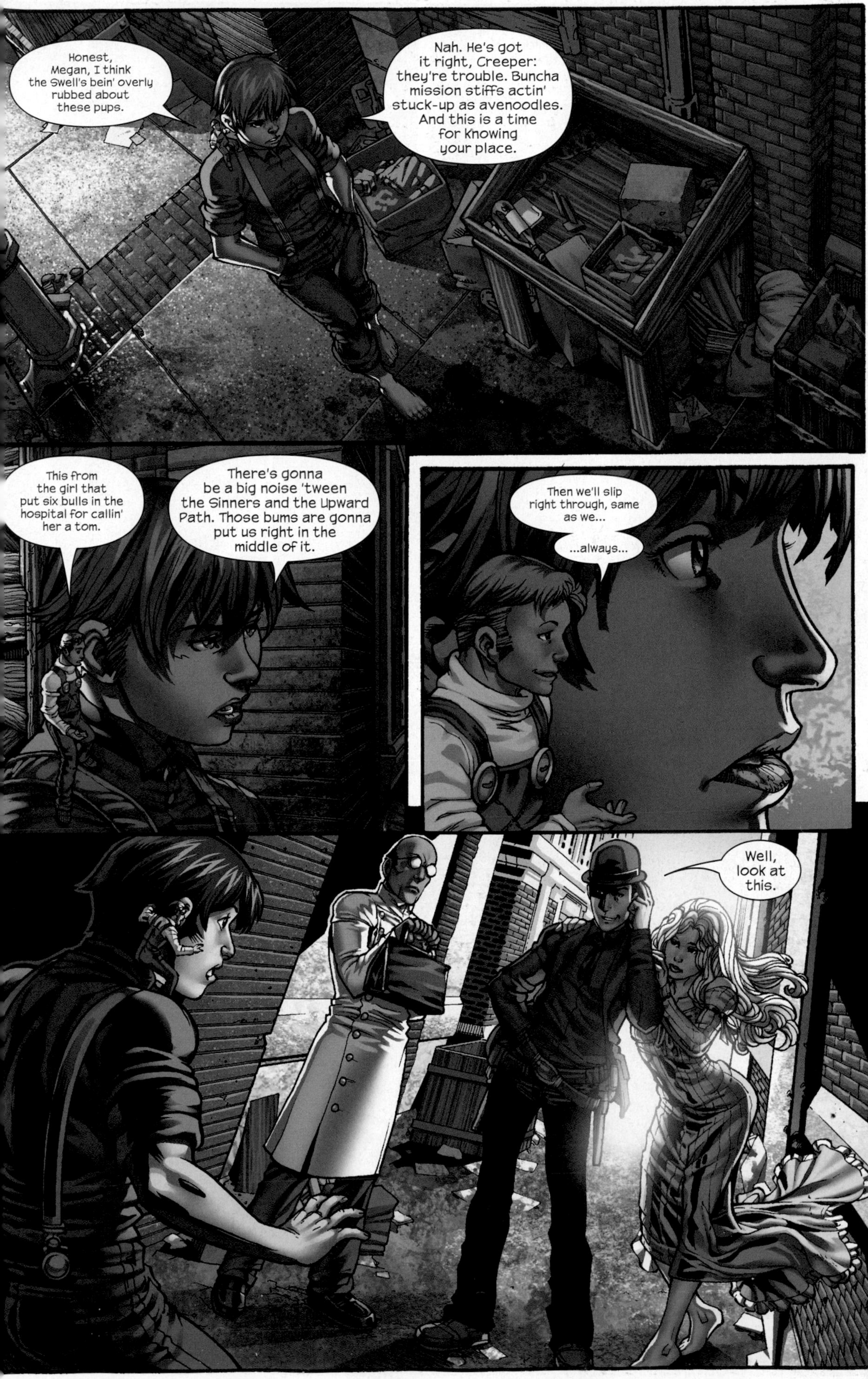
Honest, Megan, I think the Swell's bein' overly rubbed about these pups.
Nah. He's got it right, Creeper: they're trouble. Buncha mission stiffs actin' stuck-up as avenoodles. And this is a time for knowing your place.
This from the girl that put six bulls in the hospital for callin' her a tom.
There's gonna be a big noise 'tween the Sinners and the Upward Path. Those bums are gonna put us right in the middle of it.
Then we'll slip right through, same as we...
...always...
Well, look at this.

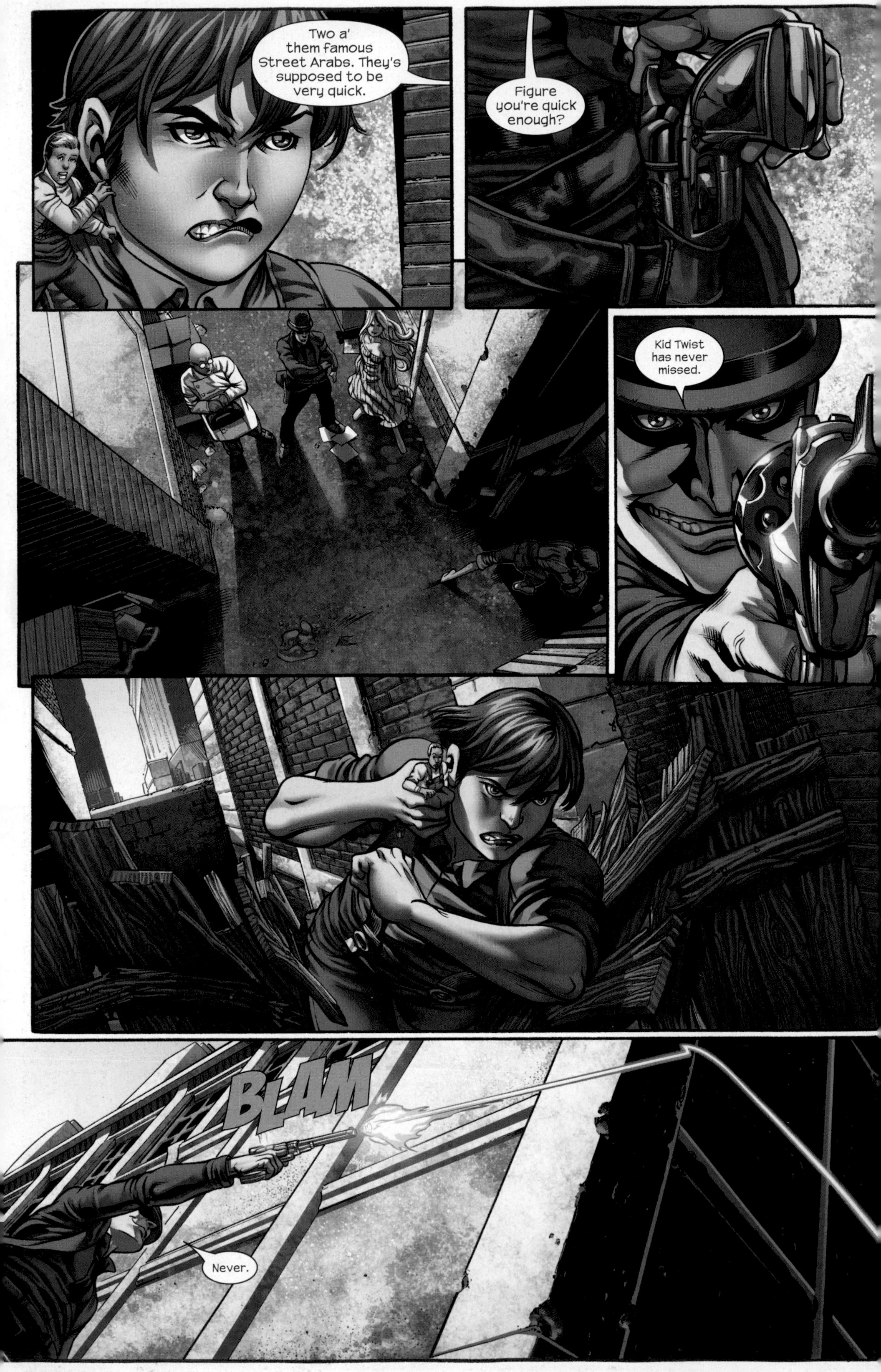
Two a' them famous Street Arabs. They's supposed to be very quick.
Figure you're quick enough?
Kid Twist has never missed.
BLAM
Never.

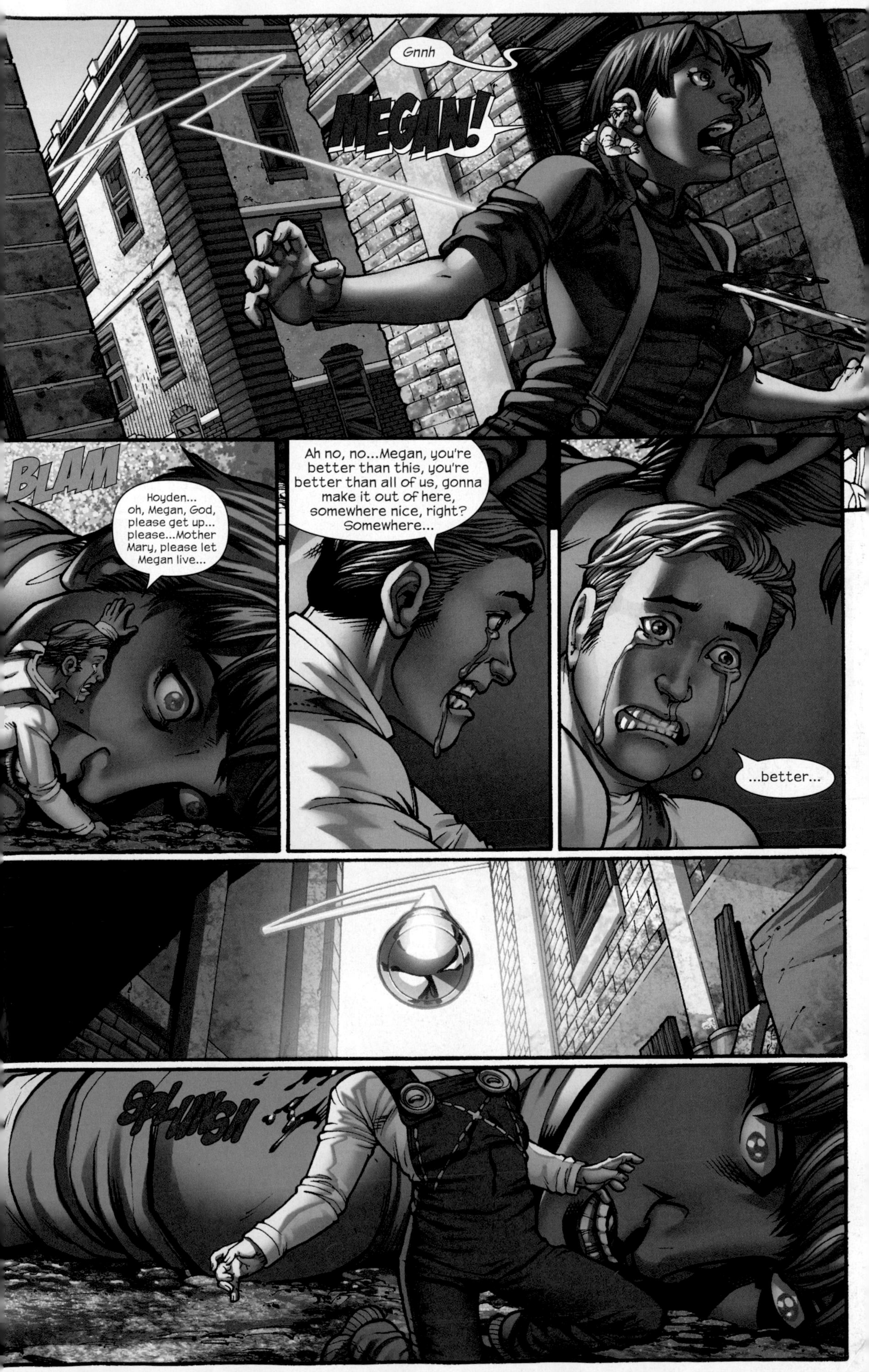
Gnnh
MEGAN!
BLAM
Hoyden... oh, Megan, God, please get up... please...Mother Mary, please let Megan live...
Ah no, no...Megan, you're better than this, you're better than all of us, gonna make it out of here, somewhere nice, right? Somewhere...
...better...
SPLUNSH

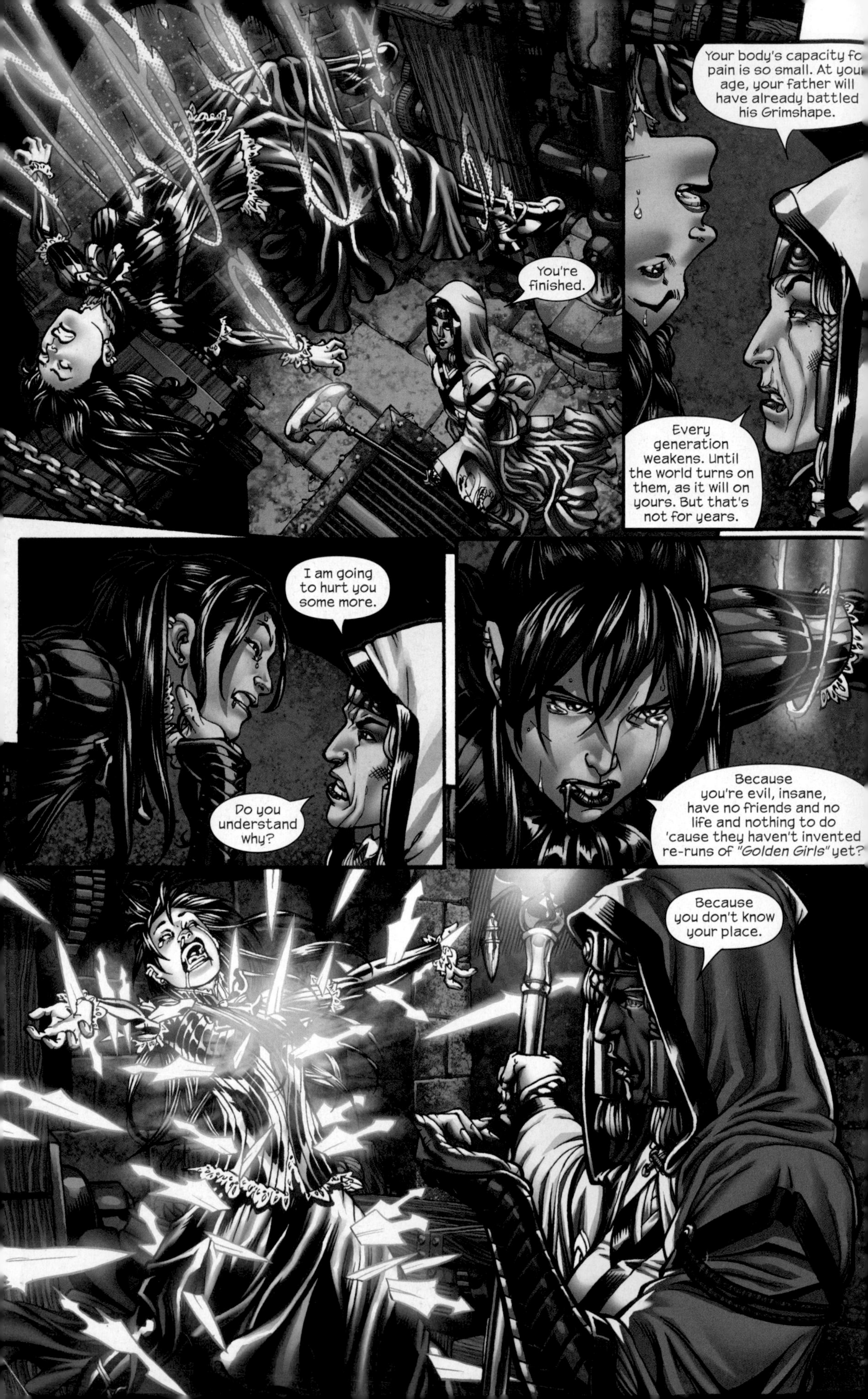
You're finished.
Your body's capacity fo pain is so small. At you age, your father will have already battled his Grimshape.
Every generation weakens. Until the world turns on them, as it will on yours. But that's not for years.
I am going to hurt you some more.
Do you understand why?
Because you're evil, insane, have no friends and no life and nothing to do 'cause they haven't invented re-runs of "Golden Girls" yet?
Because you don't know your place.

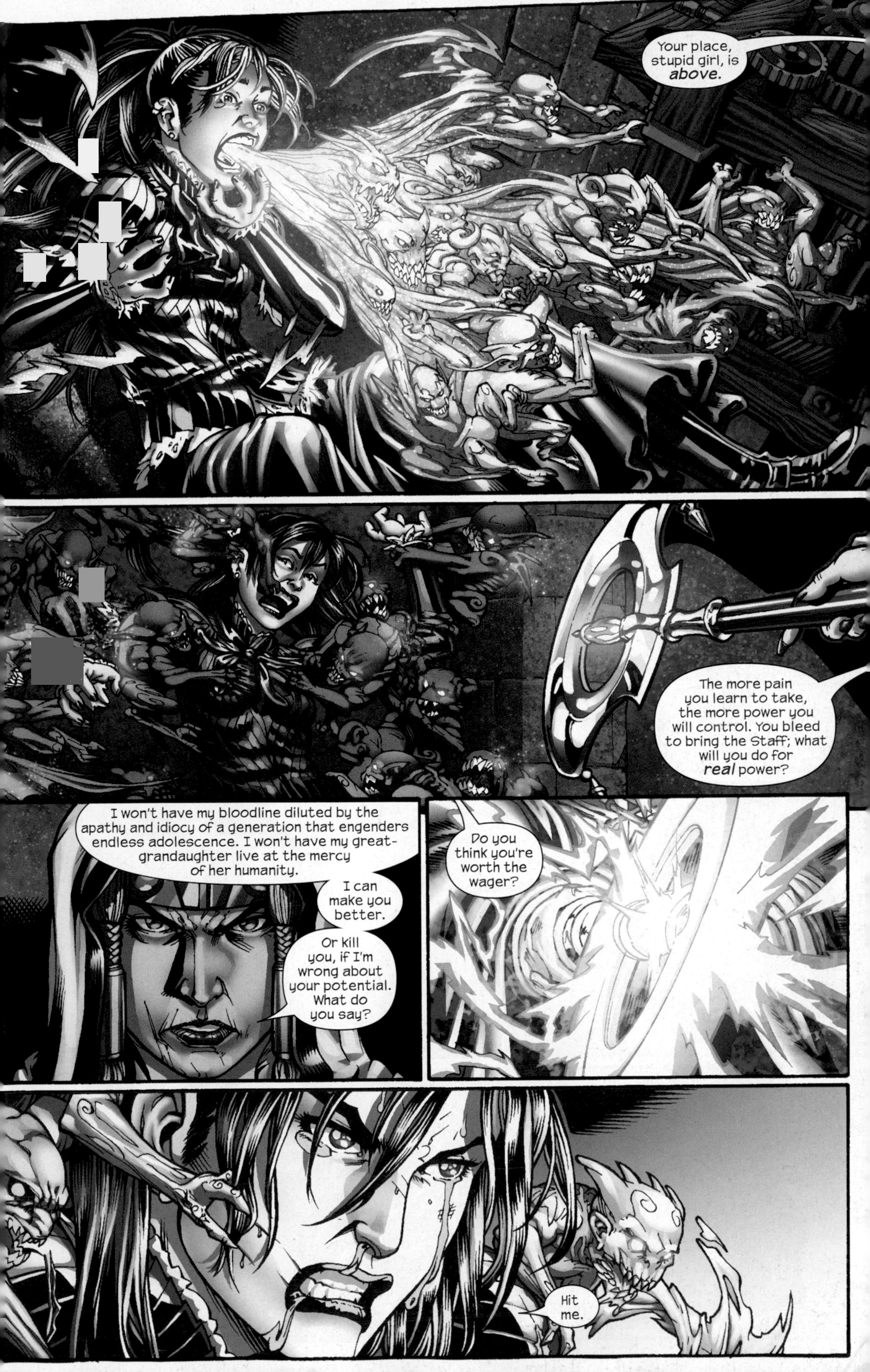

Your place, stupid girl, is *above.*
The more pain you learn to take, the more power you will control. You bleed to bring the Staff; what will you do for *real* power?
I won't have my bloodline diluted by the apathy and idiocy of a generation that engenders endless adolescence. I won't have my great-granddaughter live at the mercy of her humanity.
I can make you better.
Or kill you, if I'm wrong about your potential. What do you say?
Do you think you're worth the wager?
Hit me.

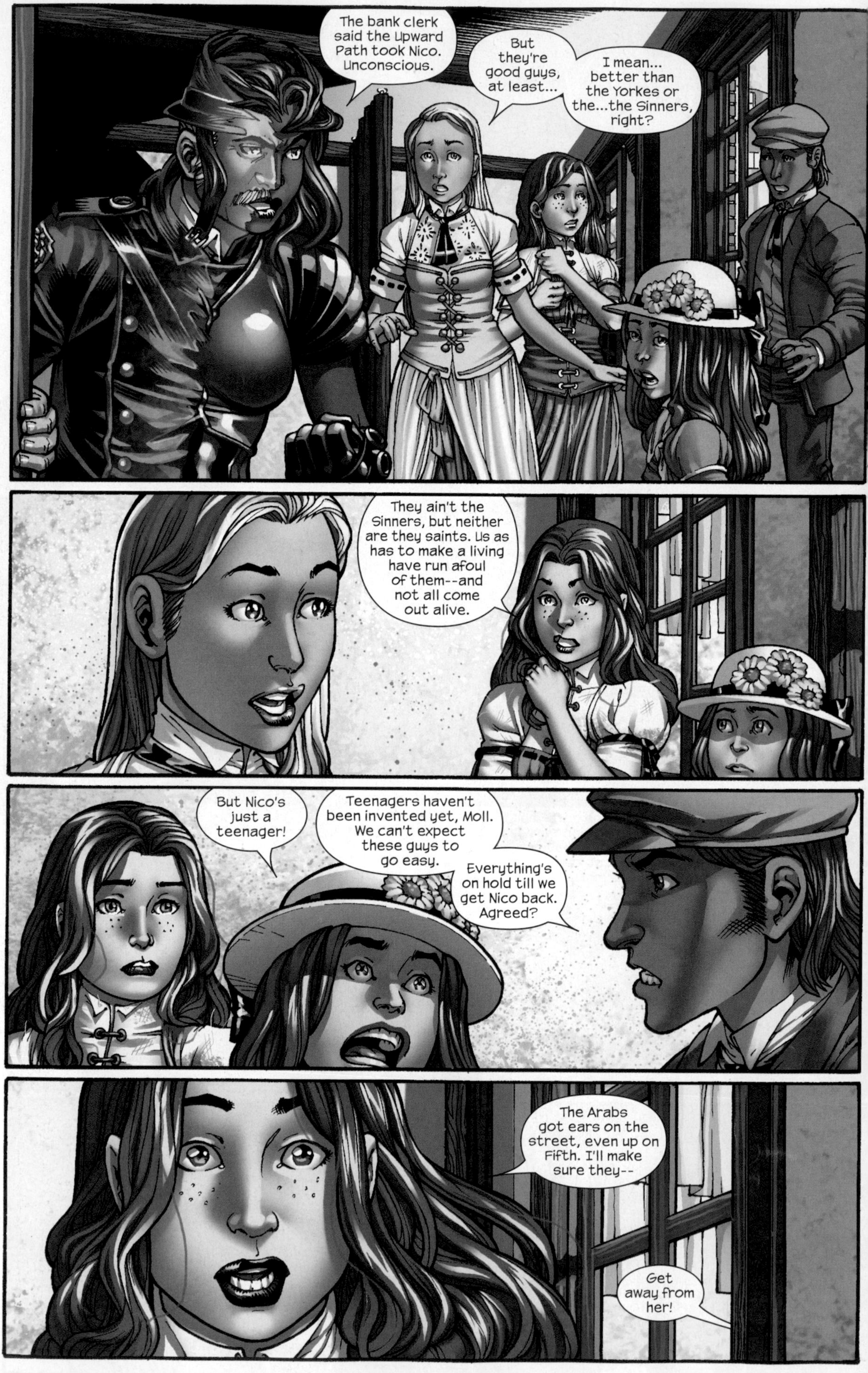
The bank clerk said the Upward Path took Nico. Unconscious.
But they're good guys, at least...
I mean... better than the Yorkes or the...the Sinners, right?
They ain't the Sinners, but neither are they saints. Us as has to make a living have run afoul of them--and not all come out alive.
But Nico's just a teenager!
Teenagers haven't been invented yet, Moll. We can't expect these guys to go easy.
Everything's on hold till we get Nico back. Agreed?
The Arabs got ears on the street, even up on Fifth. I'll make sure they--
Get away from her!

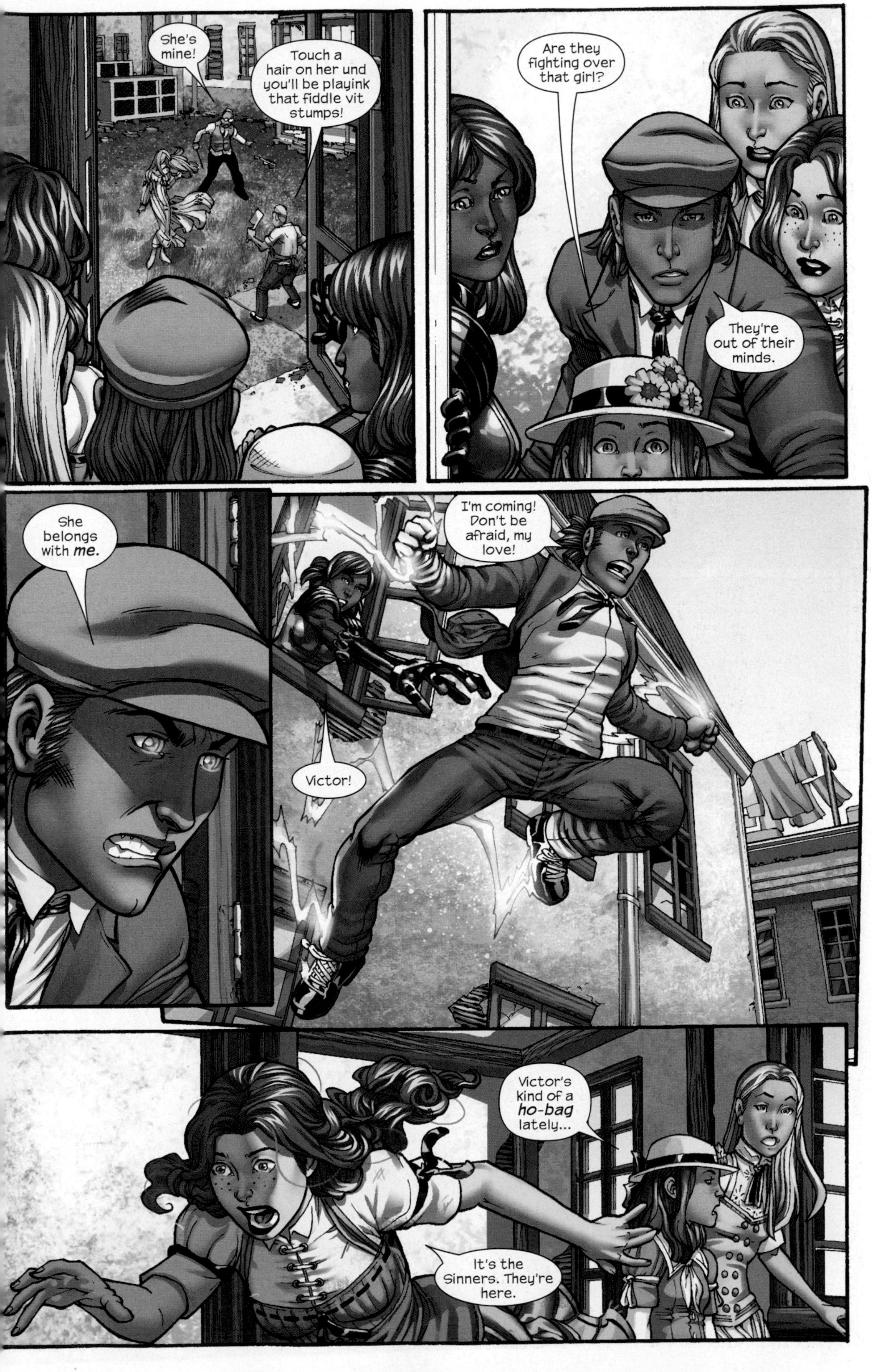
She's mine!
Touch a hair on her und you'll be playink that fiddle vit stumps!
Are they fighting over that girl?
They're out of their minds.
She belongs with *me.*
I'm coming! Don't be afraid, my love!
Victor!
Victor's kind of a *ho-bag* lately...
It's the Sinners. They're here.

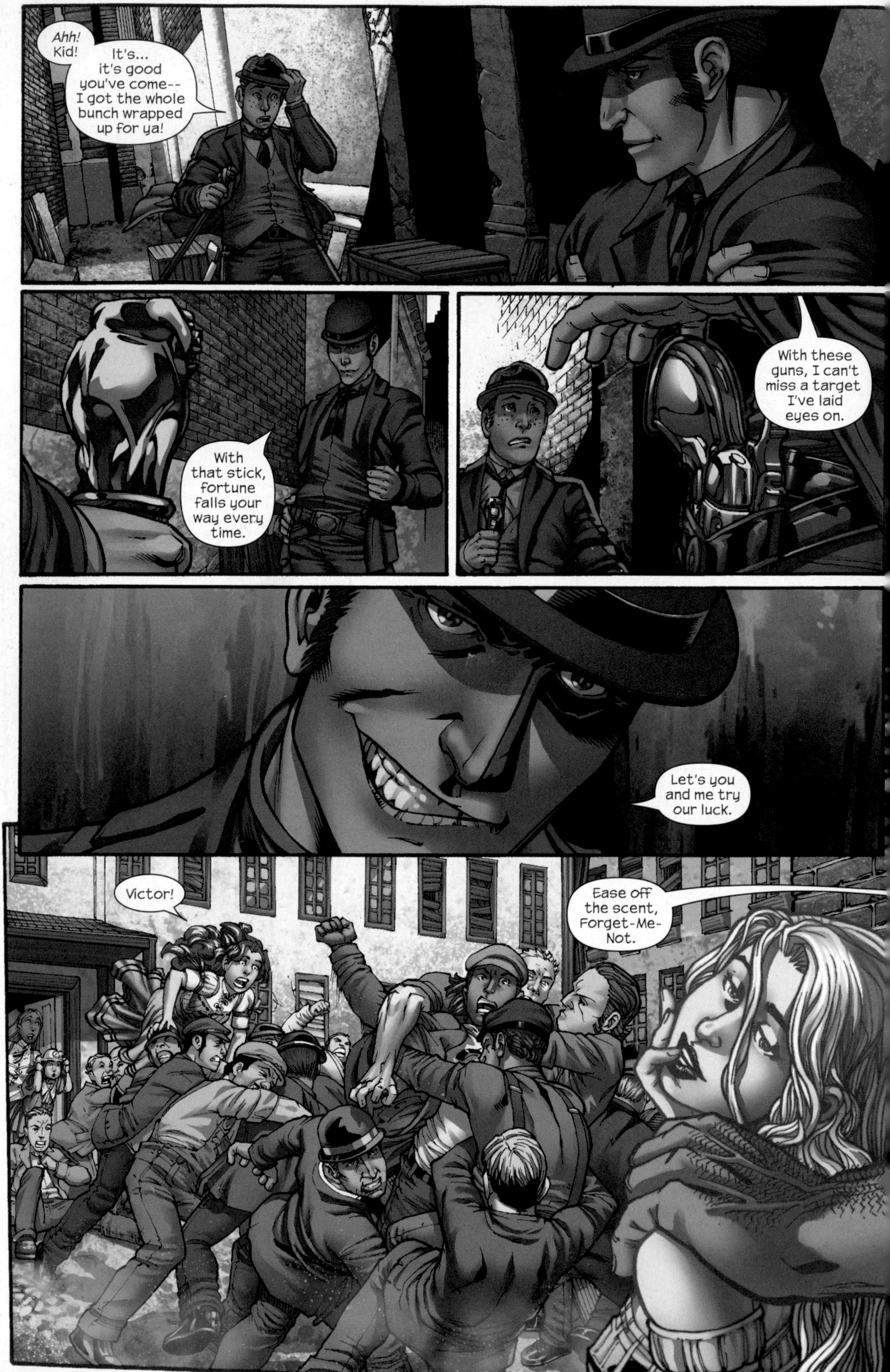
Ahh! Kid!
It's... it's good you've come-- I got the whole bunch wrapped up for ya!
With that stick, fortune falls your way every time.
With these guns, I can't miss a target I've laid eyes on.
Let's you and me try our luck.
Victor!
Ease off the scent, Forget-Me-Not.

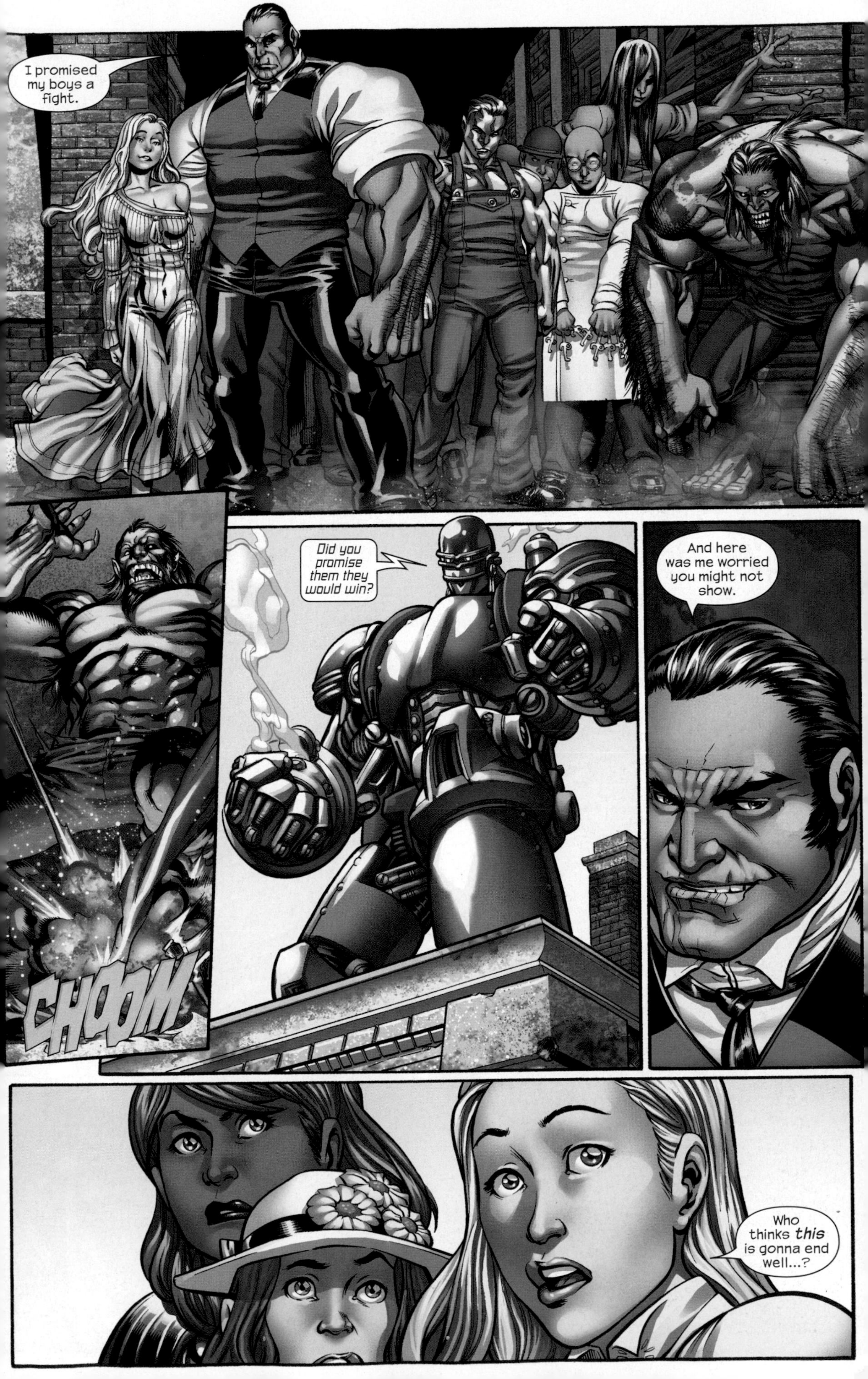
I promised my boys a fight.
Did you promise them they would win?
CHOOM
And here was me worried you might not show.
Who thinks *this* is gonna end well...?

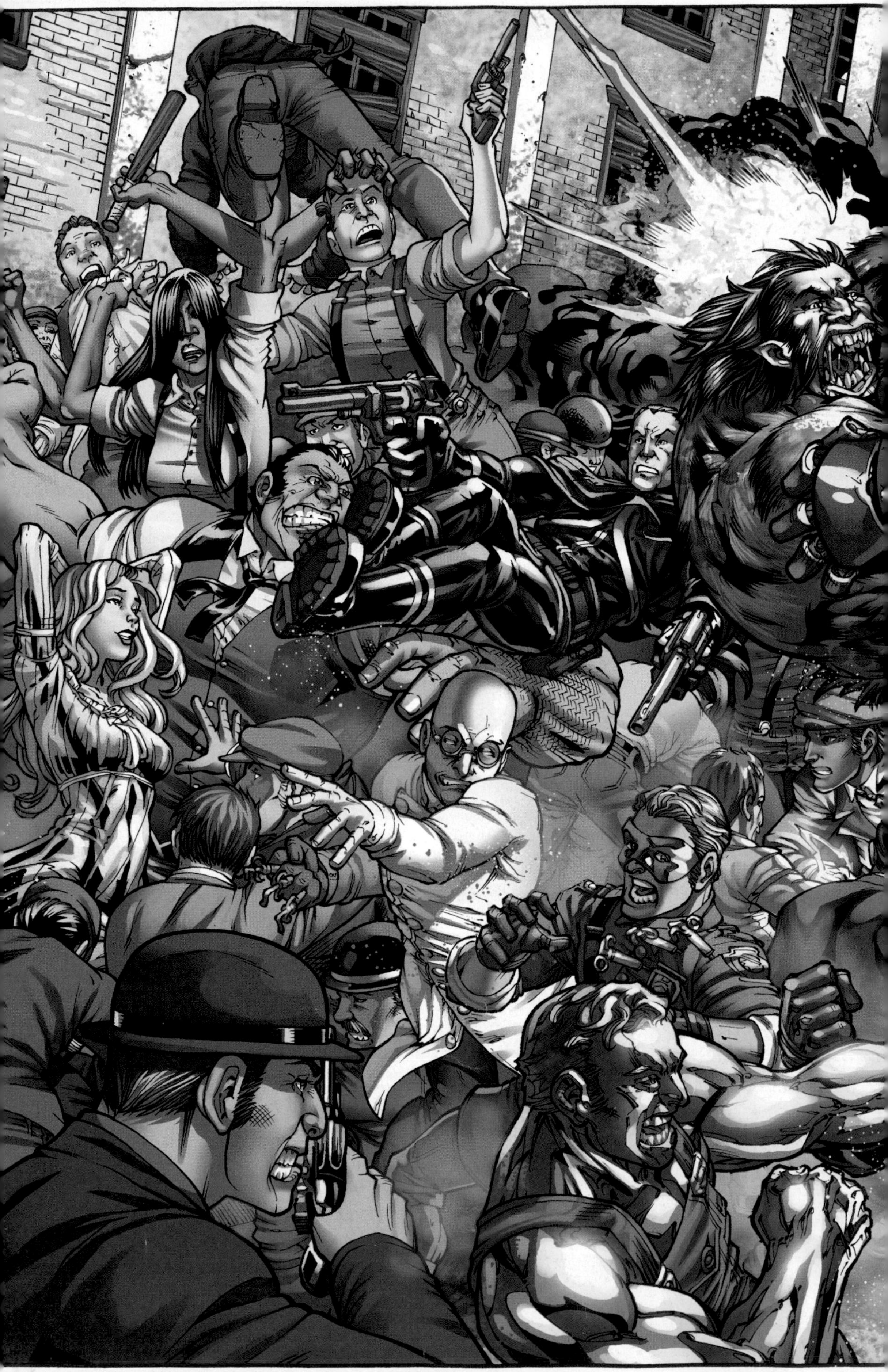

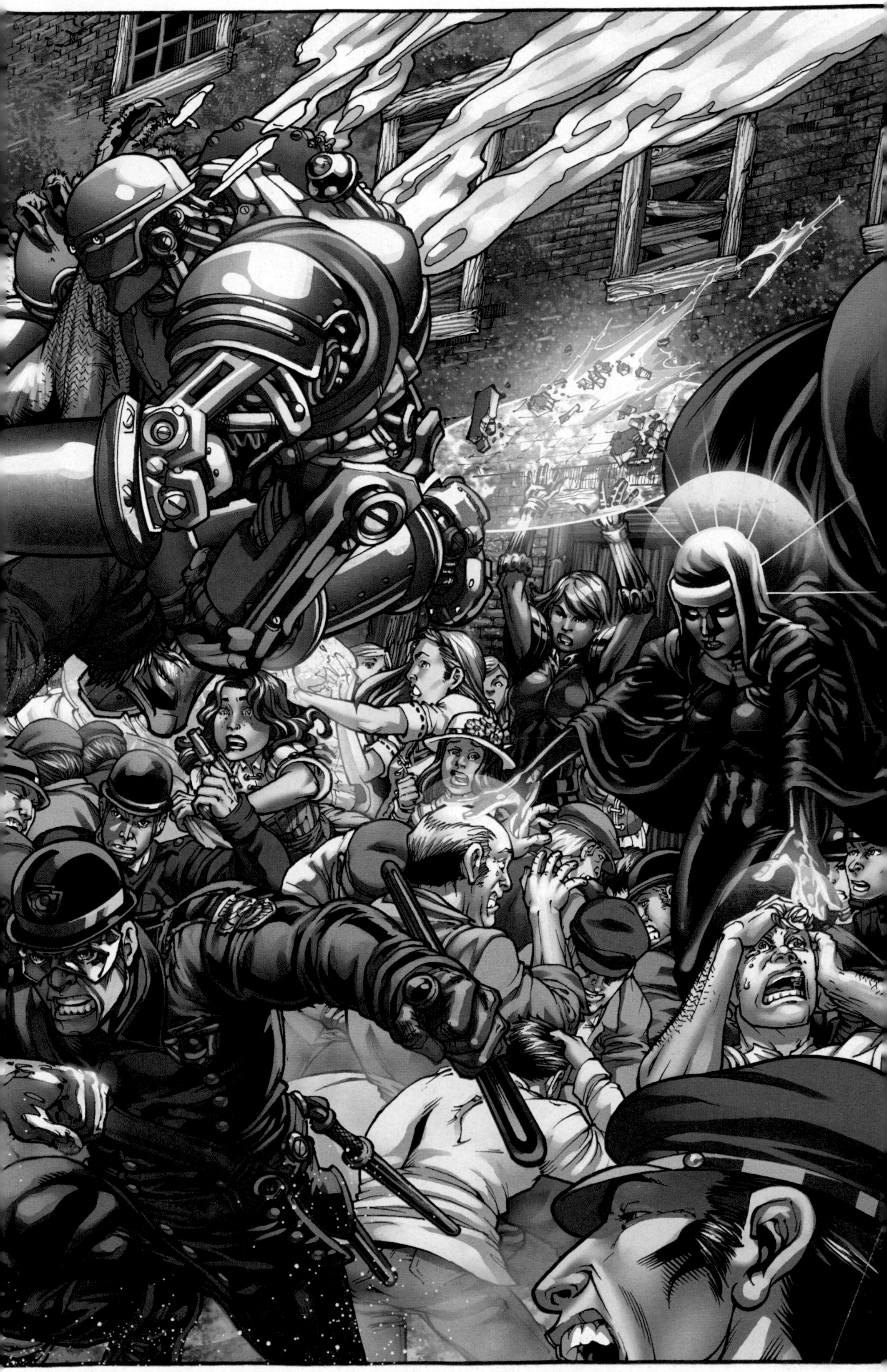

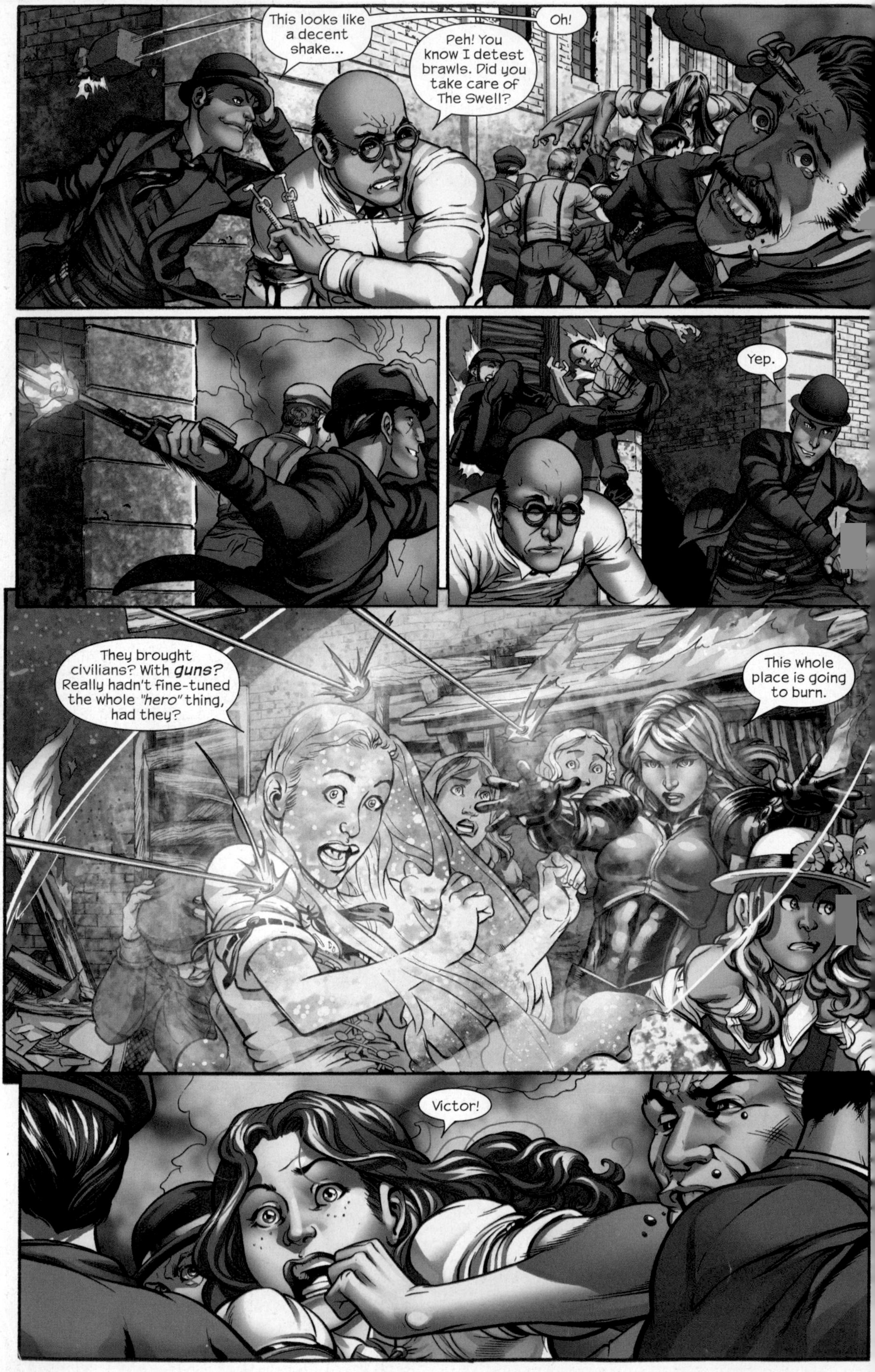
This looks like a decent shake...
Oh!
Peh! You know I detest brawls. Did you take care of The Swell?
Yep.
They brought civilians? With *guns?* Really hadn't fine-tuned the whole *"hero"* thing, had they?
This whole place is going to burn.
Victor!

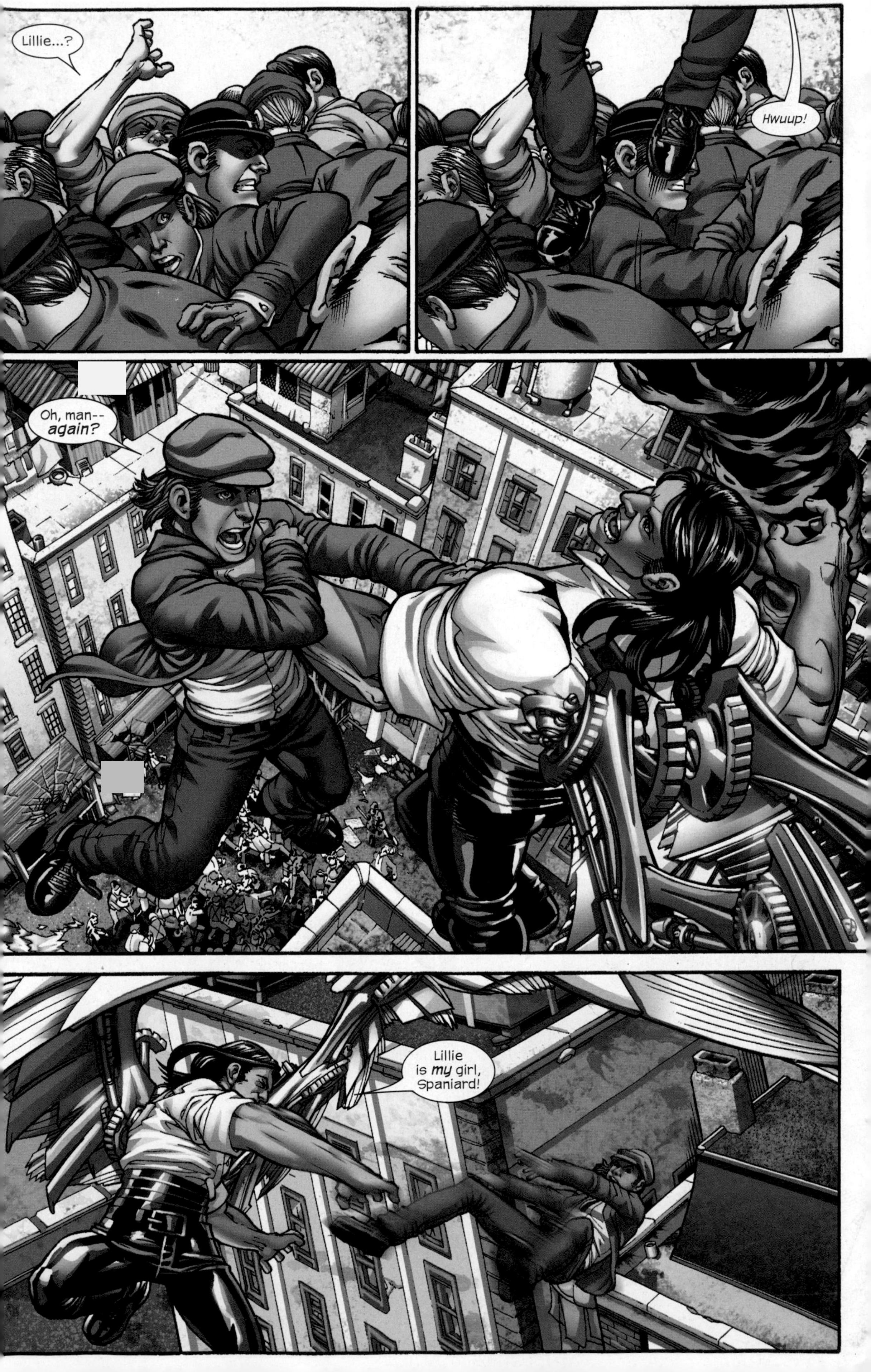
Lillie...?
Hwuup!
Oh, man-- *again*?
Lillie is *my* girl, Spaniard!

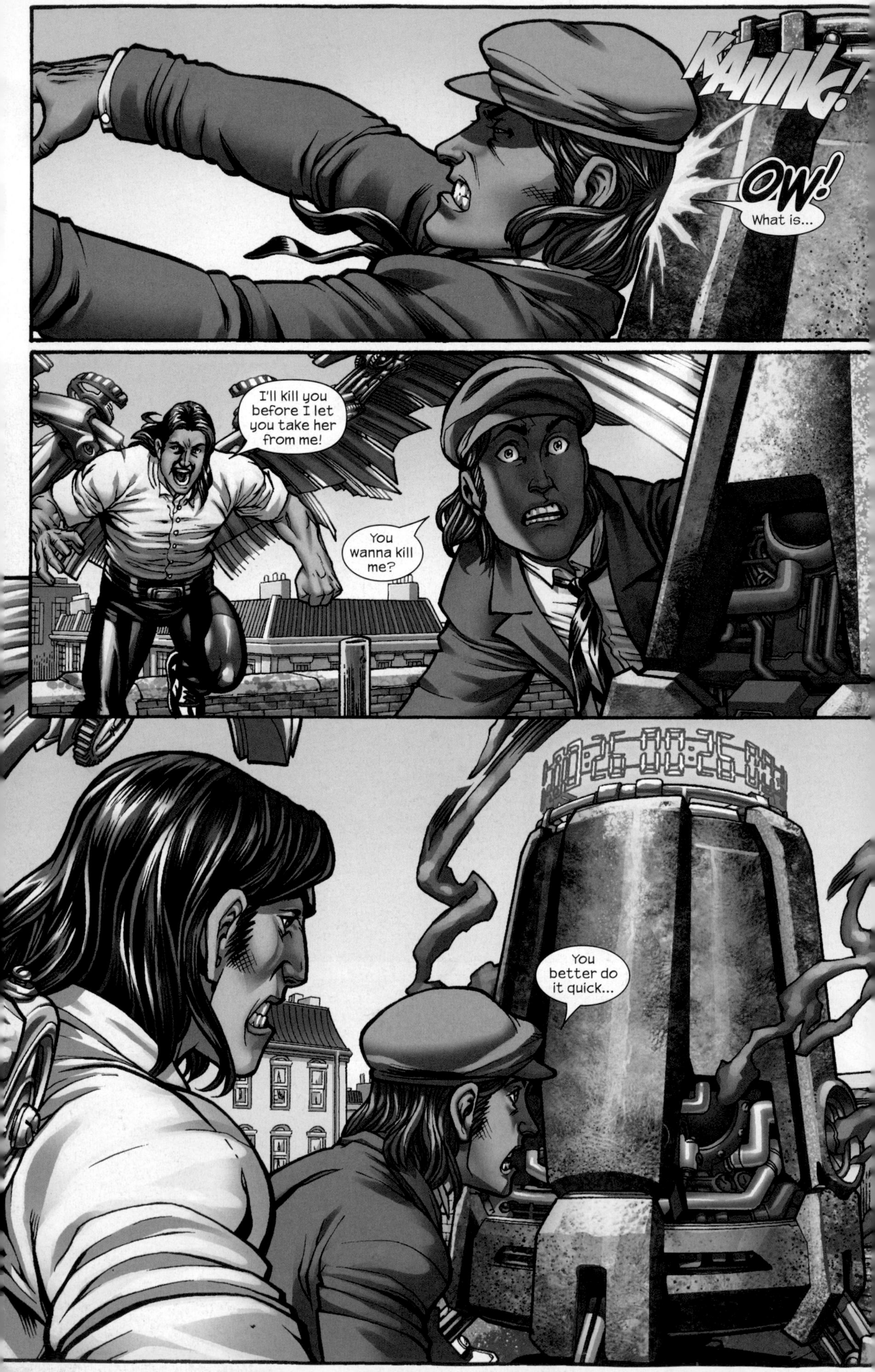
KANNG!
OW!
What is...
I'll kill you before I let you take her from me!
You wanna kill me?
You better do it quick...

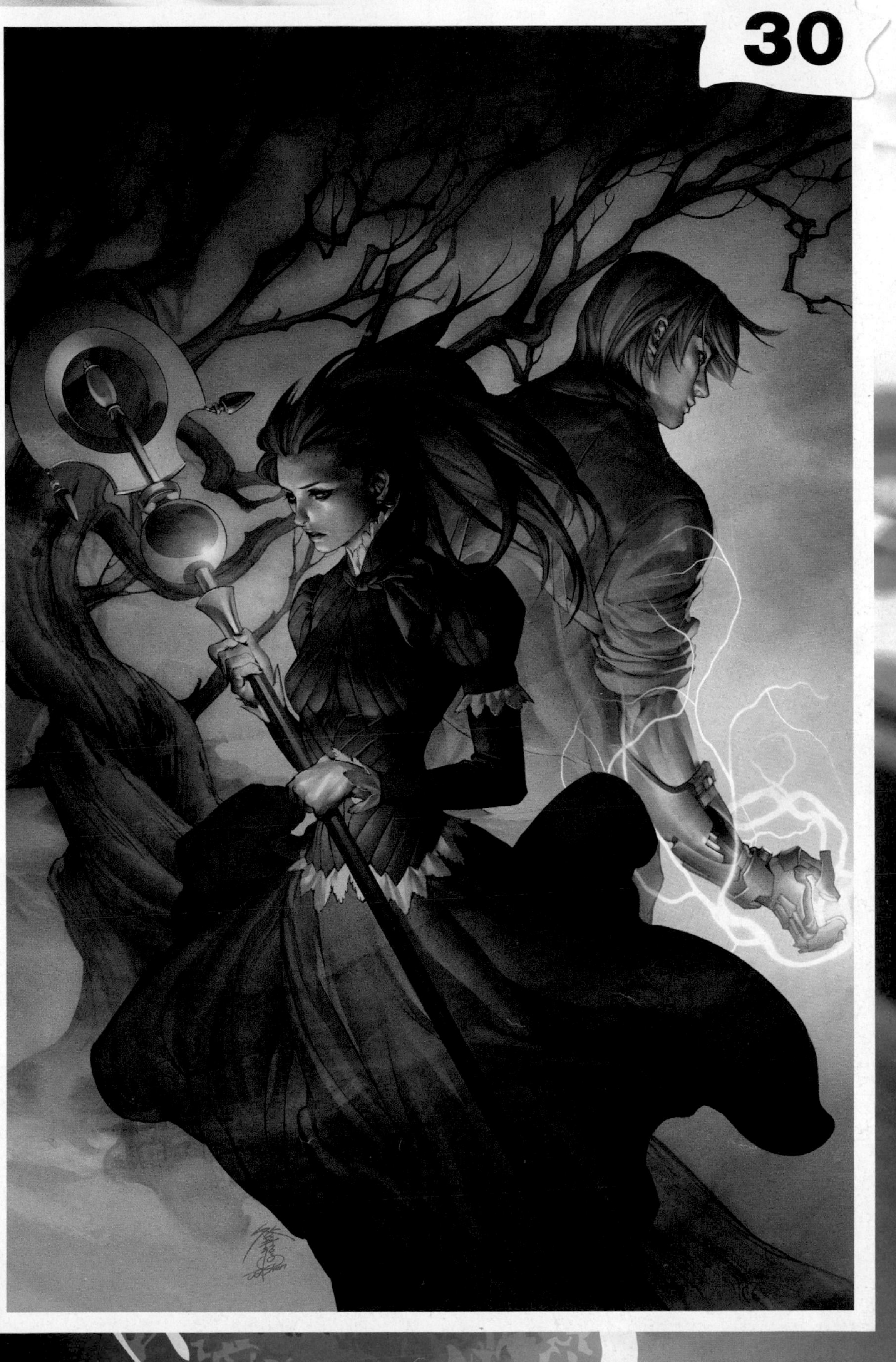
30

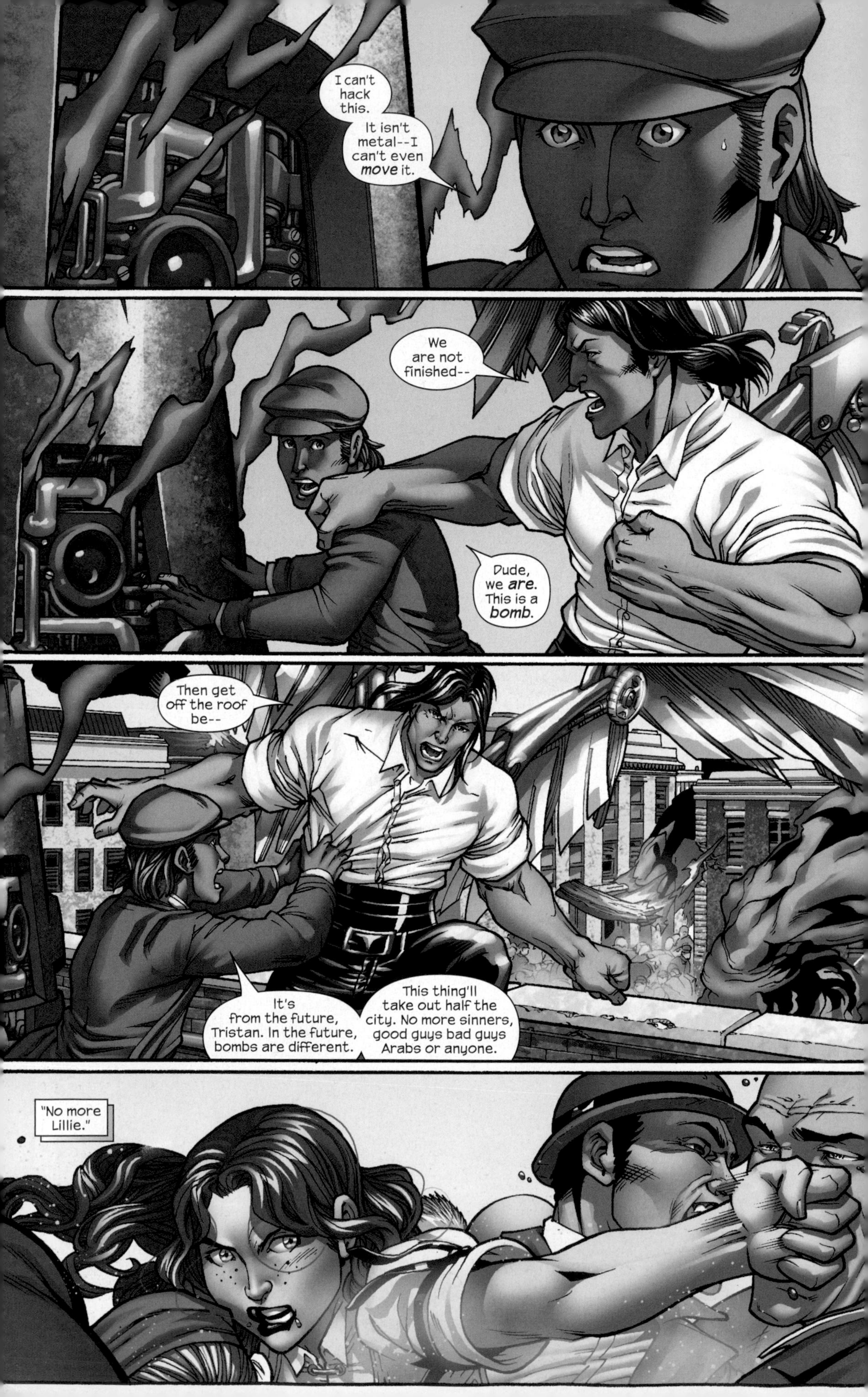
I can't hack this.
It isn't metal--I can't even *move* it.
We are not finished--
Dude, we *are*. This is a *bomb*.
Then get off the roof be--
It's from the future, Tristan. In the future, bombs are different.
This thing'll take out half the city. No more sinners, good guys bad guys Arabs or anyone.
"No more Lillie."

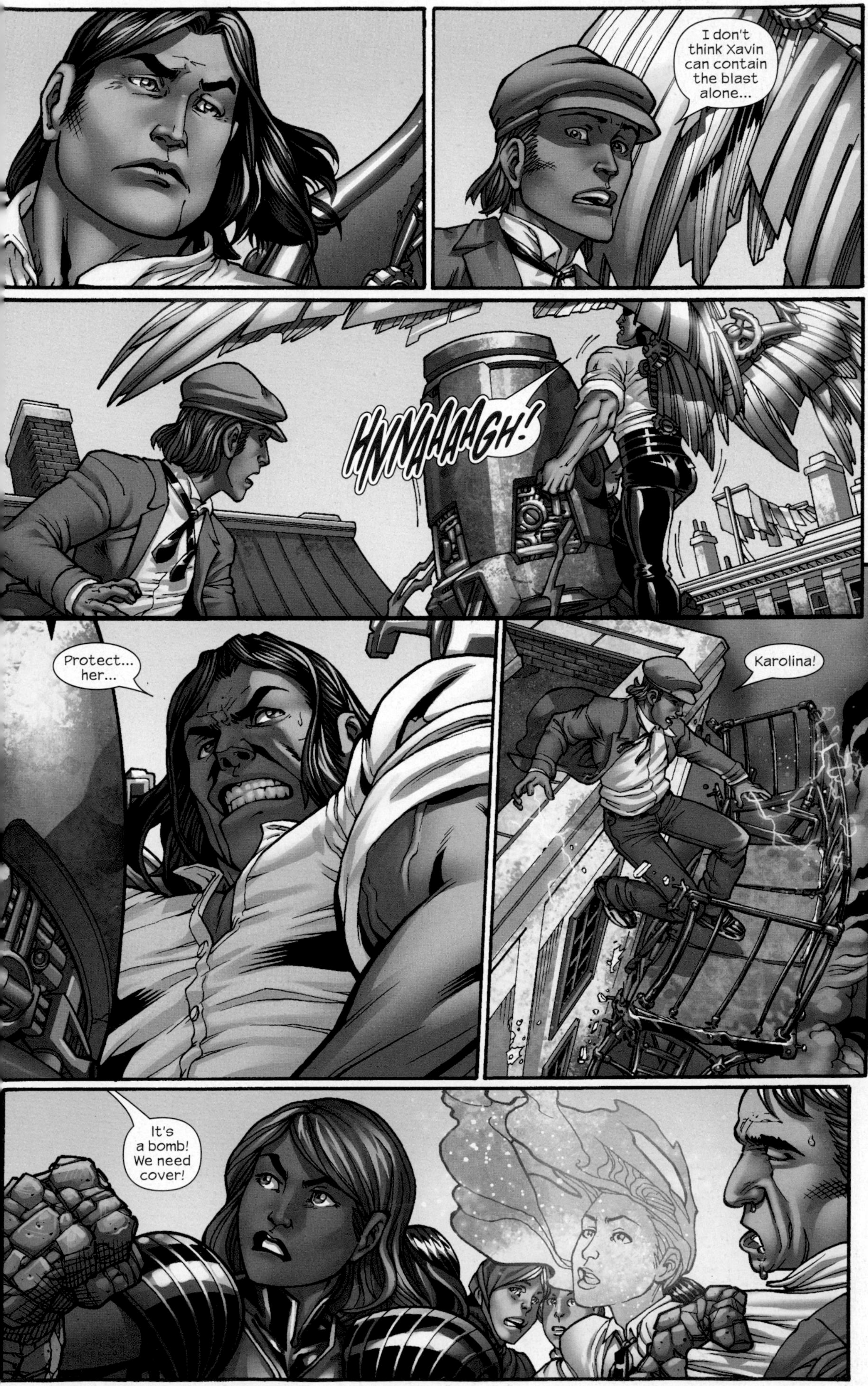
I don't think Xavin can contain the blast alone...
KNNAAAAGH!
Protect... her...
Karolina!
It's a bomb! We need cover!

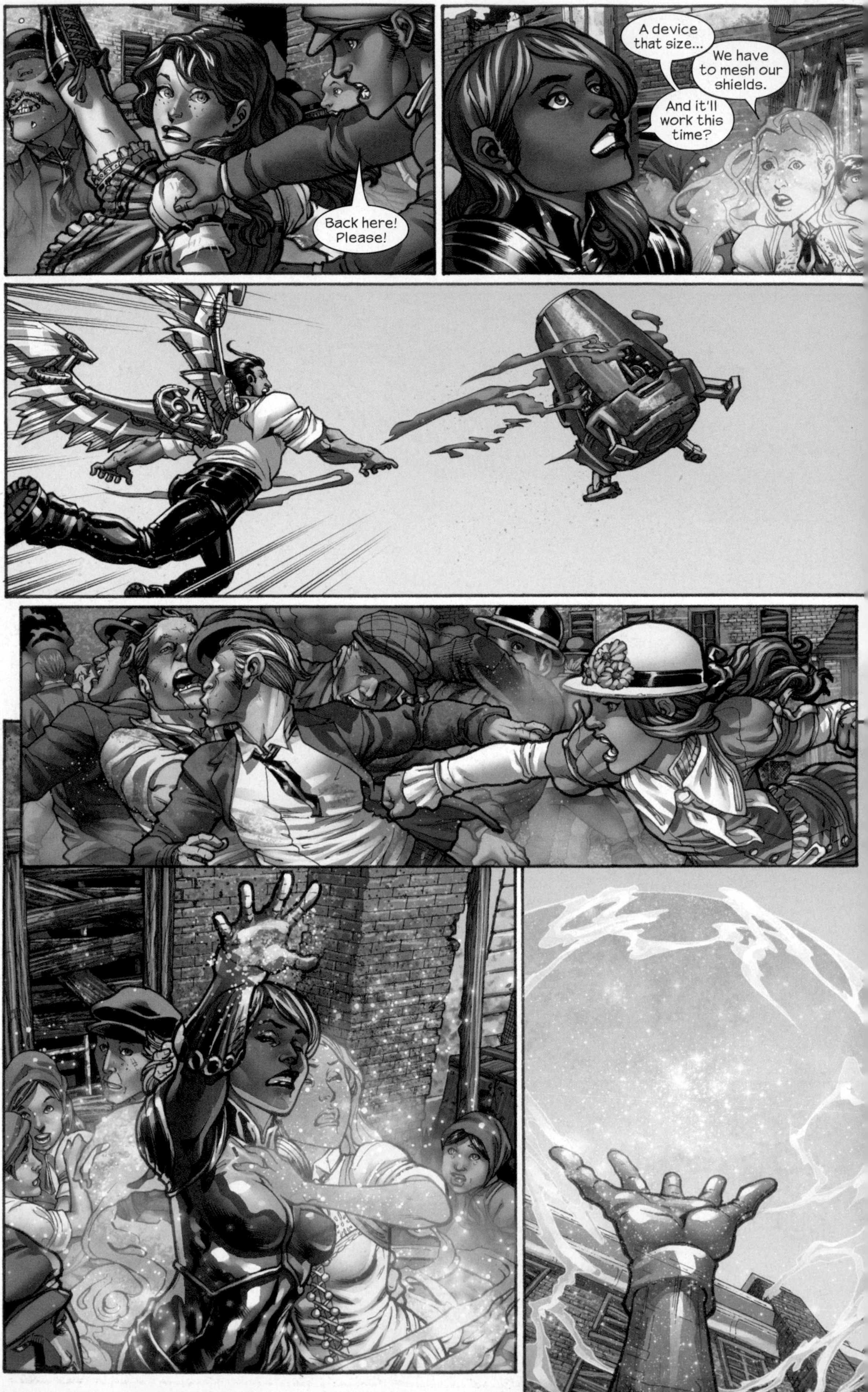
Back here! Please!
A device that size...
We have to mesh our shields.
And it'll work this time?

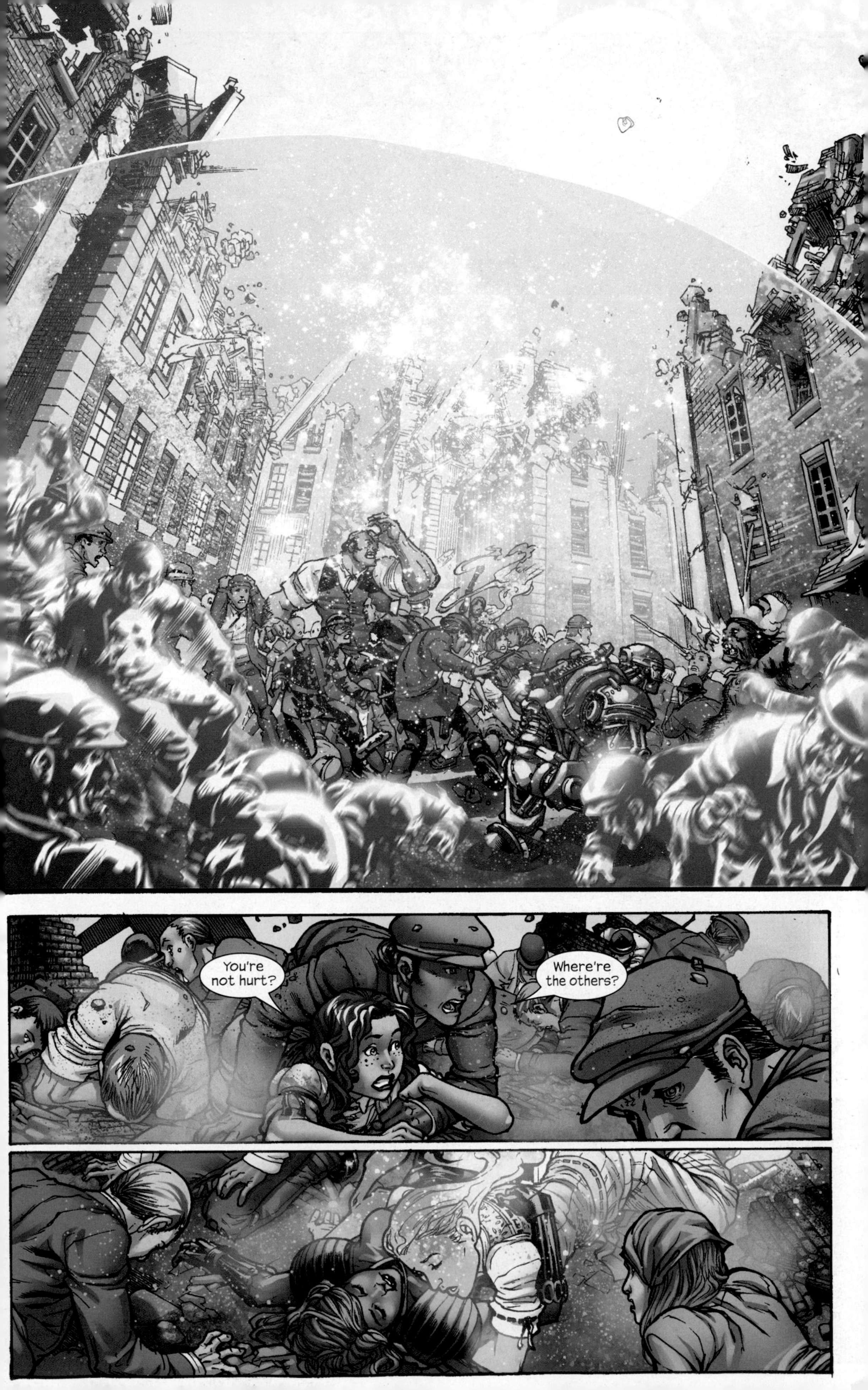
You're not hurt?
Where're the others?

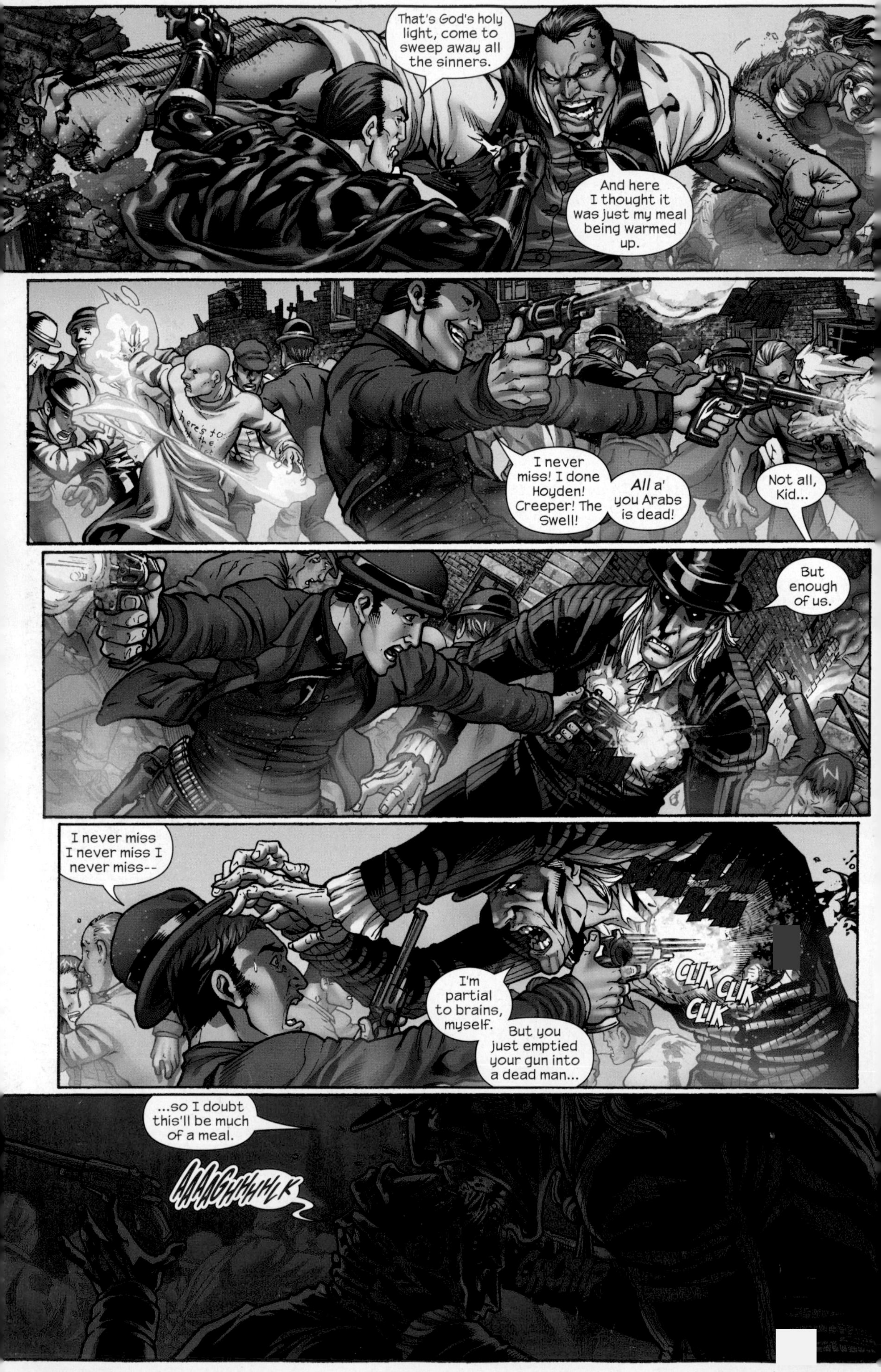

That's God's holy light, come to sweep away all the sinners.
And here I thought it was just my meal being warmed up.
I never miss! I done Hoyden! Creeper! The Swell!
All a' you Arabs is dead!
Not all, Kid...
But enough of us.
I never miss I never miss I never miss--
I'm partial to brains, myself.
But you just emptied your gun into a dead man...
CLIK CLIK CLIK
...so I doubt this'll be much of a meal.

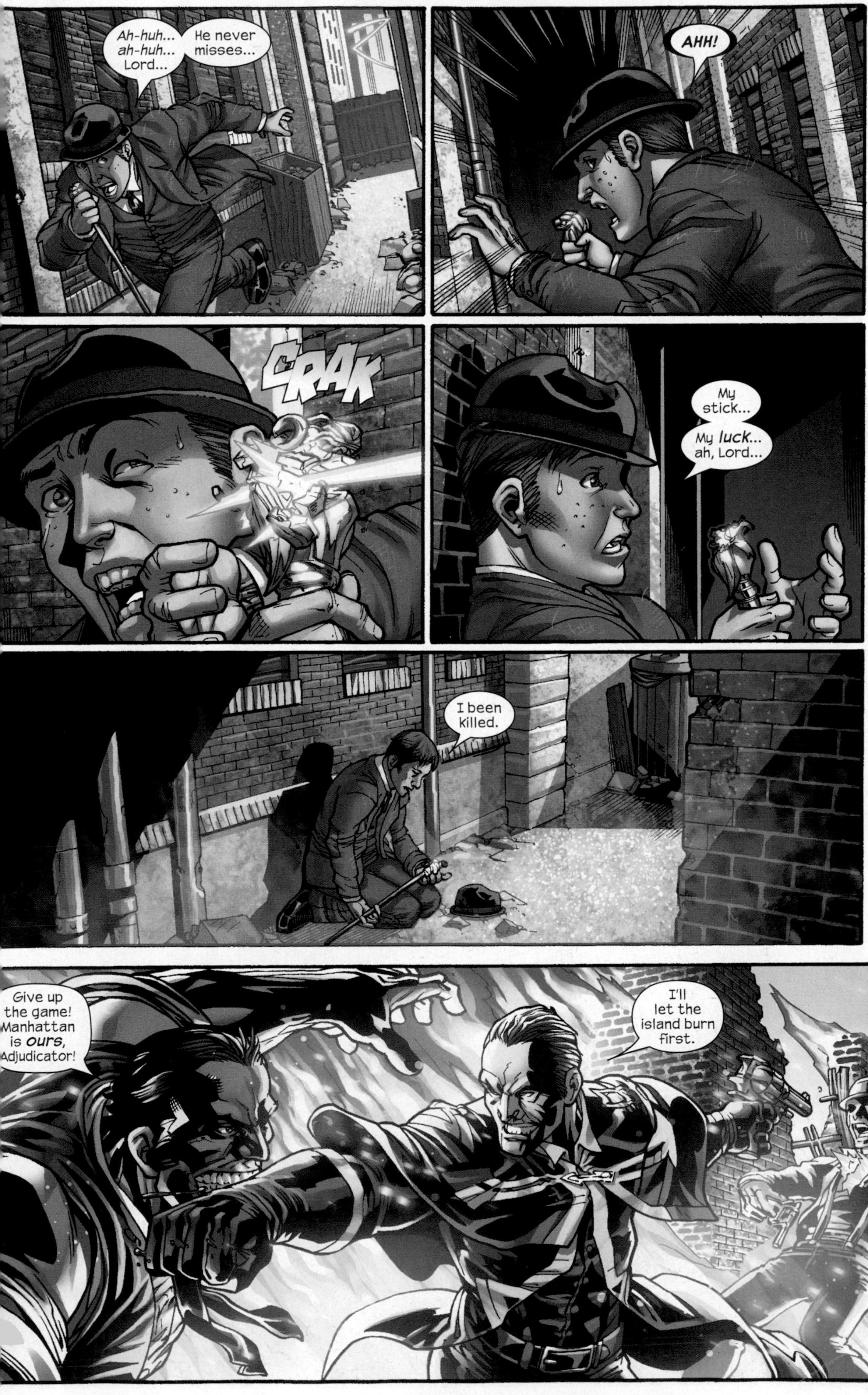
Ah-huh...
ah-huh...
Lord...
He never
misses...
AHH!
CRAK
My
stick...
My *luck*...
ah, Lord...
I been
killed.
Give up
the game!
Manhattan
is *ours*,
Adjudicator!
I'll
let the
island burn
first.

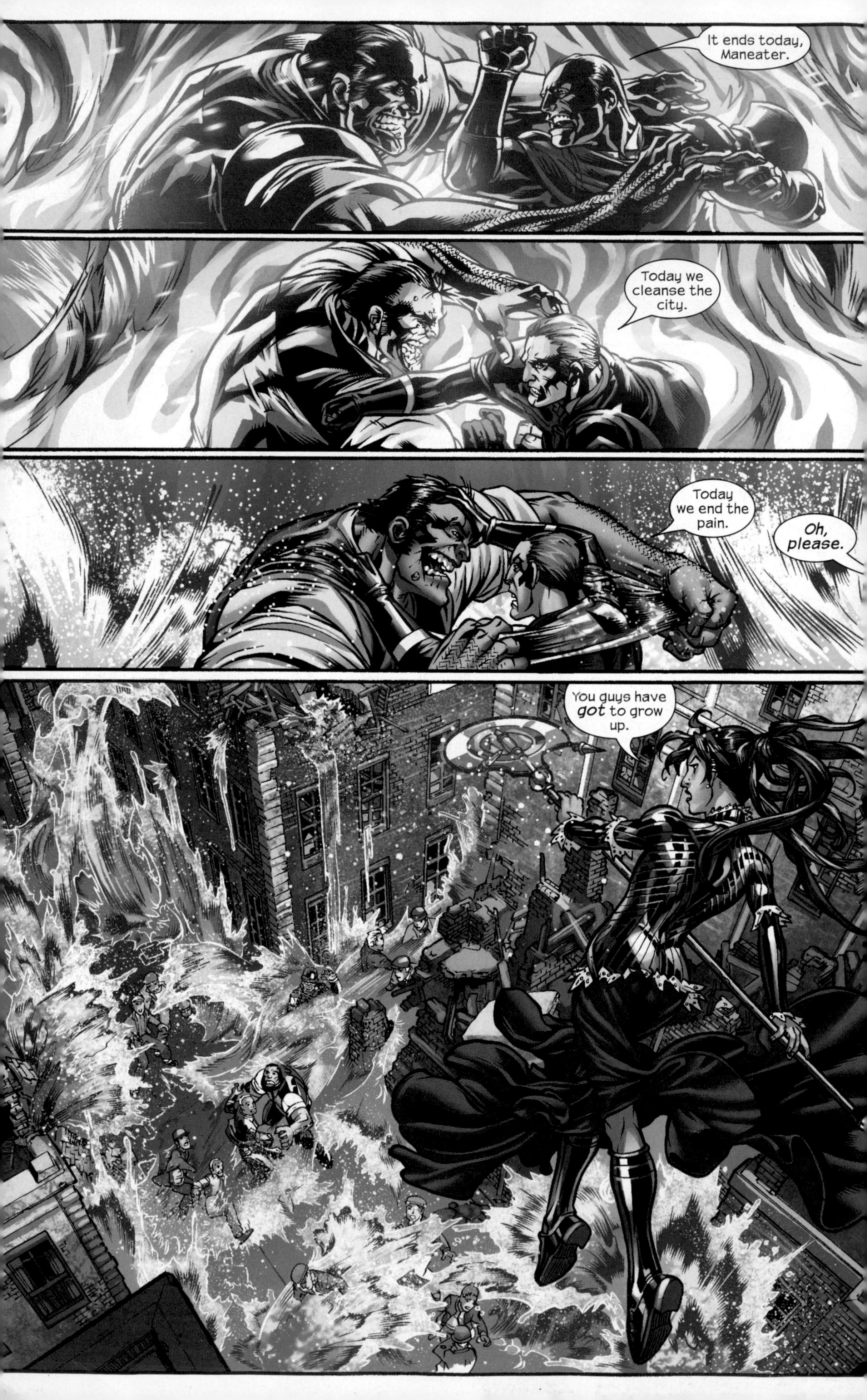
It ends today, Maneater.
Today we cleanse the city.
Today we end the pain.
Oh, please.
You guys have got to grow up.

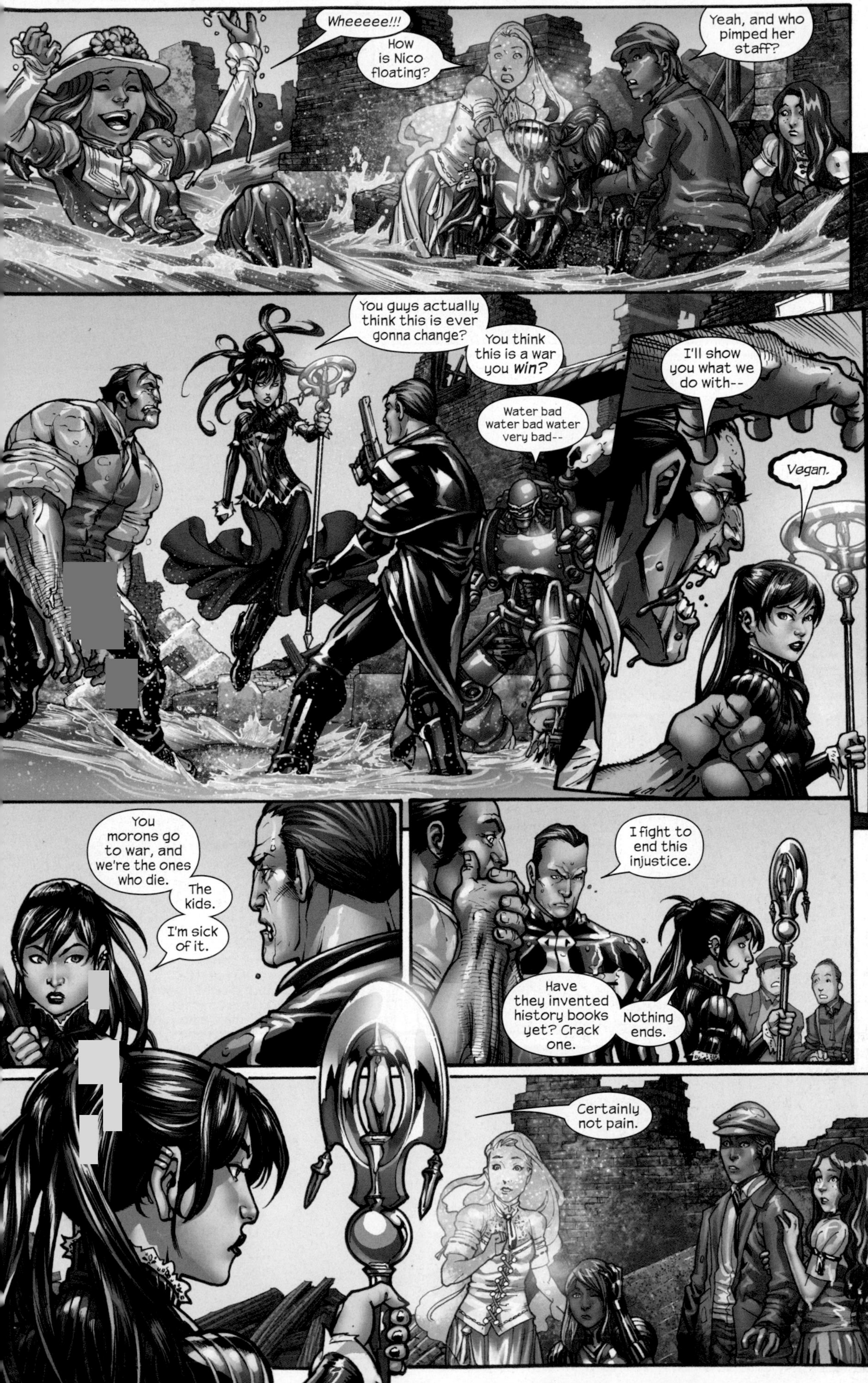
Wheeeee!!!
How is Nico floating?
Yeah, and who pimped her staff?
You guys actually think this is ever gonna change?
You think this is a war you *win*?
Water bad water bad water very bad--
I'll show you what we do with--
Vegan.
You morons go to war, and we're the ones who die.
The kids.
I'm sick of it.
I fight to end this injustice.
Have they invented history books yet? Crack one.
Nothing ends.
Certainly not pain.

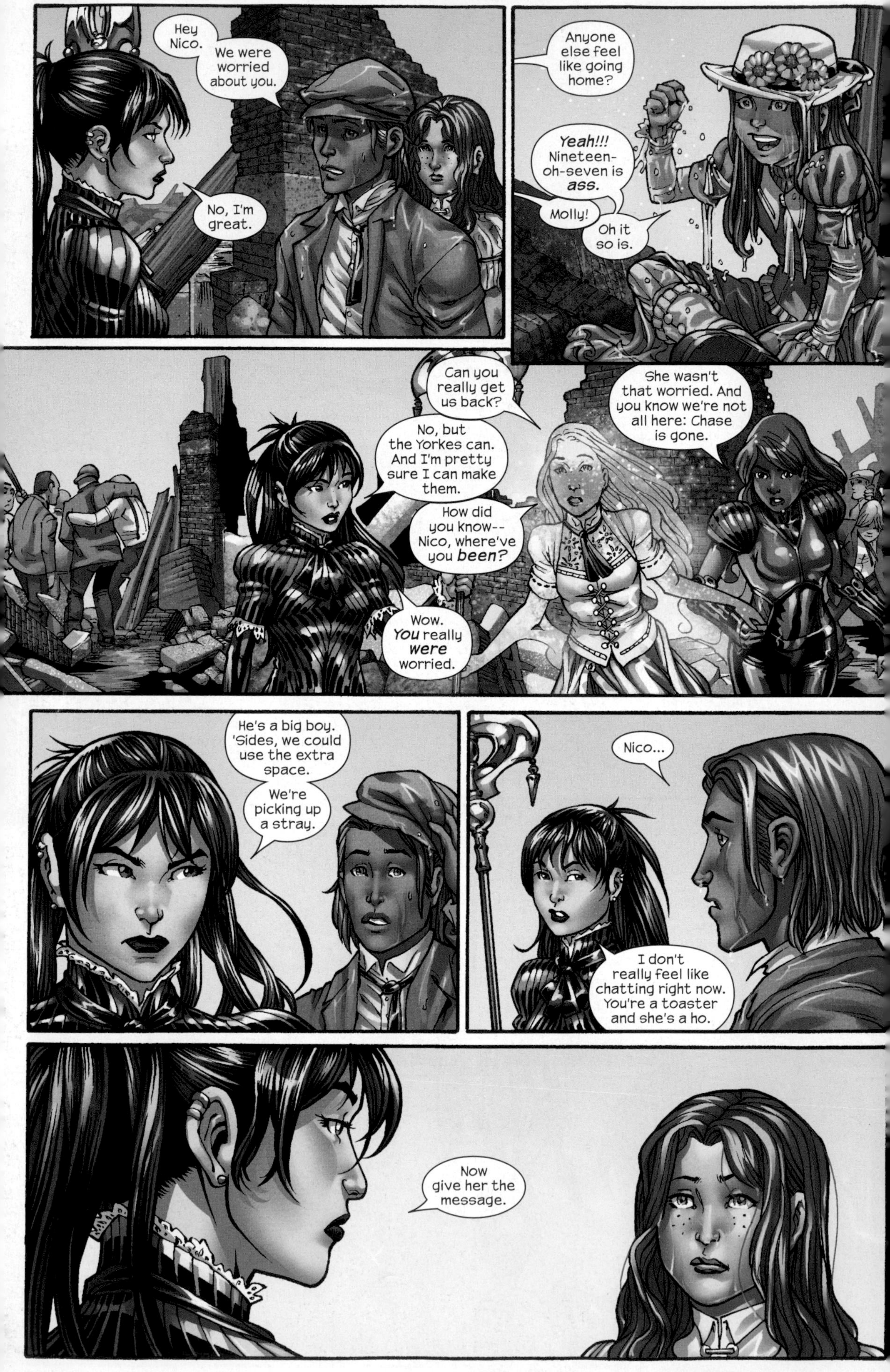
Hey Nico.
We were worried about you.
No, I'm great.
Anyone else feel like going home?
Yeah!!! Nineteen-oh-seven is ass.
Molly!
Oh it so is.
Can you really get us back?
No, but the Yorkes can. And I'm pretty sure I can make them.
How did you know-- Nico, where've you been?
She wasn't that worried. And you know we're not all here: Chase is gone.
Wow. You really were worried.
He's a big boy. 'Sides, we could use the extra space.
We're picking up a stray.
Nico...
I don't really feel like chatting right now. You're a toaster and she's a ho.
Now give her the message.

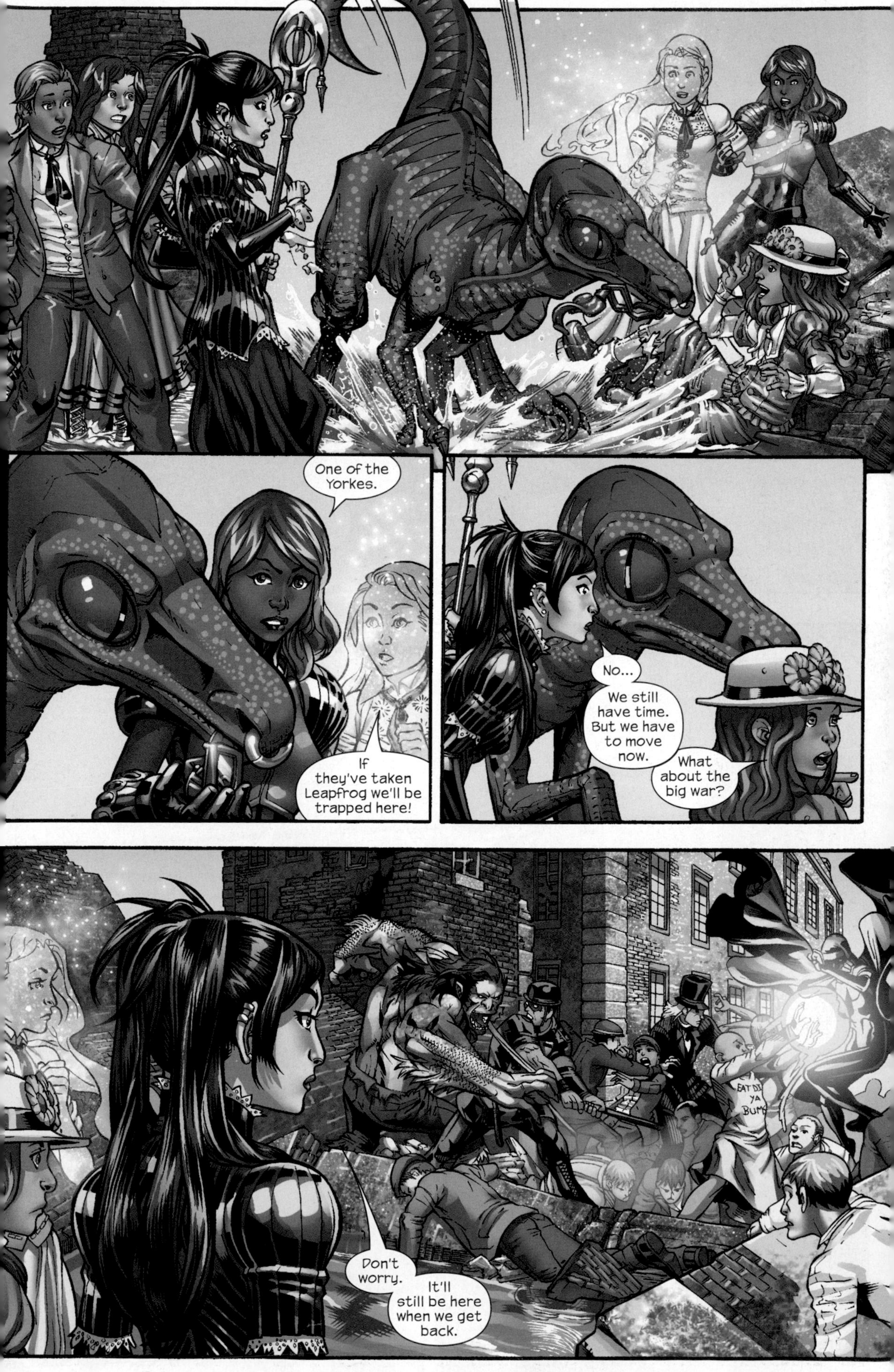
One of the Yorkes.
If they've taken Leapfrog we'll be trapped here!
No...
We still have time. But we have to move now.
What about the big war?
EAT DI YA BUMS
Don't worry.
It'll still be here when we get back.

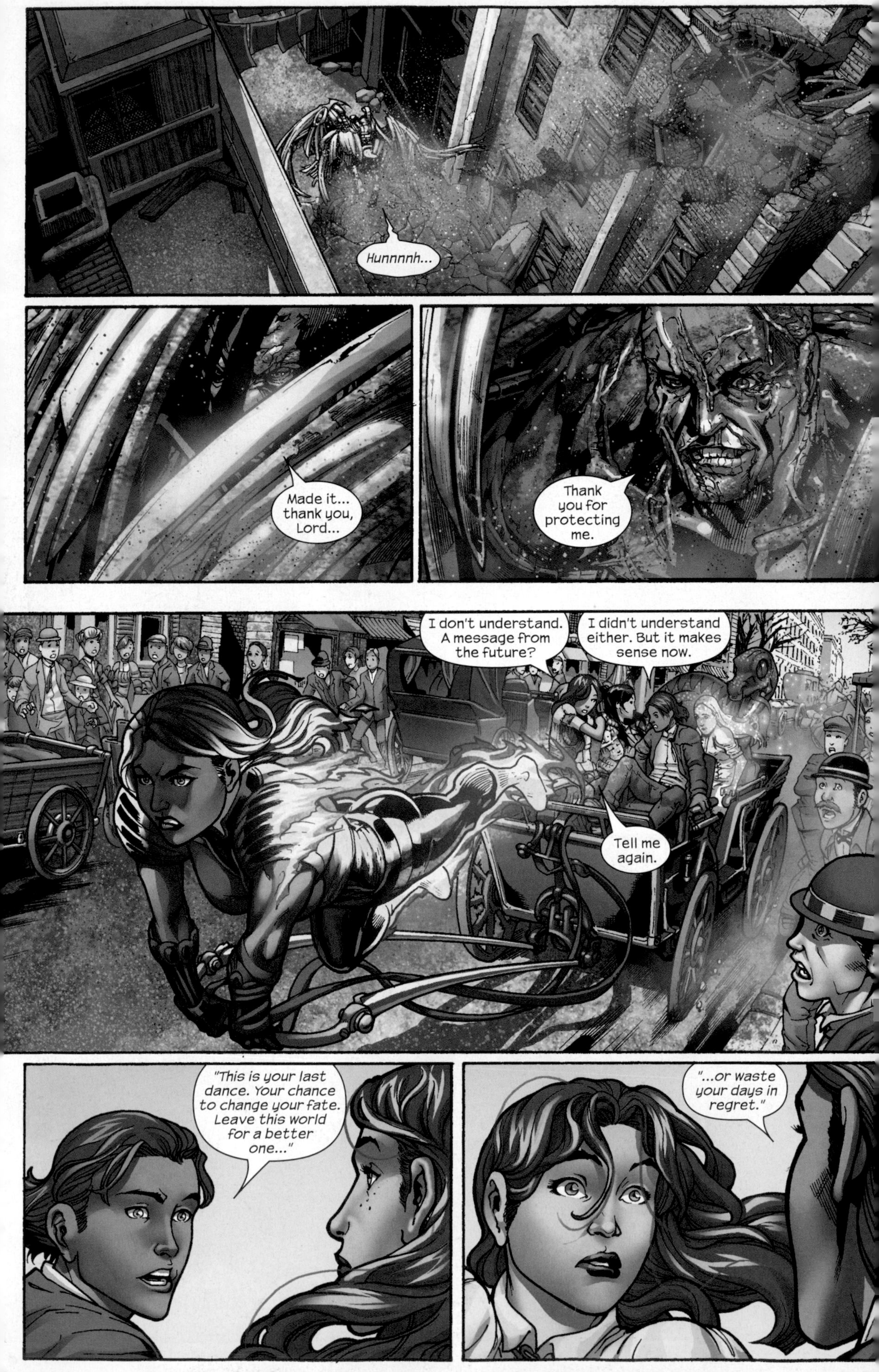
Hunnnnh...
Made it... thank you, Lord...
Thank you for protecting me.
I don't understand. A message from the future?
I didn't understand either. But it makes sense now.
Tell me again.
"This is your last dance. Your chance to change your fate. Leave this world for a better one..."
"...or waste your days in regret."

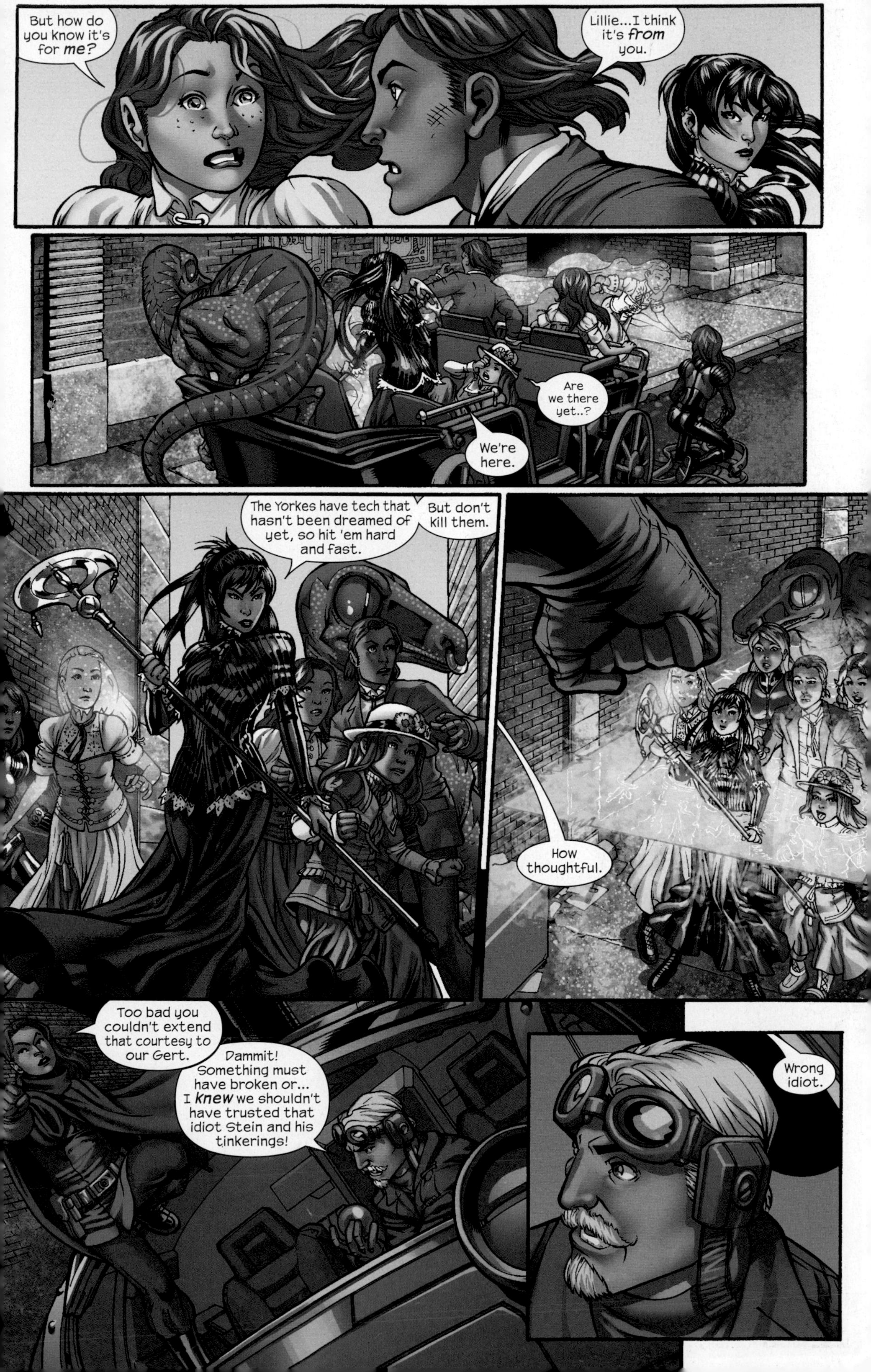

But how do you know it's for *me*?
Lillie...I think it's *from* you.
Are we there yet..?
We're here.
The Yorkes have tech that hasn't been dreamed of yet, so hit 'em hard and fast.
But don't kill them.
How thoughtful.
Too bad you couldn't extend that courtesy to our Gert.
Dammit! Something must have broken or... I *knew* we shouldn't have trusted that idiot Stein and his tinkerings!
Wrong idiot.

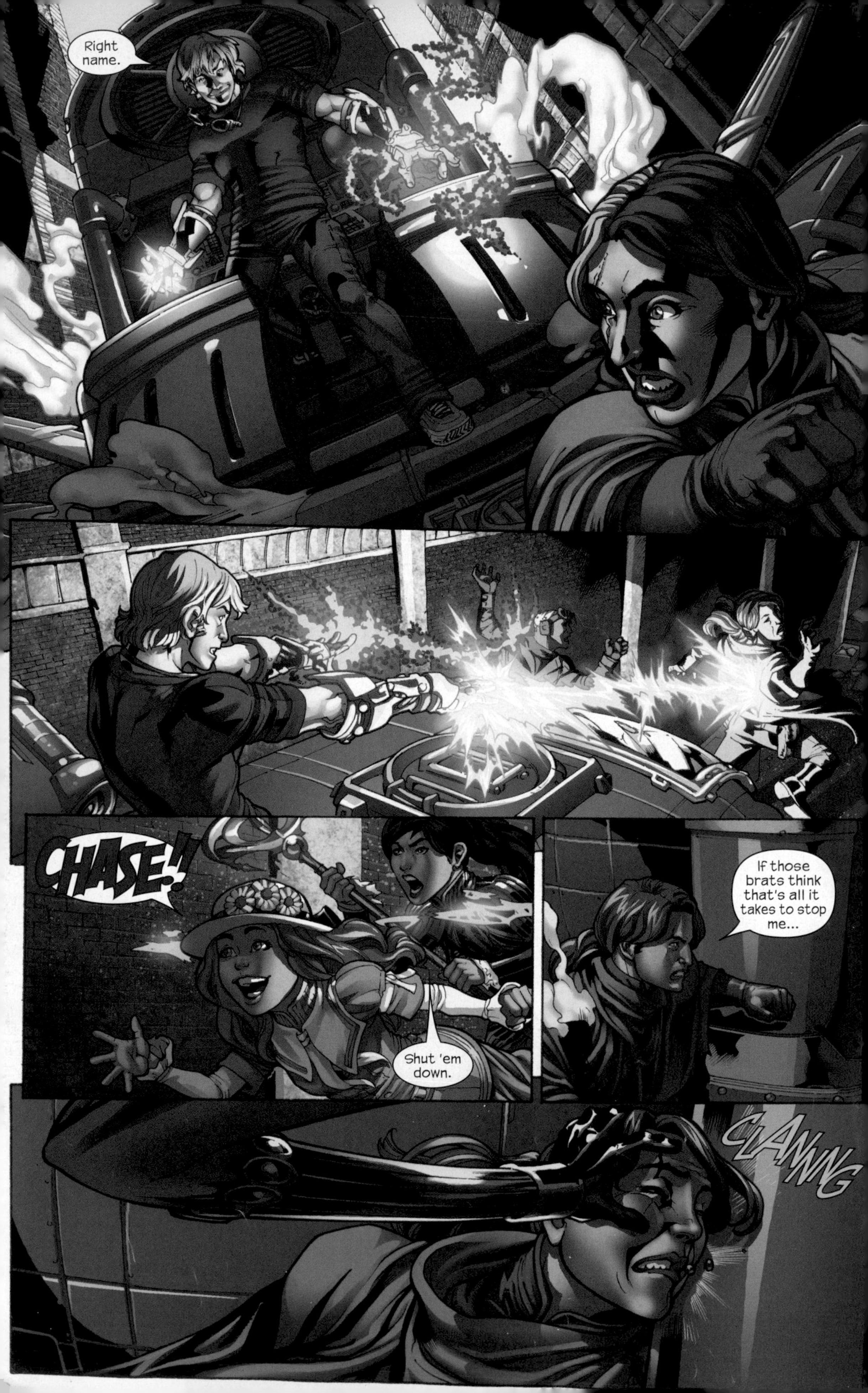
Right name.
CHASE!
Shut 'em down.
If those brats think that's all it takes to stop me...
CLANNG

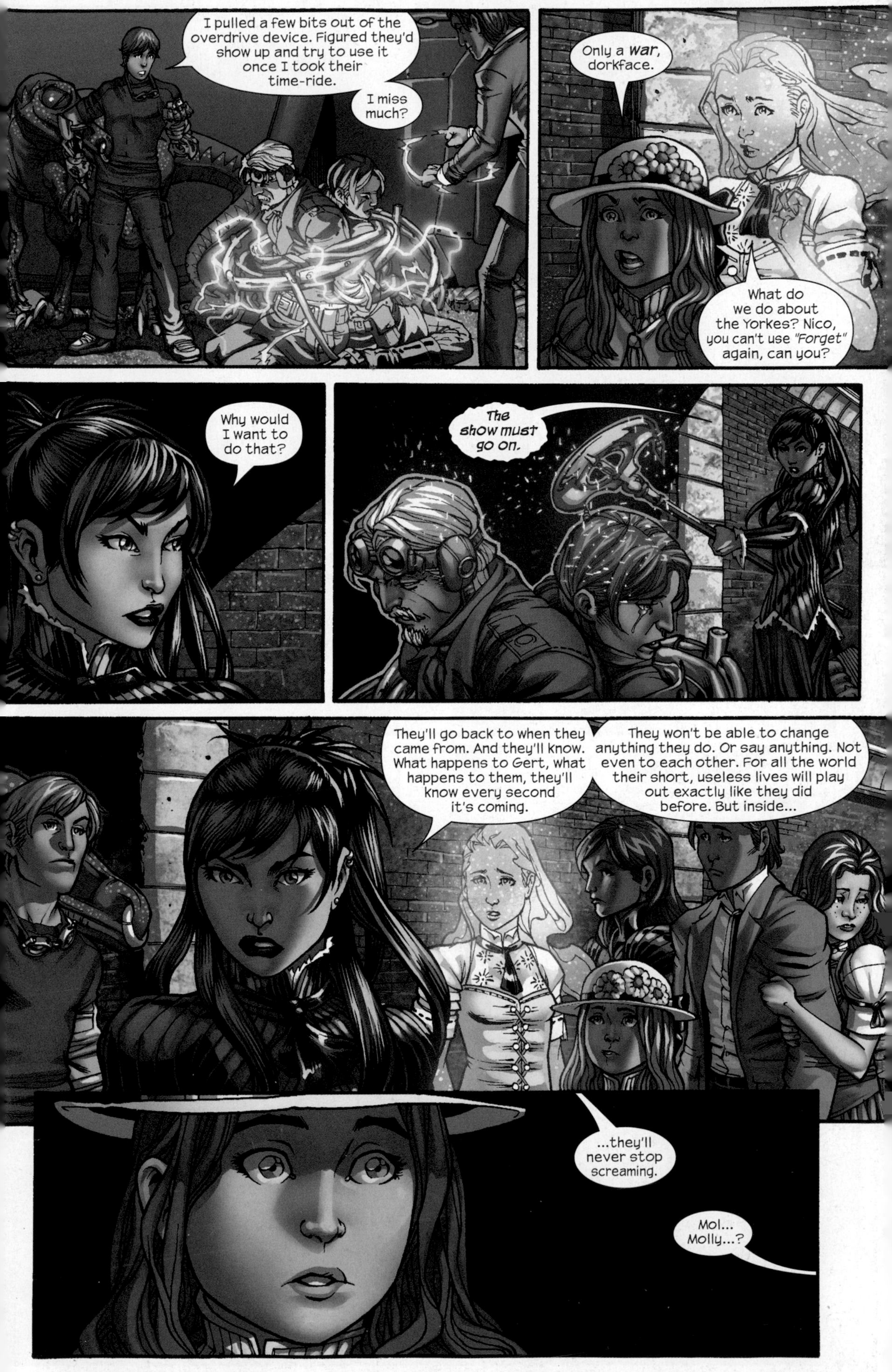

I pulled a few bits out of the overdrive device. Figured they'd show up and try to use it once I took their time-ride.
I miss much?
Only a *war*, dorkface.
What do we do about the Yorkes? Nico, you can't use *"Forget"* again, can you?
Why would I want to do that?
The show must go on.
They'll go back to when they came from. And they'll know. What happens to Gert, what happens to them, they'll know every second it's coming.
They won't be able to change anything they do. Or say anything. Not even to each other. For all the world their short, useless lives will play out exactly like they did before. But inside...
...they'll never stop screaming.
Mol... Molly...?

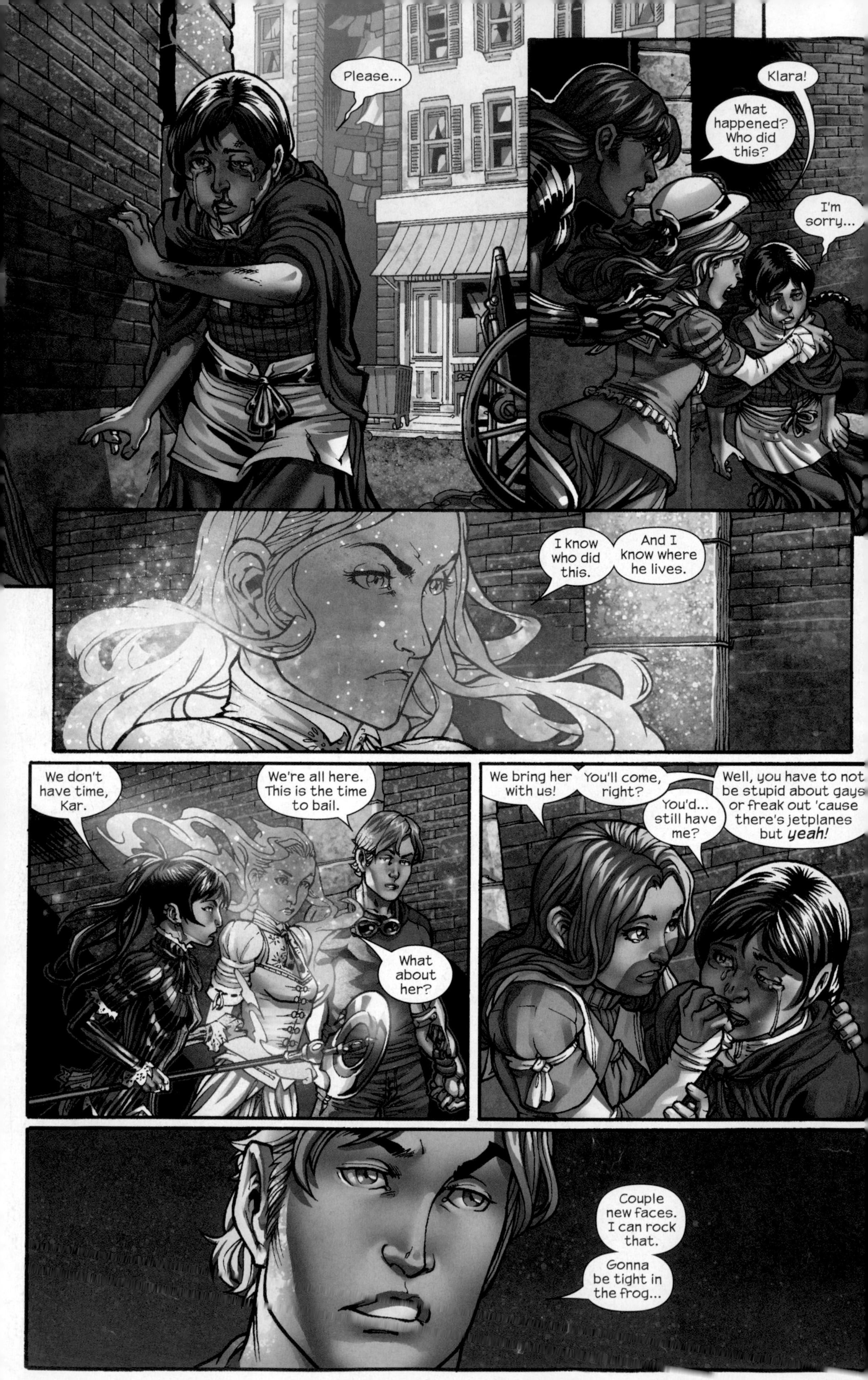
Please...
Klara!
What happened? Who did this?
I'm sorry...
I know who did this.
And I know where he lives.
We don't have time, Kar.
We're all here. This is the time to bail.
What about her?
We bring her with us!
You'll come, right?
You'd... still have me?
Well, you have to not be stupid about gays or freak out 'cause there's jetplanes but *yeah!*
Couple new faces. I can rock that.
Gonna be tight in the frog...

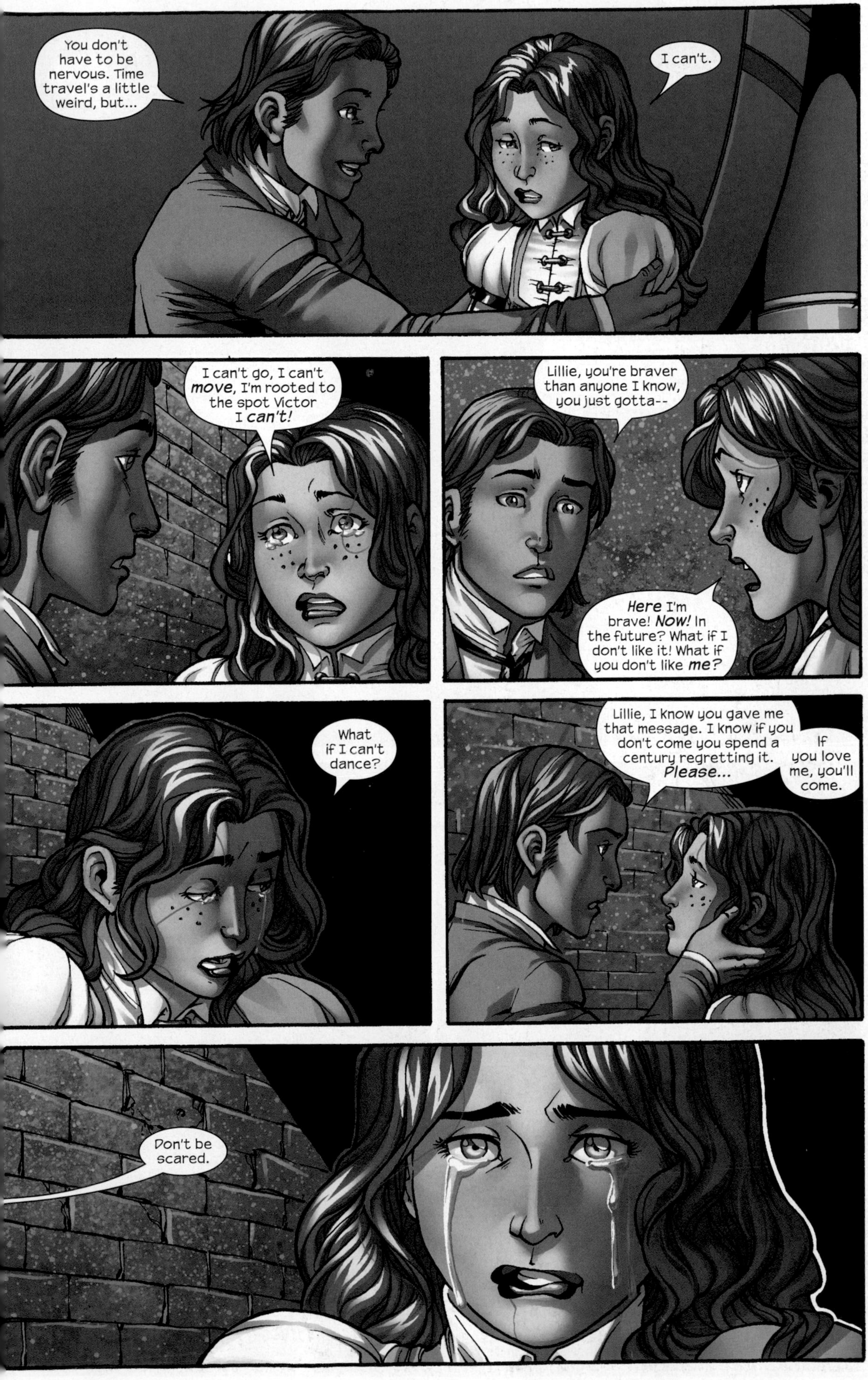
You don't have to be nervous. Time travel's a little weird, but...
I can't.
I can't go, I can't *move*, I'm rooted to the spot Victor I *can't!*
Lillie, you're braver than anyone I know, you just gotta--
Here I'm brave! *Now!* In the future? What if I don't like it! What if you don't like *me?*
What if I can't dance?
Lillie, I know you gave me that message. I know if you don't come you spend a century regretting it. *Please...*
If you love me, you'll come.
Don't be scared.

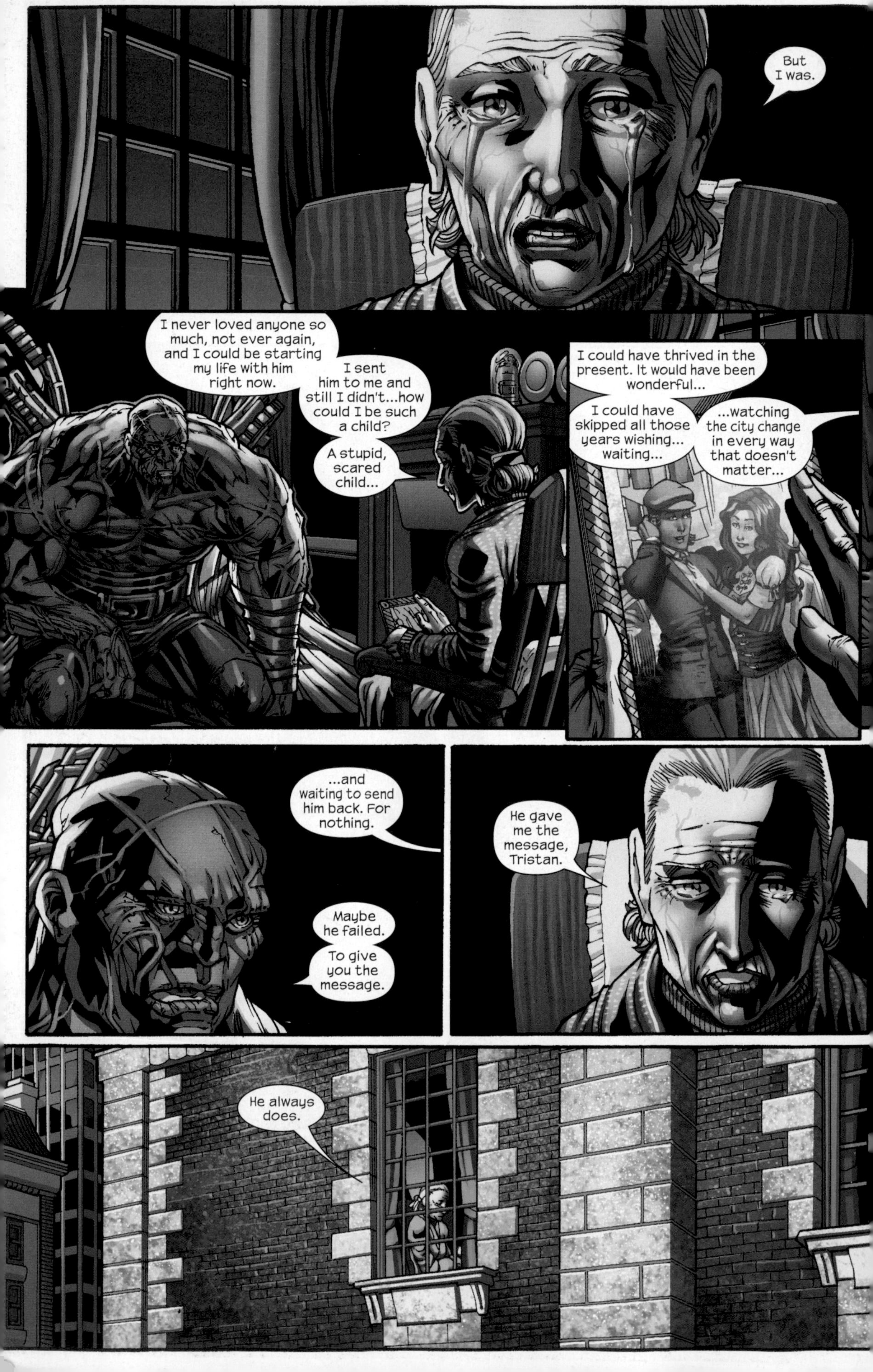
But I was.
I never loved anyone so much, not ever again, and I could be starting my life with him right now.
I sent him to me and still I didn't...how could I be such a child?
A stupid, scared child...
I could have thrived in the present. It would have been wonderful...
I could have skipped all those years wishing... waiting...
...watching the city change in every way that doesn't matter...
...and waiting to send him back. For nothing.
Maybe he failed.
To give you the message.
He gave me the message, Tristan.
He always does.

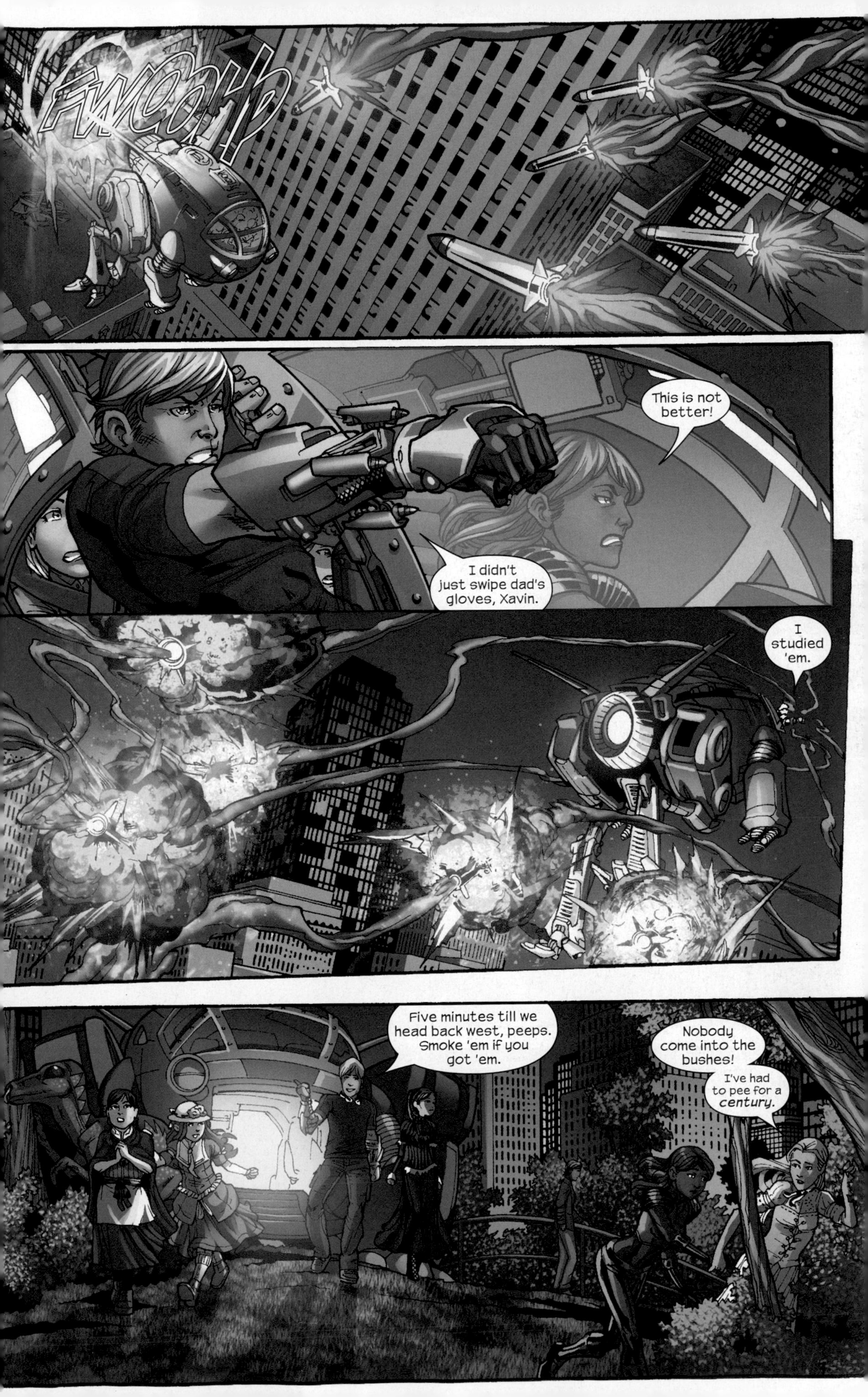
FWOOOMP
This is not better!
I didn't just swipe dad's gloves, Xavin.
I studied 'em.
Five minutes till we head back west, peeps. Smoke 'em if you got 'em.
Nobody come into the bushes!
I've had to pee for a *century*.

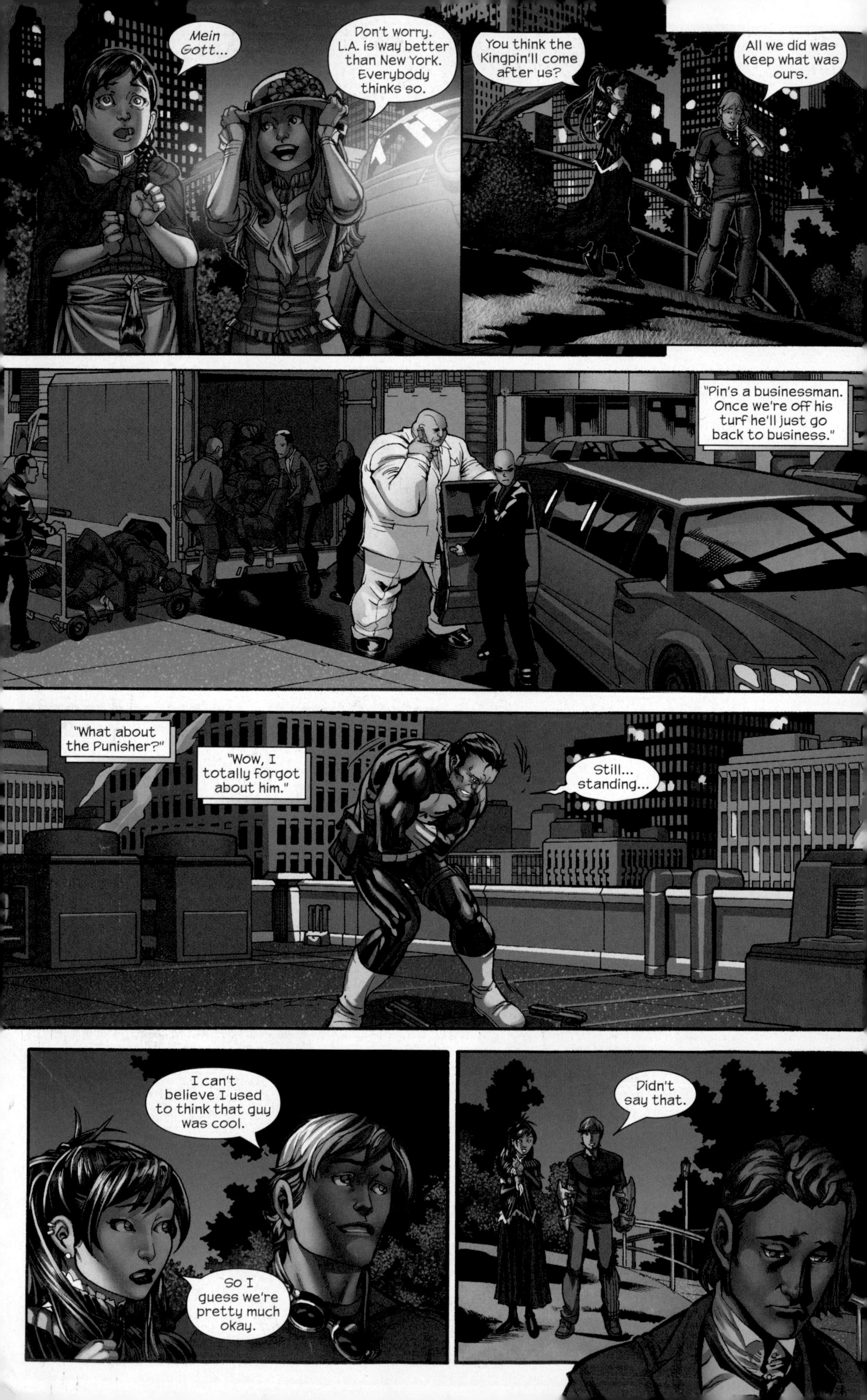
Mein Gott...
Don't worry. L.A. is way better than New York. Everybody thinks so.
You think the Kingpin'll come after us?
All we did was keep what was ours.
"Pin's a businessman. Once we're off his turf he'll just go back to business."
"What about the Punisher?"
"Wow, I totally forgot about him."
Still... standing...
I can't believe I used to think that guy was cool.
So I guess we're pretty much okay.
Didn't say that.

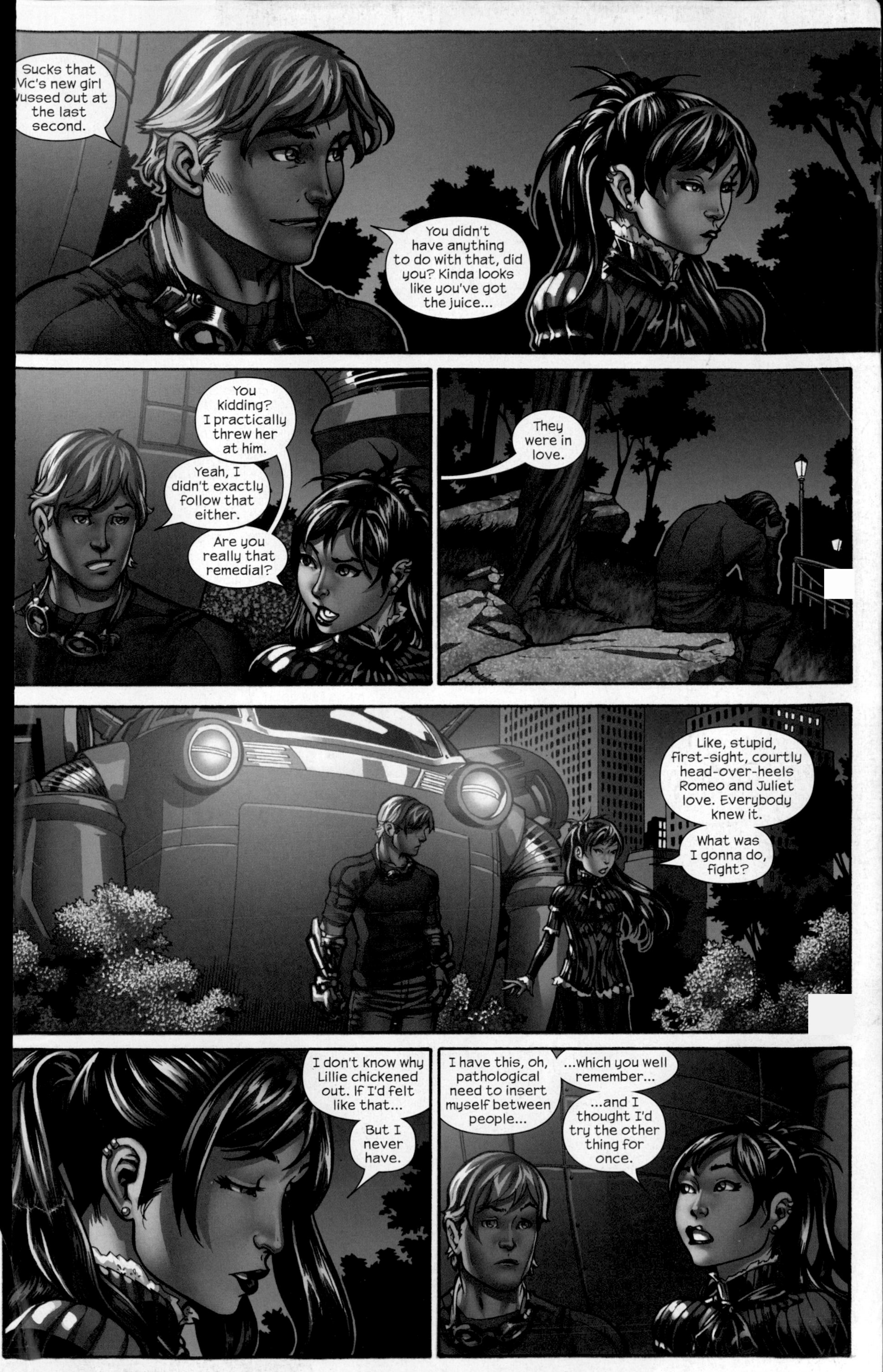
Sucks that Vic's new girl wussed out at the last second.
You didn't have anything to do with that, did you? Kinda looks like you've got the juice...
You kidding? I practically threw her at him.
Yeah, I didn't exactly follow that either.
Are you really that remedial?
They were in love.
Like, stupid, first-sight, courtly head-over-heels Romeo and Juliet love. Everybody knew it.
What was I gonna do, fight?
I don't know why Lillie chickened out. If I'd felt like that...
But I never have.
I have this, oh, pathological need to insert myself between people...
...which you well remember...
...and I thought I'd try the other thing for once.

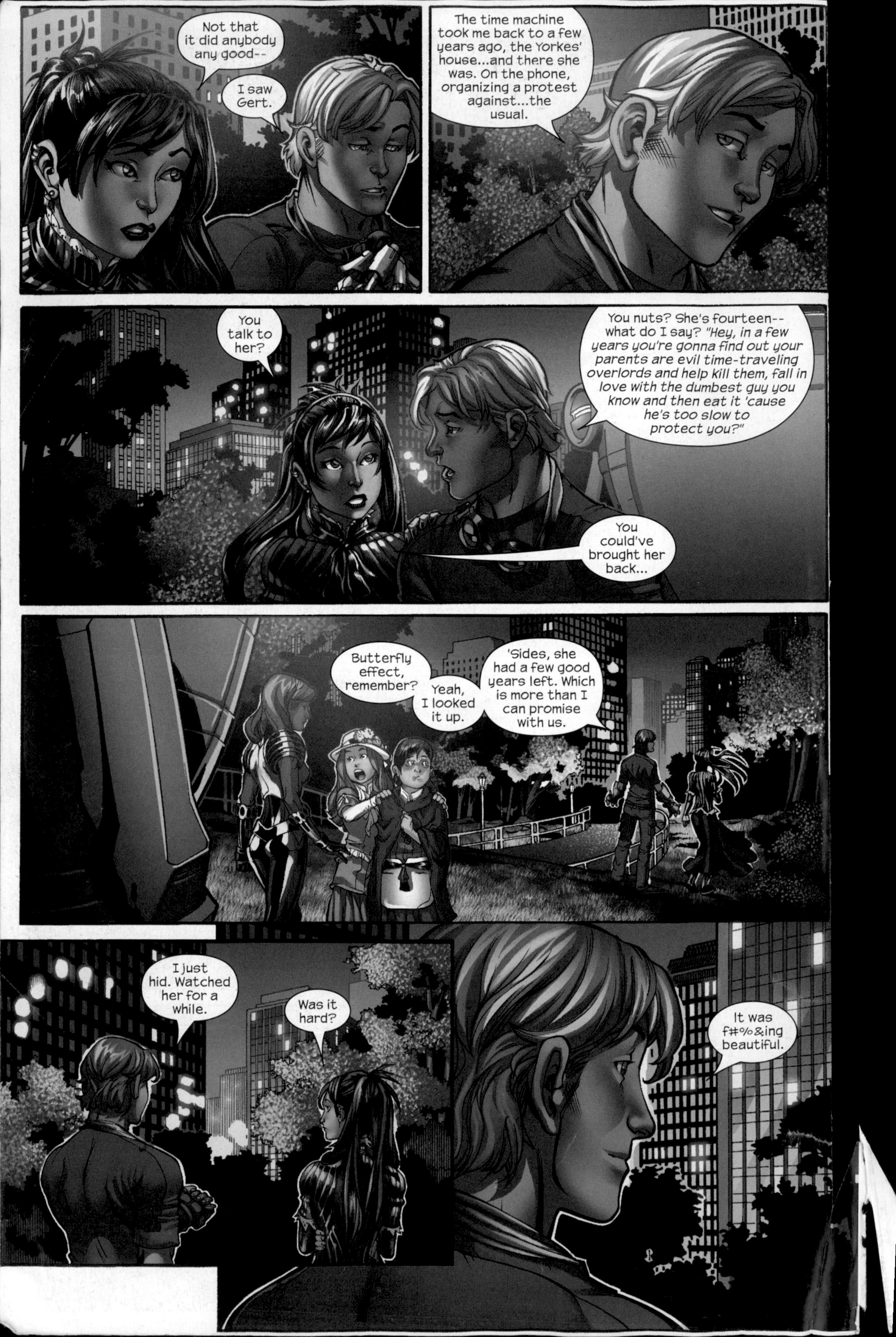
Not that it did anybody any good--
I saw Gert.
The time machine took me back to a few years ago, the Yorkes' house...and there she was. On the phone, organizing a protest against...the usual.
You talk to her?
You nuts? She's fourteen-- what do I say? "Hey, in a few years you're gonna find out your parents are evil time-traveling overlords and help kill them, fall in love with the dumbest guy you know and then eat it 'cause he's too slow to protect you?"
You could've brought her back...
Butterfly effect, remember?
Yeah, I looked it up.
'Sides, she had a few good years left. Which is more than I can promise with us.
I just hid. Watched her for a while.
Was it hard?
It was f#%&ing beautiful.

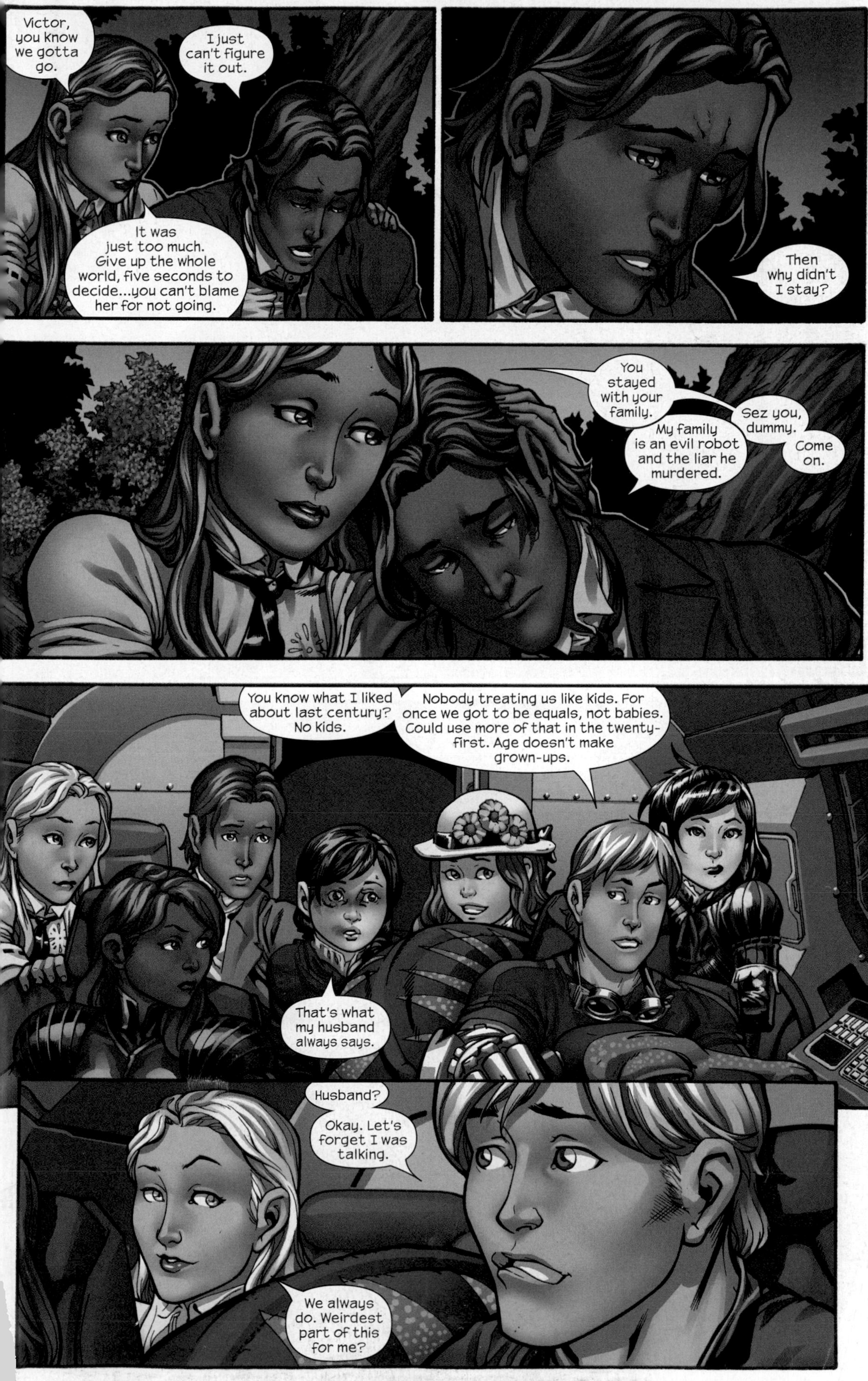

Victor, you know we gotta go.
I just can't figure it out.
It was just too much. Give up the whole world, five seconds to decide...you can't blame her for not going.
Then why didn't I stay?
You stayed with your family.
My family is an evil robot and the liar he murdered.
Sez you, dummy.
Come on.
You know what I liked about last century? No kids.
Nobody treating us like kids. For once we got to be equals, not babies. Could use more of that in the twenty-first. Age doesn't make grown-ups.
That's what my husband always says.
Husband?
Okay. Let's forget I was talking.
We always do. Weirdest part of this for me?

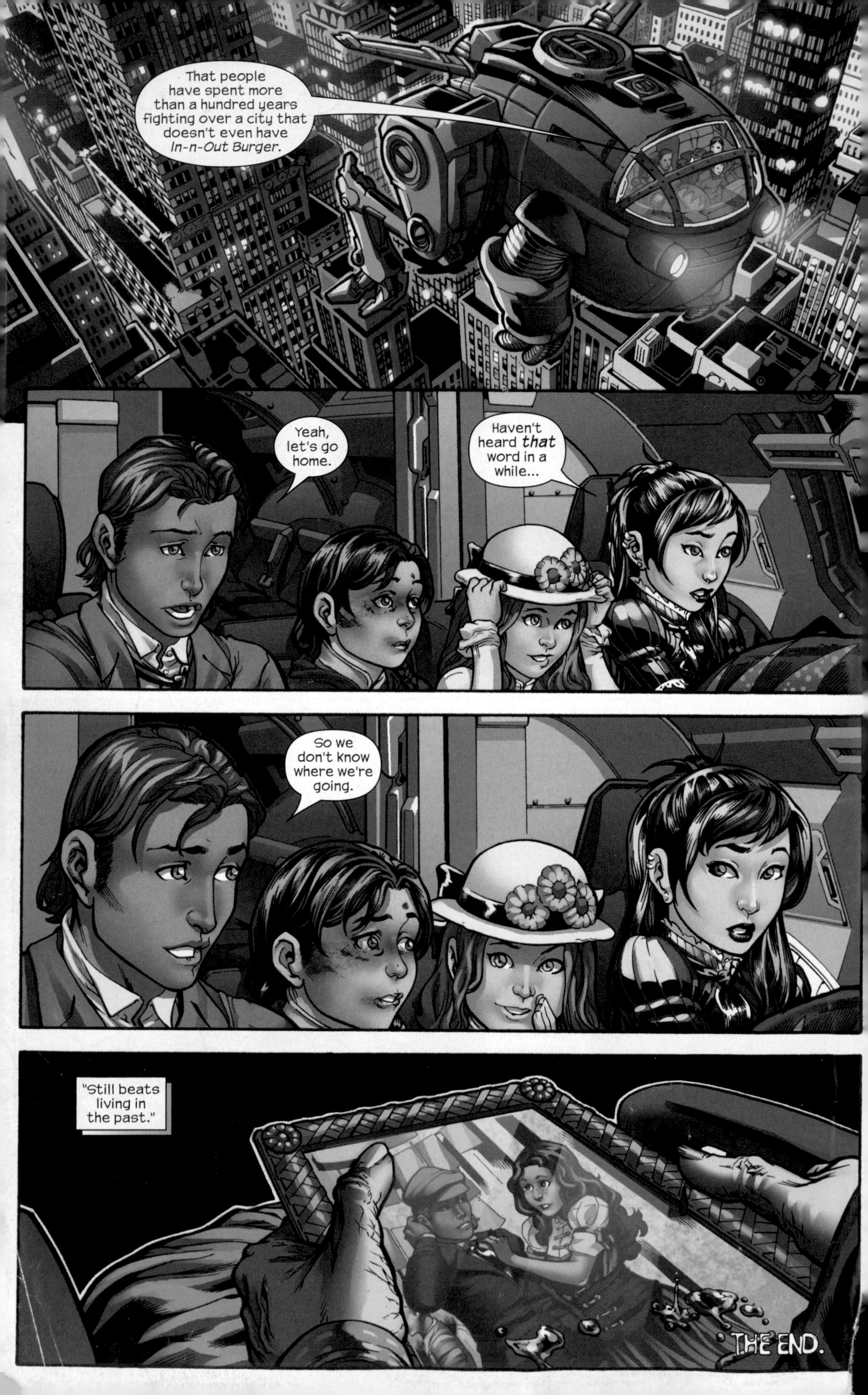
That people have spent more than a hundred years fighting over a city that doesn't even have *In-n-Out Burger*.
Yeah, let's go home.
Haven't heard *that* word in a while...
So we don't know where we're going.
"Still beats living in the past."
THE END.

NICO & KAROLINA

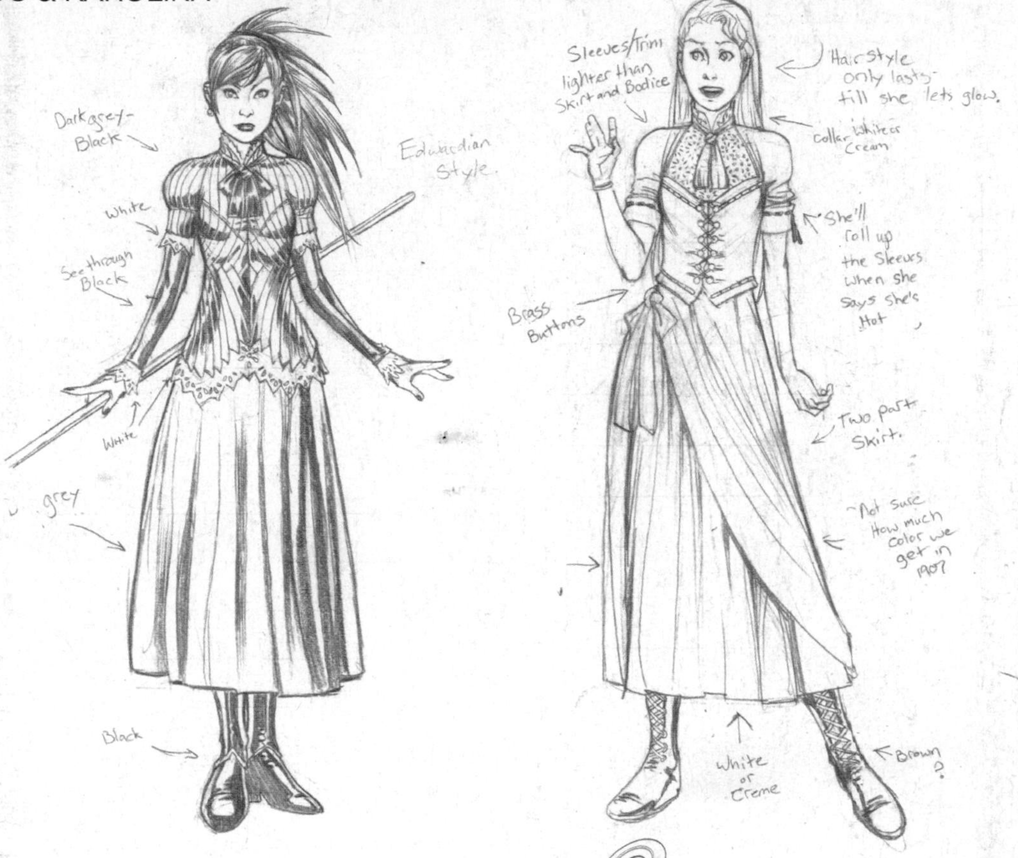
Darkgrey-Black
White
See through Black
White
grey
Black
Edwardian Style
Sleeves/Trim lighter than Skirt and Bodice
Hair style only lasts till she lets glow.
Collar White or Cream
She'll roll up the Sleeves when she says she's Hot
Brass Buttons
Two part Skirt.
Not sure How much color we get in 1907
White or Creme
Brown ?

CHASE

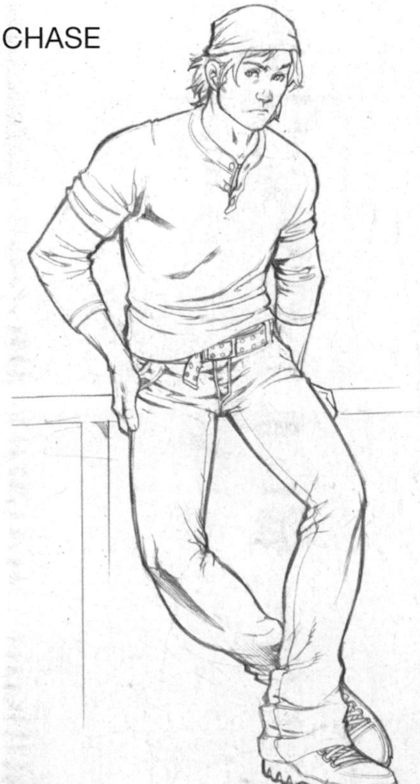

NICO

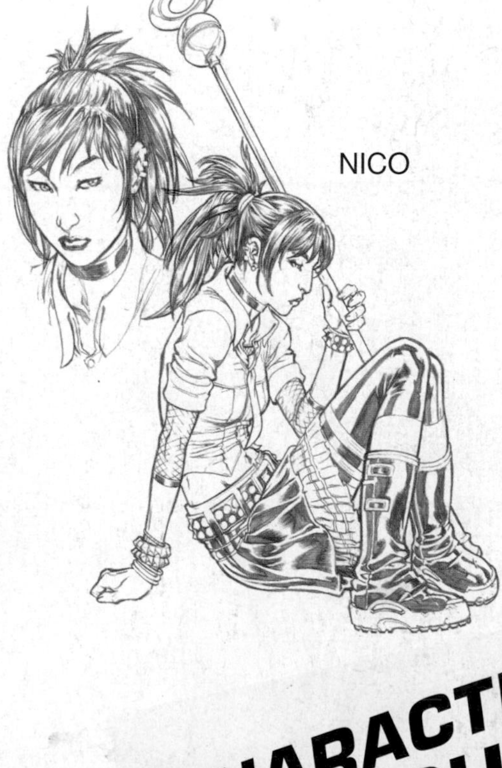

CHARACTER SKETCHES

BY MICHAEL RYAN

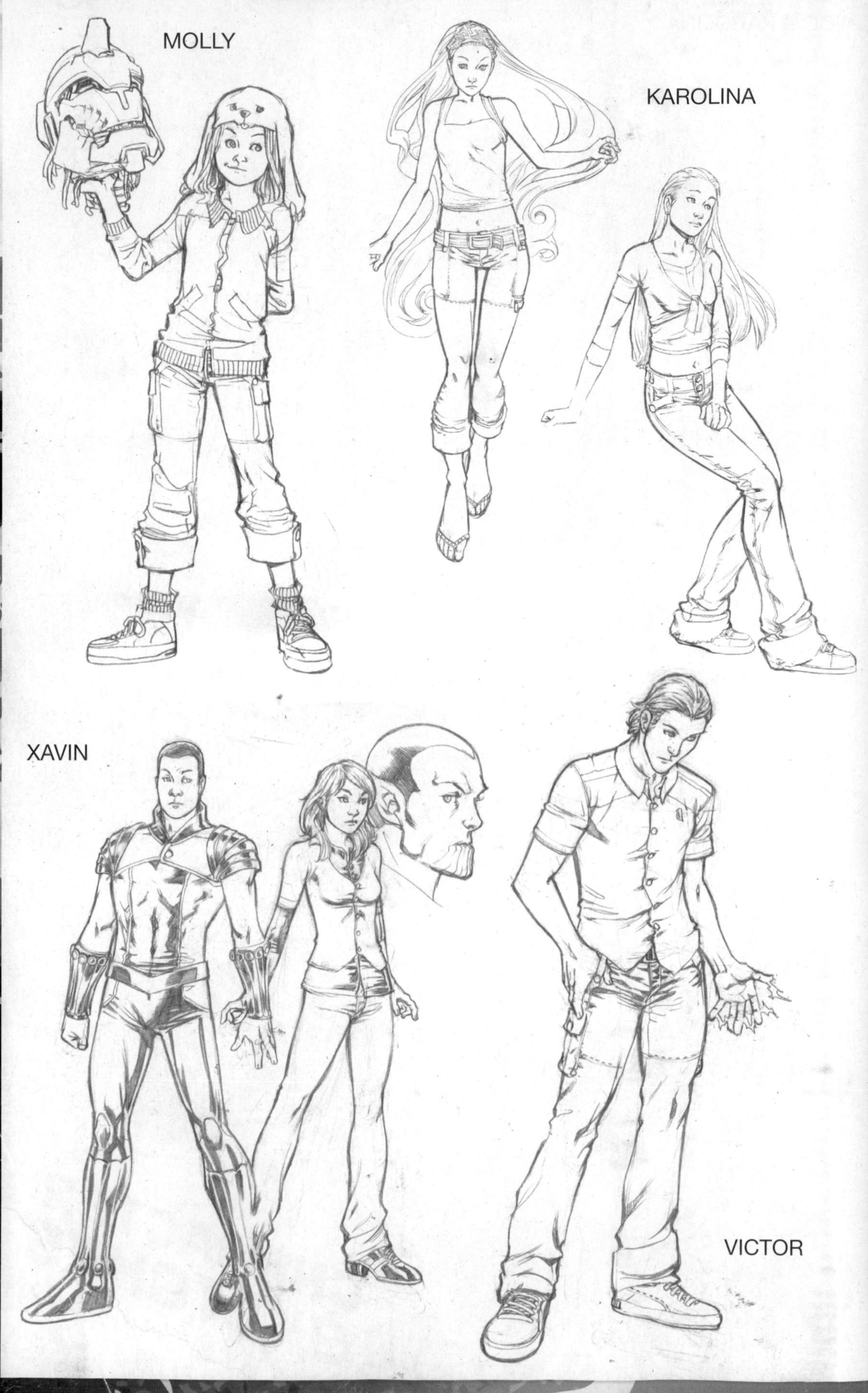
MOLLY
KAROLINA
XAVIN
VICTOR